QUESTIONING GOD

QUESTIONING GOD

TIMOTHY RADCLIFFE AND
ŁUKASZ POPKO

BLOOMSBURY CONTINUUM
LONDON · OXFORD · NEW YORK · NEW DELHI · SYDNEY

BLOOMSBURY CONTINUUM
Bloomsbury Publishing Plc
50 Bedford Square, London, WC1B 3DP, UK
29 Earlsfort Terrace, Dublin 2, Ireland

BLOOMSBURY, BLOOMSBURY CONTINUUM and the Diana logo are trademarks
of Bloomsbury Publishing Plc

First published in Great Britain 2023

A catalogue record for this book is available from the British Library

Library of Congress Cataloging-in-Publication data has been applied for

ISBN: TPB: 978-1-3994-0925-4; eBook: 978-1-3994-0923-0; ePDF: 978-1-3994-0921-6

2 4 6 8 10 9 7 5 3 1

Typeset by Deanta Global Publishing Services, Chennai, India
Printed and bound in Great Britain by CPI Group (UK) Ltd, Croydon CR0 4YY

To find out more about our authors and books visit www.bloomsbury.com
and sign up for our newsletters

This book is dedicated to Frère Marie-Joseph Lagrange
OP (1855–1938), founder of the École Biblique et
Archéologique Française de Jérusalem

Contents

Prologue

'Speak, Lord, for your servant is listening' (1 Sam. 3.9)

When the Lord first spoke to young Samuel, the young lad did not realize who was addressing him since 'the word of the Lord was rare in those days, and there was no frequent vision' (1 Sam. 3.1). Three times Samuel goes to old Eli, the priest of the sanctuary of Shiloh, asking what Eli wants until finally the priest names the one who addresses him: 'Go, lie down; and if he calls you, you shall say, "Speak, Lord, for your servant is listening"' (1 Sam. 3.9).

When he does so, the Lord responds: 'Behold, I am about to do a thing in Israel, at which the two ears of every one who hears it will tingle' (1 Sam. 3.11). The young lad receives a word which indeed sets his ears tingling, just as the disciples on the road to Emmaus will say to each other: 'Did not our hearts burn with us, while he talked to us on the road, while he opened to us the Scriptures?' (Lk. 24.32).

We too, especially in the secular West, live in an age when the Word of the Lord seems to be rare and 'there is no frequent vision'. How are we, like Samuel, to learn to hear God speaking to us a word of hope and joy in these ancient texts of the Bible, words that will make our ears tingle? Some people dismiss them as the products of long-dead alien cultures which have nothing to do with us. As with the sacred texts of other religions, others hear them as celestial commandments demanding unthinking submission. How can we respond to them with all of our hearts and intelligence? In this time of uncertainty, when the way ahead is obscure, can we, like Samuel, say, 'Speak Lord, for your servant is listening'? And how are we to make sense of the words that are given to us and receive their nourishment?

God's Word does not address us through a celestial megaphone, demanding passive acquiescence. Revelation is God's conversation with His people, through which we become the friends of God. The Second Vatican Council proclaimed that 'by this revelation, the invisible God, from the fullness of His love, addresses men and women as His friends and lives among them, in order to invite them and receive into His own company'.[1] These words of the Lord befriend us. Words of friendship are more radically transformative than orders which demand submission. Even the commandments in Scripture can only be understood aright if we see them as spoken in friendship, forming us to encounter the one who said to the disciples, 'I call you friends' (Jn 15.15).

Friendship is never one-way. It implies that words are given and received. So the Bible is filled with people responding to God's Word with expressions of their own joy and sorrow, their hopes and fears, their uncertainties, puzzlement and anger. The Word became flesh in a person who sought conversation with everyone. From his childhood, questioning of the teachers in the Temple (Lk. 2.46), until he is silenced by death on the cross, he is engaged in endless dialogues, from gentle questions to those in need – 'What can I do for you?' – to fierce arguments with his opponents. On Easter day, the Risen Word rises and breaks the silence of the tomb with words addressed to his disciples in the garden. This conversation with God will never end until we are taken up into the eternal, loving conversation of the Trinity, the longed-for home which haunts the human heart.

We chose these 18 Biblical conversations between the Lord and humanity simply because we enjoyed them and not so as to expound any systematic theory about reading Scripture. To our surprise, we discovered that nearly all of the conversations revolved around questions, from the first conversation in the Bible, in which God asks Adam, 'Where are you?', to one of the last, in which the Risen Jesus asks, 'Simon, son of John, do you love me more than these?' So we have called the book *Questioning God*, because in these conversations so often we find God both questioning and being questioned.

On the cover of this book is an image of the journey to Emmaus (Lk. 24.13–35), by Janet Brooks-Gerloff. After the Resurrection, two disciples flee Jerusalem. On the way they meet a stranger, the Risen Lord, whom they do not recognize, and who walks with them. The encounter is filled with questions. He asks them what they are talking about. They ask him, 'Are you the only one visiting Jerusalem that does not know what [things] happened in it in these days?' He responds by asking them, 'Wasn't it necessary that the Christ suffer these [things] and enter his glory?' After he disappears from their sight, they ask each other: 'Was not our heart aflame within us when he was speaking to us on the way, when he was opening for us the scriptures?'

Why all these questions? Questions, more than commandments, ignite a personal encounter. Indeed, Moses questions the Lord who is revealed in a burning bush. Job hears the terrifying words: 'Gird up your loins like a man; I will question you and you shall declare to me!' (Job 38.3). We shall grapple with some of God's questions to humanity, but not so as to solve intellectual riddles; rather, it will be in the hope that they will open us to a deeper encounter with the Lord and educate us in the art of friendship, which often leads into the happy silence of companionship.

St Paul quotes Isaiah: 'What no eye has seen, nor ear heard, nor the human heart conceived, what God has prepared for those who love Him' (1 Cor. 2.9). These questions, which God puts to us and we to God, take us to the edge of language, beyond what the human heart has conceived. This is why so often the Word of God is poetic, inviting us beyond what can be captured by literal statement. Christianity is not 'a religion of the book' but one of encounter with the Lord, and such a personal engagement with the Divine always escapes being fully captured in words.[2] Questions invite us to enter further into the mystery.

We need each other's help in listening, as the young lad Samuel needed old Eli. This is why we, Łukasz Popko and Timothy Radcliffe, decided that a good way to explore these Biblical conversations was in dialogue with each other. A fruitful conversation is more than the exchange of information or logical debate. It is an encounter of different imaginations. Of course, we share much. We are both Dominican friars who love the Scriptures, but much of the pleasure of our exchanges lies in our differences. Like Eli and Samuel, we are of different generations, Timothy in his seventies and Łukasz in his forties, not that that gives Timothy any claim to the wisdom of old Eli! Łukasz is Polish and Timothy is English. Łukasz is a Biblical scholar, teaching at the École Biblique in Jerusalem, whereas Timothy is an itinerant preacher based in Oxford. Similarity is needed for conversation to be possible, but also difference if it is to be exciting.

We have not chosen conversations that are necessarily among the most important in the Bible, just ones that appealed to us. Our aim is not to clarify their content and arrive at conclusions, summing up what they are all about. Rather, we wish to open up a little of their dynamism, of their play and performance, even, we hope, sharing a little of their fun!

For the best conversations between friends often have a ludic dimension. We hope that they will provoke discussion rather than present analyses, further questions rather than conclusions. Each conversation is probably best read slowly, meditatively, as an invitation to the reader to join in the conversation. If one tries to read this book rapidly, one will get indigestion! As Wittgenstein advises his fellow philosophers, 'Take your time!'[3]

At various points in the book we have inserted brief pauses, the occasional intermezzo. These are not summaries of what has gone before but are intended to slow the pace of reading, to help our readers digest the texts and reflect on how they might enter into conversation with them.

It is typically Dominican to believe that friendship with God is often refracted through the prism of friendship with each other. St Albert the Great, Aquinas's master, wrote of the pleasure of seeking the truth together, '*in dulcedine societatis quaerere veritatem*'.[4] St Catherine of Siena declared that there was no greater joy than talking with one's friends about God. This has been our joy, and we hope that we may share in it too.

Because of geographical separation, Timothy's illness with cancer and the restrictions on travel imposed by COVID we have not often been able to sit down together and talk face to face. Even Zoom could not be an adequate substitute. So we have communicated largely through email. This was not ideal, but we hope that, despite this limitation, which will sometimes be evident, our conversations may stimulate or provoke your own discussions with friends and opponents, in discussion groups or in prayer with the Lord of the Word.

The translations which Łukasz has prepared do not aim at elegance and fluency. They keep as close as possible to the original Hebrew or Greek, suggesting the underlying word play, with its repetition and variation, evoking the gritty foreignness of the original texts. They may seem strange, but we hope that they will break that sense of the familiarity of the texts, so that they may address us freshly and even put us on the spot.

We also offer an image with every conversation. A conversation is an imaginative act through which one enters another's view of the world, and is touched by their experience, their delight and sorrow. We hope these images may open a door into the encounter with God that is each conversation, perhaps sometimes more effectively than through the words which we, Łukasz and Timothy, exchange! Nearly all of these images show faces, faces formed in conversation with the One whose face became visible when the Word became flesh. In the image on the cover of this book, we do not see the faces of the two disciples walking with the Lord. If they were to turn around, maybe they would be ours or yours.

Łukasz Popko OP
Timothy Radcliffe OP
Jerusalem and Oxford
The Feast of the friends Sts Basil
the Great and Gregory Nazianzen, 2023

'Where are you?' (Gen. 3.8–20)

They heard the voice of YHWH God who was having a walk in the garden in the wind of the day. Then the man and his woman hid themselves from the face of YHWH God among the trees of the garden. And YHWH God called to the man, and said to him, –

'Where are you?'

He said, –

'Your voice I heard in the garden. Then I became afraid, because I was naked, and I hid myself.'

He said, –

'Who told you that you were naked? Is it that from the tree of which I commanded you not to eat from it, you have eaten?'

The man said, –

'The woman whom you gave *to be* with me, she gave me *some* from the tree, and I ate.'

Then YHWH God said to the woman, –

'What is this that you have done?'

The woman said, –

'The serpent deceived me, and I ate.'

Then YHWH God said to the serpent, –

'Because you have done this, cursed are you among all animals and among all wild creatures; upon your belly you shall go and dust you shall eat all the days of your life. And enmity I will put between you and the woman, and between your seed and her seed. He will crush your head, and you will crush his heel.'

To the woman He said, –

'I will greatly multiply your toils and your pregnancy; in pain you will give birth to children, yet for your husband *will be* your desire, and he shall rule over you.'

And to the man He said, –

'Because you have listened to the voice of your woman, and have eaten of the tree about which I commanded you, saying, "You shall not eat of it," cursed is the soil because of you. In toil you shall eat of it all the days of your life. Thorns and thistles it shall grow for you. And you shall eat the plants of the field. By the sweat of your face you shall eat bread until you return to the soil, for out of it you were taken; for you are dust, and to dust you shall return.'

The man named his wife Eve, because she was the mother of all living.

Łukasz: This is the first dialogue with God recorded in the Bible. Before then, God addressed some words to the man and woman, but we have never heard their answer nor did either of them pose a question. Before the Fall, what one would need to ask or explain? From this original human silence, we presume their tacit agreement and understanding. The unique context of the first exchange of humanity's words with God reveals the paradoxical condition of any true dialogue: there is speech because there is distance between the speakers.

The moments of deepest unity, communion, between persons – in human relationships, as well as with God – are woven with silence. The presence and immediacy are felt, experienced, expressed, lived in mind and body, through looks and gestures and through all that we are. The deepest communion is beyond words. This is how all of us begin, in wordless communication with our mothers, fathers and carers – before and beyond language.

In the Book of Genesis, the Divine capacity of speech serves to name, create, order and rule the world. First by God, and it is later shared with the man. This naming precedes conversation. What could Adam and Eve talk about before the Fall? They still were naked and without shame, in full transparency. There was nothing to hide, nothing to disagree about, nothing to attack and nothing to defend. There must have been some blessed silence before distrust crept into Paradise. We long for that silence and sometimes we get a glimpse of it.

When the deceived discover the existence of lies and the victims discover violence, their peaceful and friendly garden, which is their world, becomes immediately a very different place. Not all voices are benevolent. Not all words are what they seem to be. This first dialogue with God is born out of confusion and fearful silence, heavy with incertitude, newborn guilt and the hint of death in the long shadows of the afternoon. A known friendly voice became a potentially dangerous voice.

Timothy: I love what you say, Łukasz, about that initial silence between Adam and Eve when no words were needed, that unbroken communion that we first had with our mothers before we talked. I wonder whether you would agree that we move from an original silence, a communion untroubled by shame or blame, through words, years of conversation, sometimes muddled and difficult, towards a new silence which is much deeper, a sort of sharing in the infinite silence of God, a communion beyond all imagination, sharing in the unspeakable simplicity of the Divine life. Tradition has it that at the end of his life St John the evangelist said less and less until all that he would say in his sermons was: 'Love one another.' But he had to go through the years of complex theological reflection – writing, thinking, praying – before that simplicity could be attained.

St John of the Cross said: 'The Father spoke one Word, which was His Son, and this Word He always speaks in eternal silence, and in silence it must be heard by the soul.'[1] So we move from the simplicity of an initial almost naive human silence, in which words are not needed, through all the complex, knotty interactions of human beings to attain, with the grace of God, the untroubled calm of the Divine silence, what St Catherine of Siena called 'the pacific Ocean' and 'the boundless Ocean'.[2] In between times, we can fall – our fall! – into the false simplicity of unreflective sound bites, simplistic slogans that reject all nuance. These blunt words are not part of any journey towards understanding.

Becoming truly simple is a hard slog! So Revelation, that long dialogue between God and humanity, leads us into a friendship in which words are no longer needed, and simplicity is a Divine gift.

Łukasz: One of my Dominican friends is a composer, and with complete frankness he told me once that he is not yet good enough to compose simple music. I bet it is true also about our homilies, PhDs and dialogues! God is simple and asks simple questions.

I translated His question as 'Where are you?' In Hebrew, it is in the singular, 'Where art thou?' I love that introduction. It breaks this fearsome silence wonderfully. God gives Adam and Eve, the hiding couple, their freedom to step out and answer. He is not seeking them as one would hunt for an animal or worse for a lost object. This question gives them back their – so easily forgotten – Divine capacity of speech.

It is a terrible bother to prepare for difficult dialogues. Sometimes we spend half of the night pondering and wondering what the best opening sentence would be. 'Where are you?' is a great opening question. It is not an accusation in disguise of a rhetorical question like 'What have you done?' or 'Who has done it?' or, even worse, 'Where is my apple?!' From the very beginning, it is all about the man and woman and not about the fruit.

So let us ask our forgotten friends, our apparent enemies and angry siblings: 'Where are you now?' and let those addressed react, reflect and answer. In a complex situation – and which one is not complex after the Fall? – the interlocutor needs some space and a question to help to make sense of his or her world. The answer of the Man was partial, biased and still confused, and yet by speaking he begins to reconstruct the world that has been just shattered. With this dialogue, the slow recreation of the broken world is beginning. In her drawing *Adam*, the artist makes us see the Man incomplete, headless, as if the bright ideas of God and the matter of this earth have not matched yet. Maybe the author thought about the act of creation from Genesis 3. I think that it could also reflect Adam after the Fall: disintegrated, alone, sitting in the dirt. The humans needed another creation, another creative word.

The delicacy of God's first question makes me think about the timing. Was God waiting for Adam and Eve to get ready before he asked? They have just invented clothing, have had some time to get dressed – and how odd must that have been! Did they even have words for shame and lost dignity? Their Creator did not appear impromptu. He let the couple raise their defences, mend a bit the collapsed world, feel safer. Love is patient, isn't it?

Timothy: Yes, Łukasz, it is marvellous that this first conversation between God and humanity begins with this gentle question, 'Where are you?', inviting Adam to come out of hiding. Already we are pointed to the last conversation of the disciple with the Risen Lord in the gospels, when Jesus asks, 'Simon, son of John, do you love me more than these?' (Jn 21.15). So God's conversation with humanity begins and culminates in tender questions which break the silence of two people who have failed dramatically, Adam and Peter. Each conversation begins not with accusation but with invitation.

It is a beautiful paradox that this first conversation begins with Adam and Eve in hiding, because they do not want to talk with God. They are ashamed. Adam and Eve have made themselves garments of leaves to hide their physical nakedness, but this first conversation, when it gets going, is also a sort of hiding. It is a tissue of words to conceal their actions. God asks Eve, 'What have you done?', but Adam and Eve pretend that they have not really done anything blameworthy. 'It was not my fault that I ate the apple. Blame it on the woman whom you created. It's really all your fault, God.' Eve also flees responsibility too: 'It's all the fault of the serpent, whom you created. You must bear the blame.' So their answers are verbal fig leaves behind which they hide.

I suppose we all sometimes flee from talking to God out of shame of what we have done or fear of what we shall be asked to do and to be. We may hide by blaming someone else. We hide behind victimhood, or its the fault of my genes, my DNA, my parents, society, the Church. Not me! Certainly not me! We may resist real conversation with God by blocking our ears with long prayers and extravagant devotions, a sort of Divine filibuster, just to get out of the dangerous business of silently listening to the Divine word which will transform us into God's friends.

Adam and Eve flee God's face, and yet this is what we most long for. Israel sang, 'Let your face shine on us and we shall be saved!' (Ps. 80). In the end this face became visible in the face of a human being who only wants to look on us with love and listen with compassion. Sister Wendy Beckett said that prayer is standing 'unprotected before God', naked.[3] So I find myself wondering what cunning devices I use to clothe my nakedness in the sight of God, what evasions and fig leaves. Anything rather than listen and be vulnerable to whatever words may be addressed to me. Yet I also know, at the same time, that these are the words which I long to hear that I may live (Isa. 55.3).

At baptism, we are naked. I was only three days old and so certainly unashamed! It is a sort of restoration of our original visibility. Gregory of Nyssa wrote of baptism, that 'casting off these fading leaves which veil our lives we should once again present ourselves before the eyes of our Maker'.[4] An ancient Eastern prayer asks: 'unveil our eyes, give us confidence, do not let us be ashamed or embarrassed, do not let us despise ourselves.'[5] So much of prayer life is letting God gently unclothe us, slip off the fig leaves, like a lover who sees our beauty even when we do not. God became naked on a cross, lifted up in a baying crowd. So we can dare to be naked before God's eyes. Do we dare also to be, as it were, naked to each other, visible in our vulnerability, our doubts and questions, our hopes and failures?

There is one thing where I would appreciate your reaction as a Biblical scholar. My Hebrew was never good, to my shame! The consequences of the Fall are described in terms of dust and infertility. Giving birth will be difficult and painful, the soil will not yield fruit abundantly; the serpent will eat dust, and we shall return to dust.

Aneta Fausek Kaczanowska, *Adam*, 2018, private collection, Kraków

Interestingly, the animals are brought forth from the soil, from earth (Gen. 1.24), whereas human beings, the earth creatures (Adam as earth), are made from the dust, which seems to me to be less precious than earth, almost dirt. I know that these passages are usually ascribed to different theological traditions, but it would be too complex to get caught up in sorting these out in this sort of a conversation! But it is as if in these stories other animals have a sort of wholesome earthy quality, whereas we human beings can sink to mere dirt or rise to Divinity. We, the earth creatures, can walk with God in 'the wind of the day' (*ruah*, 'spirit') or we can share the life of the dusty serpent! Just being human is not an option! We can rise into Divinity or sink into dirt.

Even our conversations can either be life-giving or dusty and dirty, rubbishing people and creation, destructive and unsaying God's creative Word. We bless or we curse. My mind often reverts to those words seen scrawled on walls in Rwanda during the genocide: 'Kill the Cockroaches.' Or our language can be fertile and fecund, giving life and light. Humanity's first vocation was to be gardeners of Eden, and our gardening now is to converse with each other and with God in words that are radiant, fertile. Often we begin this healing conversation, as you said, by asking others, as God does: 'Where are you? There is no need to hide.' It is an invitation to unfurl in the Divine sunlight. Our faces can shine light on others too. The dawn comes in another's eyes.

Łukasz: According to Genesis, there is only a slight difference in the matter out of which we were made: for both humans and animals, it is *adama*. *Edom* means 'red', so *adama* is also suggestive of the local reddish soil, loose earth. When *adama* is dry, it becomes dust; when moist, it is similar to malleable clay. Genesis 2.7 says more precisely that we were made of 'the dust of *adama*'. You are right, Timothy, that this dust is already here looming on the horizon, a lifeless matter which is at the beginning and the end: 'to dust shall you return.' I suppose that we are the only animals who can see and understand this horizon of non-existence, one's decomposition. God revealed to us our contingency: we are a form of dust and we know it.

Genesis 3 is not what one would call a pleasant conversation. For some readers of the Bible it could even confirm a stereotype of the vengeful God of the Old Testament, and as such be summarily rejected. Indeed, there are many Biblical texts, passionate texts, boiling with Divine and human wrath, and yet this text is not one of them. Here the dialogue unfolds smoothly, calmly, without shouting or exclamations. Just a few simple repetitions of 'and God said'. Yet God's sober words have the weight of a ruling and a judgement, and of a curse ...

Children are usually taught not to curse, and in the Bible the first one to curse is God! There is something very precise in His almost understated but solemn formulas. Actually, the man and the woman are not cursed. The Divine curse reaches in their stead to the snake and the cultivable earth. On human lips, a curse can be merely the wish of an afflicted soul. That is why we have some fantastic and flowery curses of the persecuted Psalmist. A curse can also be a veiled statement or a disguised description of one's miserable state, as when Job cursed the day of his birth (Job 3). Yet in Genesis 3, and likewise in numerous other passages, a curse comes from God's lips and therefore must have some of the creative efficacy of His Word and His blessings; it does things.

Is it possible to see good news in God's curse? I believe so, and it is my experience that there is nothing more consoling than the truth, even bitter truth. Keeping up appearances, pretending that all is well, costs way too much energy and is not life-giving at all. The two curses of Genesis 3 confirm something that we suspect now and then: there is something wrong with this world. Something wrong, not just with me or even with humans. Nowadays it is fashionable to idealize nature and to demonize culture. Genesis 3 reveals that there is something wrong with nature as well. We can imagine it as less destructive, less violent, wasteful, or less deadly. The curse on the mysterious speaking snake – however one would interpret it – means that humankind is not responsible for and guilty of all the evils of the world. We may be its focal or turning point, but we are not guilty of everything.

The fact that the curse comes from God and that it was not there 'at the beginning' gives me great hope for a different world. Its woes and disasters are not intrinsically necessary. They can be transcended. The earth was cursed with bareness *because* of the man, not in itself. It is like the portrait of Dorian Gray: a painting reveals the otherwise hidden state of Dorian's soul. As much as Dorian found it terrible to behold, it was also of the greatest value for him because we long to be truly known. The image revealed Dorian to Dorian but also by implication it pointed that there is some mysterious beholder, the Author who kept working on the portrait. The earth is Adam's portrait. It means that the fertility of fields, as well as the bareness of the desert, reveal that there is some 'third party' involved. The 'cursed' earth will resist us to the end of days. Since this quality comes from the Creator, there is also some precious gift hidden in this 'bad news'. The resistance of the untamed, barren and dangerous earth should remind us what we are: beings that easily grab for themselves the right to eat all the fruit. The lack of fruit and our biological limitations, including our death, unmask this human *folie des grandeurs*, and that is why it is indeed a good word. Jesus cursed a fig tree to make of it a sign for his people (Mk 11.21–5). He wanted them to read it, to ask questions. Hopefully, we will learn to read the barren lands, the uninhabitable space, so as to learn that we are not the ultimate lords of the earth, or even of our own lives.

Timothy: This curse brings humanity back down to dust – 'to dust you shall return' – but it ends with promise; 'The man named his wife Eve, because she was the mother of all living.' The names that Adam gives are not just labels but also blessings, summons to existence. You once pointed out to me – we do talk about scripture a lot! – that the next use of the word for 'dust' is also in the context of blessing, the promise to Abraham, 'I will make your descendants as the dust of the earth; so that if one can count the dust of the earth, your descendants also can be counted' (Gen. 13.16). Dust, the symbol of sterility and barrenness, becomes the symbol of fecundity. The dust of the curse is transformed into a sign of blessing. The cursed soil will grow thorns, but those thorns shall crown the Lord of life before he is led the cross, when all sterility and aridity is overcome.

The dust of the desert and of the seashore also become a sign of the fertility promised to Abraham: 'I will indeed bless you, and I will multiply your descendants as the stars of heaven and as the sand which is on the seashore' (Gen. 22.17). Curse never has the final word, and the desert which is the home of demons and death is also the place where God reveals himself to Moses and the Israelites. The silence of the desert, which is empty and devoid of meaning, becomes the silence in which we hear God speak: 'And Moses and the Levitical priests said to all Israel. "Keep silence and hear, O Israel: this day you have become the people of the Lord your God"' (Deut. 27.9). So whatever desolation and barrenness we encounter in our lives, whenever we sit in the dust like Job, we believe that the Lord's blessing is not far away.

'Where is Abel, your brother?'
(Gen. 4.1–16)

Now the man knew Eve, his woman. She conceived and bore Cain, and said, –

'I have acquired a man with (the help of) YHWH.'

And again she bore his brother, Abel. And Abel was a shepherd of small cattle, and Cain was a tiller of the soil. It happened at the end of days that Cain brought from the fruit of the soil as an offering for YHWH. But Abel, he brought as well from the firstlings of his small cattle and from their fat. YHWH looked towards Abel and towards his offering. And towards Cain and towards his offering he did not look, and Cain became very angry, and his face fell. Then YHWH said to Cain, –

'Why are you angry, and why has your face fallen? If you do well, will it (your face) not be lifted up? And if you do not do well, is not sin crouching at the door? It desires you, but you should master it.'

And Cain said to Abel, his brother, – ...

And when they were in the field, Cain rose up against Abel his brother and murdered him. Then YHWH said to Cain, –

'Where is Abel, your brother?'

He said, –

'I do not know; am I my brother's keeper?'

And YHWH said, –

'What have you done? Listen! Your brother's blood is crying out towards me from the soil. And now you are cursed from the soil that has opened its mouth to receive your brother's blood from your hand. For when you till the soil, it will no longer give you its strength. A fugitive and a wanderer, you will be on the earth.'

Cain said to YHWH, –

'My offence is too great to bear! Behold you have driven me away today from the face of the soil, and from your face I shall be hidden, and I will become a fugitive and a wanderer on the earth, and it will happen that anyone who finds me may murder me.'

And YHWH said to him, –

'That is why whoever would murder Cain will suffer a sevenfold vengeance.'

And YHWH put a mark on Cain, so that no one who finds him would strike him. Then Cain left from the face of YHWH and dwelled in the land of Nod ('Land of Wandering'), east of Eden.

Timothy: The first conversation between God and humanity opened with God's question to Adam: 'Where are you?' Adam replies truthfully that he is afraid and has hidden himself. God's question invites him to come out into the open so that the healing conversation can begin.

The second conversation at which we look now is a step backwards. Initially it is a double refusal of conversation. God asks, 'Why are you angry?' but Cain does not answer. Instead he kills Abel, silencing his brother. Then God asks, 'Where is your brother?', to which Cain replies untruthfully: 'I don't know. Am I my brother's keeper?' It is not until Cain is desperate that he engages with God. Then God can begin the healing conversation he always wished to have.

So we move from Adam and Eve's hesitant, fearful response to God's invitation to talk to Cain's rejection of all conversation. From 'Where are you?', spoken in hope of engagement, to 'Where is your brother?', to which Cain can make no answer. The second question is implicit in the first. We have no idea who and where we are unless we know who and where are our brothers and sisters. Cain's reply – 'I don't know!' – shows he does not know himself. Abel says nothing until his blood cries out from the ground to God.

So this first murder, the beginning of violence, is rooted in this terrible silence. Your translation of the text says that Cain spoke to Abel, but no words are given, just a murderous violence. All the violence of the world, from the first murder to the dropping of the atomic bombs until today, springs from dead silence, the refusal of conversation. Think of the terrible silence of Russia today! But with infinite patience, our God offers us words that break the silence, until the Word is made flesh, embraces the deepest silence of the cross and breaks it on Easter morning.

'Where are your brothers and sisters?' This question is put to us as we enter a period of profound political and ecological instability, with rising violence, natural and political, with millions of migrants fleeing from war and poverty, dying on land and in our seas. Will we, like Cain, refuse to hear their voices: 'I do not know; am I their keeper?' The brutal words of Cain are heard today ever more loudly. 'I don't know and I don't care.'

Łukasz: The Bible is not only about dialogue, but it is definitely about relationships. You attracted my attention to the dramatic fact that there is no conversation between Cain and Abel. Or, on the contrary, there is something like a non-conversation, like a torn-out page. I marked this unusual phrase with the three dots. We would expect something after the phrase 'and Cain said to Abel, his brother, – …' Even the ancient Greek translator felt compelled to fill this crying gap with some words and many contemporary translations do the same. Cain seems to say something, but these were no-words, it was a non-conversation. Something worse than a lie, something that ultimately killed his brother …

Unfortunately, it is so true that one can have a brother, a sister, living side by side, a husband or wife, and have no conversation. Silence can be too heavy to bear, so one fills it with anything other than words that bind us to others and reveal who we are. Cain's body was made for love and not for killing but it did kill. Cain's words, like those of Abel, were supposed to name the world, to touch God and the soul of his brother and yet they disconnect, disrupt and gape like some terrifying empty eye sockets in a frame that should have been beautiful.

If I imagine heaven and some ultimate reconciliation, that must be the scene when Cain speaks to Abel. Finally. The whole of human history is needed, epochs, ups and downs, and the Cross and the Resurrection, to make these two speak to each other. It rips me apart because I realize that there are some impossible dialogues that I need to have, some conversations I would die to have.

Cain does not answer. Cain lies. Don't we? Why? Because we do not know the answers to the questions people put to us. Or we know the answers and we do not like them. We do not feel free to ask for an explanation. We feel intimidated, we do not trust enough that the conversation can be meaningful, or important enough… You name it.

The main character of this narrative is Cain, not Abel. The way the story is told places us in his position and perspective. The Bible invites us into the role of Cain. If it comes from this source, from God, its purpose is not to manipulate or make us feel guilty. Reading the story with Cain's eyes should be a life-saving or maybe even a life-giving experience. Deep down we run away from the Word of God for the same reasons that we avoid other humans and ourselves.

Timothy: I am glad you say that we should place ourselves in the shoes of Cain, because I feel some sympathy for poor Cain, whose sacrifice has been rejected by God. Of course, he is hurt! In John Steinbeck's novel *East of Eden*, one of the characters claims that this is the story of humanity:

> The greatest terror a child can have is that he is not loved, and rejection is the hell he fears. I think everyone in the world to a large or small extent has felt rejection. And with rejection comes anger, and with anger some kind of crime in revenge for the rejection, and with the crime guilt – and there is the story of mankind.[1]

So, as in the first conversation, we might be inclined to say, like Adam and Eve, 'God, it is all your fault. You, God, created that woman; You, God, created that serpent.' If God had not preferred meat to vegetables, Cain would not have been so hurt and enveloped in silence, and become a fugitive and a wanderer. Whose fault is that? What is going on?

Łukasz: Anyone who is jealous or lives in deep resentment enters Cain's logic, which proposes an illusionary solution. First, I realize that there is something wrong in the relationship between me and X. Second, I note that the relationship between X and Y flourishes. Conclusion: getting rid of Y will improve my relationship with X. This reasoning is, of course, absurd and conceals plenty of false presuppositions.

Cain thinks that people are interchangeable, that God will simply have to look at him when there is no more Abel. From Cain's perspective, Abel is replaceable, but so is Cain! The root of Cain's sin is not his pride but his lack of appreciation of his own person. He thinks that God has to choose between the two brothers. Just to be clear: God does not have to reject or choose either; one cannot be manipulated into loving somebody.

Not only children but also many adults enter this destructive logic: if I do not win this game, this game is stupid. Maybe this was Cain's problem, that he thought of his relationship with God as a type of game? Something one can win or lose, or something once can win back. God is not perceived here as a free protagonist, someone to whom one can talk. Wouldn't it be the simplest thing if Cain asked God why He didn't look at his sacrifice? Why not? He had a chance to do it. Did he not trust the answer he might have received? Did he not believe he would receive one? These are all questions to Cain and to all of us who do not ask God fair and square questions. Why do we instead naively attempt to manipulate the Creator of Heaven and Earth and of all that they contain?

Was Cain indeed rejected by God? I do not think so, and even if he *felt* rejected, such a sentiment was not justified. We know he was sad. It was God who came to Cain asking what was wrong. This was a perfect moment to get things straight. There was no Abel around, just God and Cain. God did not reject or neglect Cain; He came out to Cain, noted and named his sadness. There is only so much one can do from the outside.

I am here not that interested in defending God; I am too poor an advocate and He does not need one. I am rather speaking to us who are Cain: stubborn and refusing to react to the attempts of communication, to a fair word of concern, to an inconvenient truth.

Timothy: Let's try to dig a little deeper into the nature of this drama, so that we can understand what it might teach us about how to break the silences that undermine our communion with God and with our brothers and sisters. First of all, it is all about faces, having and seeking recognition in the face of the other. Second, perhaps Cain embodies a way of being human which tends towards the silencing of others.

Łukasz, your translation brings out better than any other that I know, that the text is saturated with references to faces. It is the drama of Cain being seen or feeling invisible. God does not 'look towards' Cain's sacrifice, and so 'his face falls'. God promises that if he does well, his face will look up again.

Also the face of God and the face of the soil seem to be intimately linked. The earth shuts her face against Cain, who complains, 'Behold you have driven me away today from the face of the soil and from Your face I shall be hidden.' His exile from God and his exile from the earth are felt to be the same. God does not look favourably on his offering of the fruit of the earth, and the earth becomes fruitless.

So this drama of the first murder is about our profound desire to be looked at, to be smiled at by the eyes of our God. If we are not at home in God's gaze, can we be at home anywhere? Coming home to God's kind eyes is the ultimate homecoming.

The theme of the face will recur throughout our book. We saw it already in the conversation with Adam, who must stop hiding and become visible to God's kind gaze. We saw how the history of salvation leads to that Divine gaze becoming flesh and blood in the face of a Jewish man two thousand years ago, a face that was banished outside the city walls, and whose eyes were closed at death but opened again on Easter morning. This is the gaze we are called to embody as we look at each other, even on Zoom!

I wonder whether the mark of Cain may not actually be his own face. This fugitive still carries the face of one on whom God looks protectively. His sin does not make him invisible. He is settled in the land of Nod because God has his eye on him, and his story is open for future surprises. He is not doomed to be trapped in the endless cycle of violence which closed the eyes of the murdered Abel. Blessings lie ahead.

Whenever we feel locked in silence, feeling as if we are expelled from the sight of God, God's loving gaze still falls on us, however far we flee. All our conversations with each other should embody that look which lifts up the face of the other, which invites him or her to show their face. Conversation is rooted in mutual gaze, for the face of the other always proclaims that they are marked by God, God's own possession. In Marilynne Robinson's marvellous novel *Gilead*, the protagonist says, 'Any human face has a claim on you, because you can't help but understand the singularity of it. The courage and loneliness of it.'² Can you really hurt someone if you see with clarity their face?

Recent research suggests a rise in the incidents of prosopagnosia, the inability to recognize and read faces. Is the rising violence in most cultures today linked to an increasing inability to decipher the faces of strangers?

In the Book of Revelation, at the other end of our Bible, the angel cries out, 'Do not damage the earth or the sea or the trees, until we have marked the servants of our God with a seal their foreheads' (Rev. 7.3). When we truly see the face of our brothers and sisters, how could we possibly silence or ignore them? Every human face is marked as God's possession.

Łukasz: The mark of Cain was understood by some interpreters as a curse. Some preachers even used this text to promote slavery because they identified it with dark skin. What a terrifying case of using a text in support of such a cause, a dreadful exegesis! Actually, the text intends the opposite: it is a protective sign. According to Genesis, Cain thrived, settled down and had children. God protected the murderer and gave him a second chance. Rashi, a Jewish scholar from the Middle Ages, gives a very interesting exegesis of the mark. Hebrew grammar allows us to read verse 15 simply as 'He placed *YHWH* on Cain as a sign.' That means simply that God placed his Divine name on Cain. Rashi precisely interprets 'a sign' as letters from the Divine name, Tetragrammaton.

Julius Paulsen, *Cain*, 1891, Statens Museum for Kunst, Copenhagen

I do not think that Rashi knew the Christian Apocalypse, but this is precisely what Revelation 22.4 promises us! 'And they will look upon His face. And His name – on their foreheads.'

The congregation of the saved are like the children of Cain. They returned home and can see the face of the Lord again. The mark of Cain commemorates their guilt but at the same moment is a witness to God's forgiveness and fidelity to the repentant sinner. It becomes a mark of love, election and belonging. *Felix culpa*!

Timothy: Yes, again we can see how what looks like a curse conceals a blessing, just as you argued that the curse of the earth at the end of that conversation with Adam and Eve also bears a quiet promise. It is interesting that both Eve and her son Cain have something like a serpent lurking in enmity which they will conquer! Like mother, like son! Eve was promised that her seed would crush the serpent. This might have been Cain, but he failed to do so.

There still remains a puzzle. Why does God not look favourably on Cain's offering of the fruit of the earth? Why is it inferior to Abel's offering 'from the firstlings of his small cattle and from their fat'? Maybe it originates in tensions between farmers and shepherds. Maybe it is a justification for the animal sacrifices of the Temple. But our concern in this book is not with exegesis for its own sake, but with seeing how we are invited by the Word of God to enter into dialogue with God and each other. What has this odd story about God's preference for meat over vegetables, not at all fashionable today, got to say to us?

The great Jewish thinker Jonathan Sacks offers what may be a fruitful point of entry into its drama. He claims that Cain's name points to ownership and possession. When Eve names him, she says, 'I have acquired [*kaniti*] a man.'³ His very name suggests possession, ownership. Abel's name, Sacks asserts, means 'breath', God-given breath, which is the Divine gift to all living breathing beings.

Sacks does not explore this, but the difference between their sacrifices could be that Cain offers what he claims to own, plants which are given to us to sustain all that lives, but Abel offers back to God what is most intimately Divine in us, the breath – *ruah* – that gives life to us and all animals. This breath belongs to God, given and ultimately returned, when to dust we return. Cain offers what is in us all that we may live. Abel returns to God what is Divine. His sacrifice is a recognition that life is a gift, given and to be returned.

So maybe even his sacrifice suggests Cain's assertion of ownership. He sacrifices to God what he owns! He denies ownership of his brother's life: 'Am I my brother's keeper?' But he has taken possession of his brother's life. The one thing that God commanded him to rule, the evil lurking at his door, has mastered him for a while. So in claiming mastery he loses it, and becomes a fugitive and a wanderer.

So maybe Cain uncovers humanity's temptation to take ownership of other living breathing beings which belong to God, and even to take possession of other human beings, made in the Divine image. Just think of the innumerable ways in which people take possession of others, from the oppression of one's spouse, domestic violence, to the enslavement of whole peoples. This continues today, from the trafficking of woman and children for sexual exploitation to the sweatshops which produce so many of our clothes. Thus are people silenced. The voices of those who are reduced to property are not heard.

In the spirit of Cain, everything can be appropriated on the market. Even our own God-given bodies, breathing with the Divine breath, are seen as properties with which we can do what we like. Yet when we look around at the suffering of the world, do we say, 'Am I my brothers' and sisters' keeper?' while actually taking possession of their lives. Their blood calls to us from the ground and from the sea.

Łukasz: The conflicts between the pastoralists and the farmers are as old as the first villages and are still going on in Africa. The ancient rabbis had the same intuition preserved in the collection of their homilies:

> What were they arguing about? They said:
> 'Come let's divide up the world, one will take the land and one will take
>   the moveable property.'
> This one said:
> 'The ground you are standing on is mine.'
> The other one said:
> 'What you are wearing is mine.'
> This one said:
> 'Take it off!'
> The other one said:
> 'Fly!'
> Because of this 'Cain rose against his brother Abel and killed him.'
>   (*Bereishit Rabbah* 22:7, *c.* AD 300–500)

Nevertheless, I would still seek the reason of this brotherly conflict in the relationships and not in possessions. The name *Qayn* was given by the mother. If indeed the matter of possession is here central, it is rather Eve that declared that she *owns* her firstborn, and it is not a good beginning for any mother–son relationship.[4] We do not know what the age difference between the two sons was. There is, however, a significant difference in the experience of the two children. When the younger son is born, from the beginning of his existence he is already born as a brother. Indeed, most often the narrator says 'Abel, his brother', as if for Abel being Cain's brother was simply the part of what he was, his innate identity. It is not the case for the firstborn, Cain. For the older son, it is an altogether different story. The firstborn must *become* a brother, recognizing the other. We all know family stories about funny or dramatic ways in which the firstborn receives the younger usurper!

In the story, as it is given to us in Genesis, Cain looks at Abel only after God looks at Abel, at Abel's sacrifice. I may be reading too much into this story, I admit, but it seems that only at this moment, as if only by following God's gaze, did Cain look and see his brother. Unfortunately, instead of recognizing the value of his brother's gift, as God did, he only recognized him as a rival and an obstacle to be removed.

Timothy: Łukasz, what you say about the challenge to the firstborn son to become a sibling is most perceptive. Perhaps that is because you are the firstborn son, though you have an older sister. I am merely a third son and fourth child! Maybe it is precisely as one who was originally an only child that Cain reaches out for ownership not just of his mother's love but also of God's.

This brings us to the very lifeblood of any fruitful conversation, which is that neither interlocutor one can own it. When we open ourselves deeply to another, neither should claim completely to steer the direction of their dialogue, or to impose their vocabulary or agenda. A good conversation is unpredictable, freely going where we did not expect. The silence of Cain is of one who is not willing to take that risk. If he had talked with Abel, where might it have taken him? If he had talked with God when God addressed him, things might have been so different.

Do we flee from really conversing to people because we do not want to lose control of our lives? Do we silence people with our words, beating them into silence, depriving them of oxygen, as Cain did to Abel? The metaphors that haunt our debates are often implicitly violent. We squash our opponents, wipe the floor with them; we dismiss their ideas as ridiculous, absurd. All these aggressive metaphors are heavy with the violence of Cain.

Conversations become alive when we beget them together, emerging freely and surprisingly out of our humble seeking of words together, leading us beyond our habitual pastures. The Dominican Academy of Human Sciences in Baghdad had as its motto: 'Here no questions are forbidden.'[5]

In conversation, we receive the gift of the other and discover who we are too. Conversation at its best is a sort of shared breathing, whereas Cain stopped Abel's breath. Every profound friendship leads to conversations one could never have had with anyone else, as one enjoys the play of different minds, allowing each in turn the chance to guide and direct, as in chamber music, in which each instrument takes its turn, first the violin and then the cello.

In the Scriptures, God does not boom at us, crushing us with oppressive Divine words, but invites us to speak: 'Where are you?', 'Why are you angry?', 'Where is your brother?' Each question is an invitation to speak rather than a request for information. The Bible is filled with our passionate responses, our disappointment and anger, even that of Cain the murderer. We are given freedom to express our fragile hopes, our joy and our resentment. God does not silence us, but embraces all of humanity's fumbling words in the dialogue of God and humanity which is the Bible. It does not end even when we silence our brothers and sisters and flee the face of God. God awaits with another question and another blessing, as we shall in the next conversation.

3

'Where is Sarah, your wife?' Welcoming the strangers (Gen. 18.1–16)

YHWH made Himself seen to him (Abraham) by the terebinths of Mamre. He was sitting at the entrance of the tent in the heat of the day. He lifted up his eyes and saw, and behold: three men standing facing him! And he saw and ran to meet them, from the entrance of the tent, and he prostrated himself on the ground. And he said, –

'My lords (*Adonay*), if then I have found favour in your eyes, do not pass by your servant. Let a little water be brought, wash your feet and lie down under the tree. And then let me bring a morsel of bread so that you may refresh your heart, and after that you shall pass on – for because of this you have passed by your servant.'

And they said, –

'Thus you may do, as you have said.'

Then Abraham hurried to the tent, to Sarah, and said, –

'Hurry! Three *se'as* of fine flour. Knead and make cakes!'

And to the cattle Abraham ran. Then he took a young one of the cattle, tender and good, and gave it to the young man and he hurried to prepare it. Then he took curds and milk and the young one of cattle that he had prepared and set it before them. And he was standing, facing them, under the tree, and they ate.

Then they said to him, –

'Where is Sarah, your wife?'

And he said, –

'Here, in the tent.'

And he said, –

'I will certainly return to you about a year hence, then behold: Sarah, your wife, will have a son.'

Now Sarah was listening at the entrance of the tent, and it was behind him. Abraham and Sarah were old, advanced in days. Sarah ceased to have 'a path like the women'. So Sarah laughed inside herself, saying, –

'After I have become worn out, shall I have delight? And my lord has grown old.'

Then YHWH said to Abraham, –

'Why is it so that Sarah laughed saying, "Shall I indeed bear a child" and "I grew old"? Is there a thing too wonderful for YHWH? At the appointed time I will return to you, about a year hence, and Sarah will have a son.'

But Sarah denied, saying, – 'I didn't laugh' – for she was afraid.

And He said, –

'No, you did laugh.'

Then the men rose from there, and they looked down on the face of Sodom, and Abraham was walking with them to send them [on their way].

Timothy: A third text which revolves around the question 'Where?', in this case relating to Abraham's wife. This is not why we chose it; we chose it because this wonderful text shows us the blessings of welcoming strangers. It is a diptych with the following scene, the destruction of Sodom, showing us the curse resulting from abusing them. In welcoming strangers, we open our lives to the Lord. 'I was a stranger and you welcomed me' (Mt. 25.35). St John Chrysostom tells us that every parish should have its *xenon*, its place of welcome for the stranger. Today millions of strangers are fleeing war, poverty, social collapse, ecological disaster. Pope Francis insists ceaselessly that they should be welcomed as our brothers and sisters, especially in his marvellous encyclical *Fratelli Tutti!*

Before we look at how Abraham offers hospitality, let's acknowledge the widespread fear of welcoming strangers today, those who feel threatened by immigrants and do not wish to welcome them into their homes. Walls are being erected along frontiers all over the world. Millions of Christians feel deeply uneasy about the Pope's insistence on a welcome for the poor and the stranger. Do we dismiss people who are nervous of this hospitality as unenlightened, with closed hearts, unlike superior people like ourselves?

So let me make just a tiny point to start with: how can people welcome strangers into their homes if they feel homeless themselves, as so many do today? Maybe literally homeless, living on the streets. Or those who never get to own their own house, forever renting, never able to afford a mortgage. Or those who feel deracinated and without value in their own lands, culturally alienated. It is good to understand why they see immigrants as a threat. They must feel at home if they are to have homes to open.

Łukasz: You are right that this is a scene of hospitality and it is known as such in the Greek iconography as *xenodochia*, 'entertaining strangers' – in other words, hospitality – and yet it is quite clear that, although the visitors are veiled with mystery, they are not unknown. There is no moment of recognition, as when the disciples recognize the Risen Jesus in the pilgrim they meet on their way to Emmaus. The patriarch seems to know from the very beginning that he is not dealing with ordinary people.

The narrator depicts the scene as if through Abraham's eyes, half-open and dozing in the heat of the day. The three men appear as from nowhere, they do not walk up; Abraham suddenly perceives them as standing in front of him, as if expecting him to wake up from his slumber. One may even get the impression that it was the Three who waited for him to wake up. Abraham's hurry and running hither and thither are indeed like a reaction of someone who has overslept. Then he prostrates himself before them, and this is the same verb that elsewhere we translate as 'to worship'. He is not surprised in the least when his guest turns out to know the name of his wife.

Maybe you will agree, therefore, on a compromise that the three visitors and the host know each other pretty well. They are known strangers, or 'his strangers'. It is less paradoxical than one may think. A meeting or a dialogue with a total stranger would be simply impossible. Abraham and the three men share the same language, customs and even cuisine. To be fair, our contemporary challenges are far greater and the strangers we meet nowadays are far stranger than the aliens whom Abraham might have ever met in ancient Palestine. Ancient refugees were able to move to the neighbouring country, at most, and not thousands of miles away to a different continent, climate and model of family. That would have been not far away from a planetary trip or time travel. We have also more means to overcome this distance, but the conviction that the distance from some strangers will be eliminated within a few months of schooling and plenty of money is an ingenuous illusion. Some strangers will remain strangers forever.

Whom to recognize as a guest is a very complex matter, as complex as human relationships can be. We will receive a friend, a friend of a friend, even a friend of a friend of a friend ... But the more distant the relationship, the less there is an obligation of hospitality. One needs supernatural inspiration, as in Matthew's Gospel (Mt. 25.35), to believe that *all* hospitality will be reciprocated at the end. We believe that even if our guests will never answer with the same openness of heart, God will do so at the end of time. That can make us Christians look naive or even stupid if we are open to complete strangers, but Jesus' judgement does not leave us much space for excuses. Being hospitable is placed among other deeds of mercy: visiting the sick or prisoners and all people who cannot pay us back with the same. Still, we do count on the reciprocity that comes from the Lord, for his hospitality on the day of judgement. Those who receive strangers now – although strangers themselves – 'will come from the east and the west and from the north and the south and will recline at table in the kingdom of God' (Lk. 13.29). Universal hospitality opened to all, good and bad, makes sense in this eschatological Christian perspective, like meekness, humility, acts of mercy, or martyrdom, and evangelical poverty.

Timothy: Yes, Łukasz, I see what you mean, how the welcome of the unknown stranger, which we must offer today in our global village, only makes sense in terms of the end of time, when the Lord will welcome us all. It is an act that looks mad, a holy madness. This meeting of Abraham and Sarah with these strangers is just a step towards that crazy openness.

Let's look at how these 'known strangers' and Abraham talk to each other. When God addresses people in the Bible – Abraham, Moses, Samuel and so on – the usual response is 'Here I am!', the lovely Hebrew word *hinneni*. But the first three conversations at which we are looking point not to presence but to the absence of someone. Where are you, Adam? Where is your brother, Abel? Where is Sarah, your wife? These conversations each circle around an absence. The most anguished words in the Bible are Jesus' own groan at the apparent absence of God: 'My God, my God, why have you forsaken me?' Listening to the Word of God requires of us a presence. 'Here I am!'

This implies an active listening! But our deepest conversations, with God and each other, may also bring to light who is absent, or not there in some way. Who is missing? Who is left out of the conversation or absent themselves?

At the heart of this text is the hidden Sarah: 'Where is Sarah, your wife?' Her invisibility is not mere matronly modesty surely, otherwise why would it be remarked upon? She is betrayed by her laugh. Let's come back to that laughter later. The communication is veiled, through the walls of the tent which separate them. I suspect we can detect here a reluctance to welcome the strangers and talk with them and doubts about the promise they bear.

Łukasz: What a peculiar way to begin a dialogue with the host! No 'Thank you for the meal', or 'That was really some delicious veal.' The visitor asks where the wife is. He must have expected her to be there. It was not a request for information. This question expressed God's desire to communicate directly with her. The One who knew that Sarah was laughing hidden in her tent most certainly knew as well where she was. I think it was rather God's discreet tactic to make the absent-but-present Sarah listen attentively. Everybody around Abraham's table knew that tents have thin walls. It does not seem that Sarah finally showed herself. The Lord and Abraham's wife spoke without seeing each other. On the one hand, the Lord does not demand that Sarah appear; on the other, he lets her know that hiding from him does not make any sense.

Convincing you, Timothy, that meeting a stranger is a great adventure and a valuable experience is like preaching to the converted. I am not too different. One of my friends laughed at me, saying that at a party I would always approach the only person I do not know. Our extrovert nature helps us, so we have no merit in being open. We are both more like Abraham, who runs to the three men and invites them over for a meal and immediately throws this work on his wife!

If I may propose a bit of a psychologizing reading, Sarah seems to be the opposite, an introvert who needs the mediation of her rather erratic husband. God created us all with different predispositions, so there must be some value in this variety of attitudes. Ultimately, Sarah is no less hospitable than her outgoing husband. She must have done a lot of the work as well. This tandem worked perfectly at Mamre, and is true for so many couples I know. Without Sarah, Abraham would not have a home where he could invite his guests. Without the outgoing Abraham, Sarah would not be troubled: she would be without guests but also without the blessing of a new life.

In the modern world we move so much more than the ancient nomads that it is not always evident that one will find someone at home without an appointment. One of my brethren shared his most significant memory of his deceased mother. It was simply that she was always at home. Whenever or from wherever he would arrive, it was enough to knock at the door and the same voice would welcome him in. She *was* this home. Abraham was a nomad, had no stable house or locality, yet with Sarah hidden in his tent he was not homeless.

Usually the people that go through some crisis find it difficult to welcome guests. They are already strained by trying to keep their family or community together. Having a guest, a stranger, costs them so much and makes it so much more difficult to preserve this fragile balance. As you said, how can one be hospitable if one is homeless? I do not mean here a physical lack of building to live in but the lack of stable relationships. We can meet at a pub, but a pub is just a place. To be a host, one needs to have a home.

Timothy: I was struck, Łukasz, by the first sentence of your translation: 'YHWH made himself seen to him (Abraham) by the terebinths of Mamre.' God did not just appear, but actively showed himself in these three strangers, seen by Christians as a glimpse of the Triune God. In an Italian song, Abraham says, 'Non per caso siete passata oggi davanti a me': 'it is not by chance that you have passed before me.'

The distinguished head of a French publishing house lamented to me that, although his wife believed, and although he wished to believe, he had never encountered God. But we trust that God actively seeks to disclose His presence to us and so we must keep our eyes peeled in confident expectation. God seeks out the lost sheep, knocks on the door, appears at the entrance of our tents. We must be expectantly alert to the Divine coming to us in unexpected strangers!

There is a wonderful Inuit word: *iktsuarpok*. It means the feeling of anticipation while waiting for someone to arrive at one's house and intermittently going outside to check for them, scanning the horizon for their arrival. Abraham was sitting at the entrance of the tent and not sheltering in the interior with Sarah. He does not see them from afar, like the father who spots his prodigal son in the distance. As you say, suddenly they are there, standing before him. Then he unhesitatingly runs to meet them and prostrates himself, as if he had gone to sleep while waiting for them to come. When people come to me, do I give the impression that I can reluctantly spare them a moment of my precious time, or that I am eager to be with them? An English Dominican Provincial, Bede Jarrett, always wrote his letters and books in a drawer of his desk so that if someone came in, he could slam it shut and seem as if he had been doing nothing but waiting for them!

Philip says to Jesus before his death, 'Lord, show us the Father and we shall be satisfied' (Jn 14.8), but he has! We are more likely to have these blessed encounters if we go to the entrances of our tents, the gates of our cities, the places where our lives are open to those who are different, eyes peeled with expectant attention, for these are the places of epiphany. As you say, this is more natural for extroverts like you and me! We also need the home builders who remain inside, keeping the home going.

God may come in a grumpy teenager, or someone covered with alarming tattoos or a strange hair style, or the family of asylum seekers just arrived from Ukraine or the apparently uninteresting person next door. So I need to pray daily, 'Show yourself to me today', and sit at my tent door with my eyes open for the Lord who will surely come today!

Surely the Lord also shows himself to us when we receive hospitality from strangers. Driving through the northern Algerian Sahara with our brother Jean-Paul Vesco, now the archbishop of Algiers, after a long and difficult day, we were looking for a road to an isolated community of religious where we could spend the night. We spotted what seemed a possible road and asked a father and his sons in an oasis if it would take us there. The father looked amused and said, 'Not in that car!' But we could see no other way and so tried and after a while the road ran out into the sand. We looked and saw that they had followed us. The father said: 'We told you so, come and stay with us!' In fact we didn't, because they showed us another route, but I felt I had seen the face of God in the faces of these three unknown Muslims.

Abraham says to the strangers that he will offer them 'a morsel of bread', but in fact he prepares a celebration with the best he has and stands before them like a servant, awaiting their bidding. Our hospitality should not offer merely enough on which to survive. Ideally it should have a certain extravagance! The best food and drink. Our Spanish Dominican brother Pedro Meca was chaplain to the homeless in Paris and often slept on the pavements in solidarity with them. Every Christmas he celebrated the Vigil Mass for them in a vast tent and invited the best chefs of Paris to prepare a marvellous feast. Nothing is too good for the Lord when he comes to us in the poor!

There is also a marvellous extravagance in Abraham's language of welcome.

> My lords (*Adonay*), if then I have found favour in your eyes, do not pass by your servant. Let a little water be brought, wash your feet and lie down under the tree. And then let me bring a morsel of bread so that you may refresh your heart, and after that you shall pass on – for because of this you have passed by your servant.

His welcome is profuse, almost over the top! Contrast this with the thin and untruthful exchange with Sarah: 'I didn't laugh'; 'No, you did.'

So we should reach out to the stranger with the best of our words, the richest of our poetry, the most beautiful music, for the stranger brings blessings beyond our imagining.

Łukasz: We often abuse the word 'guest' and rob it of its fundamental meaning, which is close to 'friend'. The hotels and tourist industry will speak of guests whereas they simply mean 'clients'. We have in Polish the saying 'Guest at home, God at home.' I suppose most cultures will have the same quasi-sacred notion of a guest. We do not simply *feed* our guests, for one can feed an animal or a starving enemy. With a guest we eat what is best and kept for feasts; we celebrate, create or reinforce this relationship. That is why having guests costs us so much: attention, a certain diplomacy, creativity, energy, time and sometimes also money. We all know people who hate having guests, even family members. Often our guests give us double joy when they arrive but also when they leave. St Benedict, who had hospitality at the centre of his Rule, prudently asks the abbot to get rid of a guest who would be overbearing and full of bad habits. He also designates after how many days a guest should be put to work together with the rest of the community, and when he turns from being a venerable guest to a vagabond and a parasite. I suppose, as in so many social games, one can only receive a guest who wants to behave as a guest.

Hospitality is a free gift whose importance goes well beyond its market value. Receiving a gift as a gift – not a payment! – intends to reinforce the relationship. That is why, like any grace, human and Divine, a gift demands some reciprocity and response. As in a dance, friendship and love, there is a sequence of movements. It is less important who took the first step. I say a word, write a letter and wait … A response, gratitude, gift, invitation or word functions like an engagement ring: its real value goes well beyond its gold and its precious stone. It is a token, a promise that this relationship will continue and grow.

The three men never said they were hungry! Abraham, like a Polish mother (or Jewish – in Israel I learned that they are very much alike), invites them just for 'a morsel of bread' and treats them with a calf and cakes! They are not at all surprised with this generosity but play along the game of hospitality by answering with an even greater gift of a child: the one only God can give. This gift is also accompanied by a promise of another visitation: 'At the appointed time I will return to you, about a year hence, and Sarah will have a son.' In this manner, also the God-given son, Isaac, becomes something more than a beloved child of Abraham and Sarah. He will be a living proof of the Lord's generosity in the past, but also a token of the future ongoing relationship, an obligation of friendship which the Lord accepted of his own free will.

Timothy: Well, Łukasz, these three strangers will certainly count as excellent guests, since they do not outstay their welcome but are swiftly on their way. Let us return to Sarah's laugh. Is it a bitter laugh or filled with joy? Most laughter in the Old Testament is bitter, laughing with scorn at the downfall of one's enemies. And Sarah comes across sometimes as a bitter person. When Isaac is born, she is scornful of Hagar and Ishmael, 'Cast out this slave woman and her son' (Gen. 21.10). So it could be a scornful laugh that bubbles up inside her. For all these long years, this promise of a son has been repeated, four times, but nothing happens! Empty words! So, of course, confronted with her bitter laugh, she denies it.

But I am not so sure. For Abraham also laughed to himself when earlier the Lord announced that Sarai would be named Sarah because she would give rise to nations (Gen. 17.15f.). The Sarah who laughs here has her new name which is a promise even before she bears a son. Laughter is a quiet theme running through this part of Genesis, and the promised son will have a name which is etymologically connected with laughter. So might it be that in these chapters we see the laugh of bitterness and sterility transformed into the joyful laughter of the promise? This picks up the theme we saw in the two previous conversations, in which even the curse points to a sort of blessing.

And there is a detail which supports this. When Sarah says, 'After I have become worn out, shall I have delight?', I am told that in some Middle Eastern cultures it was believed that there could only be conception if there was orgasm. Fertility, it was believed, went with pleasure. Maybe she was doubting that old Abraham could give her pleasure again!

We might add that the fertility of our encounters with strangers also goes with pleasure. In the best encounters there can be a sort of flirtation, a playfulness. This is what Abraham anticipates when he sees the strangers. Sarah does not, but she will come to have it in Isaac, the one who laughs with joy. Do we laugh with joy when we listen to the Scriptures? Or do we behave like grim academics?

Łukasz: The text is quite clear that Sarah laughed 'inside her'; it was internal laughter. A fleeting moment and a very discreet one too. We have to look into her introverted world. Our emotional reactions are so complex, so I suppose if we asked Sarah why she laughed she would have to think quite a bit to discern what a peculiar mixture it could be; was it a bittersweet memory of fondling babies of other mothers, a self-deriding, stubborn hope that refused to die? I am not surprised she was afraid when the Lord asked, 'Why did Sarah laugh?' Maybe she barely realized she had laughed with a voiceless laughter in the tent. Her heart proves to be as transparent to the Lord as the curtains of her tent. *Omnia nuda et aperta oculos eius*: 'All is naked and open to his eyes' (Heb. 4.13).

Who would not fear? The fear of God is different from the fear of death or any natural danger. It is a witness of a true experience and depth of meeting with God. Because Sarah and the Lord met beyond the curtains. The hospitality, shared table, conviviality, all these did not lead her to the impression that these strangers are now somewhat domesticated, tamed and thus controllable. Quite the opposite! The closer one gets to the Lord, the more one knows Him, the more one discovers His 'strangeness'. Truthfully, in true and deepening relationships with human persons, a similar awe, respect, amazement and the unceasing experience of strangeness will never be eliminated by growing familiarity. Sarah's fear is a witness to the veracity of her meeting with the Divine guest she did not see.

It is unfortunately true that a party organized for a guest does not guarantee that we meet him or her truly. There is a risk of superficiality, of multiplied words that cover up the lack of meaningful words. The very famous icon by Andrei Rublev helps us by freezing the scene for contemplation. The painter places us in the perspective of Abraham: 'And he was standing, facing them, under the tree, and they ate.' We are slightly higher than the heads of the Three; we can see the surface of the table, the exchange of looks between the mysterious guests, their gestures. The perspective is open to the viewer: the table has four sides, it is my table and I can take my place at the table.

Andrei Rublev, *Trinity*, 1411 or 1425–7, The State Tretyakov Gallery, Moscow

Timothy: Wonderful, and it is usually thought that the chalice on the table represents the Eucharist, the ultimate banquet for all strangers in Christ. Here is the promised Son, son of God and, yes, of Abraham and Sarah. Here is the gift, which is Himself.

Intermezzo: Three Absences

Łukasz and Timothy: Our first three conversations have revolved around absences: *Where* are you? *Where* is your brother, Abel? *Where* is your wife, Sarah? We did not plan this sequence, but it is worth pausing briefly and asking how these three questions engage our lives differently. This is just to help us briefly digest what has emerged before we move on.

'Where are you?' is an invitation to Adam to come out of hiding so that God may engage with him and Eve in a healing and truthful conversation. Shame and fear hold them back. It is also our own absence that is in question. Our response to this invitation lies at the beginning of our listening to God. We are invited to come out of hiding and show ourselves before the face of God, which we both long for and dread. We want to talk with God but maybe are afraid of where it will lead us.

The second absence, of Abel, is a sort of consequence of this primordial disruption of our unashamed transparent presence before God. The overcoming of sibling rivalry will be the main theme of the whole Book of Genesis. Can we converse with God without being open to our brothers and sisters? The Revelation of God lights up their absence. We cannot become apprenticed in the delicate art of talking with God if we do not talk to each other: 'Those who say, "I love God", and hate their brothers, are liars: for those who do not love a brother whom they have seen, cannot love God whom they have not seen' (1 Jn 4.20).

What of the third quasi-absence, Sarah nearby behind the thin tent wall, but not showing herself? Sarah in many ways is unique. Her pregnancy stands at the beginning of a genealogy that will, Matthew will claim (Mt. 1.1–17), include all sorts of strange and unlikely characters, from Judah, who slept with his daughter-in-law Tamar by mistake, to David, who was a murderer and adulterer and so on. Herbert McCabe notes that 'God's plan is worked out not in pious people, people with religious experiences, but in a set of crude, passionate and thoroughly disreputable people.'[1]

So, then, how are we like her? We may hesitate to engage with God's fertile Word. What can it have to do with me? I might also hide in the tent, and listen, with a mixture of bitterness and hope, to the promises. But however barren, sterile or unsuitable I feel, I can experience how the fertile Word of God becomes alive in my life, in my body too, having my small and God-given part in the coming of the Kingdom. If we welcome strangers, who knows what will happen?

4

'What is your name?' (Gen. 32.23–33)

And he rose up that night, and took his two wives, and his two handmaids, and his eleven children, and he passed over the Jabbok ford. And he took them, and made them to pass over the *wadi*, and he made all what he owned pass through. And Jacob was left alone; and a man wrestled with him until the raising of the dawn. He saw that he did not prevail against him and he touched the hollow of his thigh, and he dislocated the hollow of Jacob's thigh, as he wrestled with him. And he said, –
'Let me go, for the dawn has risen.'
And he said, –
'I will not let you go unless you bless me.'
And he said to him, –
'What is your name?'
And he said, –
'Jacob.'
And he said, –
'No more "Jacob" your name will be called, but "Israel". For you contended with God and with men, and prevailed.'
And Jacob asked him and said, –
'Say then your name.'
And he said, –
'Why this? You are asking for my name?'
And he blessed him there. And Jacob called the name of the place Peni-el (The Face of God).
'For I saw God face to face and my soul was preserved.'
And the sun rose for him as he passed over Penu-el [*sic*], and he limped on his thigh.

Łukasz: Jacob's nocturnal encounter and struggle by the ford of Jabbok are mysterious, to say the least. The scene will always keep some of its oneiric mood and symbolism, and yet the event was not so confusing to Jacob himself. To get closer to his perspective one should keep in mind that this is not the first time that Jacob fought for a blessing. He was born as a second twin. The struggle with his brother, Esau, had begun in Rebecca's womb. Jacob seems to be predestined to this conflict as if he was set up by God, even before his birth, in a difficult situation and an unavoidable conflict. While still in his mother's womb, the second twin received a rather curious name, *ya'aqov*, which means 'he will supplant' or 'he will follow the heel' or 'he will assail insidiously'. Jacob was born grasping his brother's heel, *'eqev*. His fate and his very identity seem to be defined by the relation to Esau, his dissimilar twin.

At first, Jacob seems to be the main trickster in the story. Inspired and helped by his mother, he gained the right of the firstborn from his brother and later even Esau's blessing from his father. Isaac always preferred the firstborn, Esau, as Rebecca preferred Jacob. Blind Isaac had some doubts and before he gave his blessing he had asked the supposed cook of his favourite dish: 'Are you really my son Esau?' (Gen. 27.24). How bitter Jacob's victory must have been! He got a kiss from a disabled father by imposture. Isaac intended to kiss Esau not Jacob. The cheat got the blessing and yet had to flee abroad and to pay dearly for his success for 14 years. Even when his service to Laban, his father-in-law, finished, he had to use another ruse as if stealing his own family and property.

How could Jacob understand his relationship with the God of his father in this complex experience of life and his complicated relationship with his father? He cheated his father. Did it mean that he also cheated the God of his father? During his flight from Esau, he had this peculiar dream in Bethel in which the Lord repeated his blessing (Gen. 28.12–21). Jacob, though, responded to this experience with a conditional statement: 'If God is with me …, and I come back to my father's house in peace, then the Lord shall be my God' (Gen. 28.20–21). Before his return, some questions must have remained open: was the stolen blessing valid? Who was he to his father and who was he to God? Was he even living his own life or was he living a stolen life, maybe the life of his brother? Was his success his, or perhaps it was like a victory under a false name? Ultimately, who was he, Jacob?

By the ford of Jabbok, Jacob is about to enter the land of his father and face the reality he ran away from as a youth. He must have been afraid. That is why he first sent to the other side his possessions, his slaves, his wives and children. Now he is alone again, like the night of his flight from Esau, as if going back in time.

It is fascinating that Genesis states clearly that Jacob wrestled with a 'man'. It is a puzzling statement because further on, having won the fight and already in daylight, Jacob will say that he 'saw *God* face to face' (Gen. 32.30). An important strand of Biblical interpretation tried to solve this gap between wrestling with a man and seeing the face of God by imagining an angel (Hos. 12.5), as if a being somewhere between a human and a god could explain this.

Nevertheless, this disparity seems to be precisely the main point of this text of Genesis.

In the past, Jacob won his blessing via treachery, by hiding his identity in front of his father. He ran away from his wronged brother to avoid a face-to-face confrontation. Now, at Jabbok, he embraces an encounter with a man standing in his way. I do not know if Jacob is the patron saint of wrestlers – he should be – and of anyone who dares to face his fate in the darkness of crossing to another stage of life. There is no cheating this time. In this nocturnal encounter I can also see Jacob wrestling with himself, his past, his identity. Jacob's request for a blessing – once more! – seems to suggest that Jacob wants to be blessed this time as Jacob and not as someone else. Years ago he lied about his name; this time, asked by his opponent, he answered truly: *ya'aqov*, as if saying, I am what I am, a cheat – let's be honest – a trickster.

He fought honestly as Jacob, and this became a way to a new identity, something he did not ask for! He received another name: *yisra-el*, 'God will fight' or 'he will fight God'; of course, the ambiguity of this phrase is anything but accidental. The mysterious adversary explains the new name by shedding some light on Jacob's life. Behind all Jacob's struggles, with his brother, father, father-in-law and with himself, the second twin was ultimately wrestling with God, even if the Lord kept his face in darkness, remaining hidden behind human faces.

It is telling that, on the next day, when Jacob/Israel finally meets Esau, he says, 'to see your face is like seeing the face of God' (Gen. 33.10). By meeting God, Jacob learned something about meeting a man. Wrestling with a man led him to see God's face. I find Rembrandt's painting truly revealing in its depiction of the two opponents (see FIGURE 1).

Jacob seems to be stronger, because he manages to lift the angel. Even if the patriarch's face seems to be asleep, he keeps the angel in his clutches. And the angel? This one, by contrast, seems rather to embrace peacefully and lovingly the struggling Jacob, as one would a child.

Do our fights with God look like that to Him? For Him, all is simply love, while for us everything seems to be much more complicated. I think that actually the greater trickster is God and not Jacob. The subject in the name *ya'aqov*, 'he will trick', is God, not Jacob.

The face-to-face encounter leaves Jacob victorious, with a blessing, a new name and ... a limp. Was this scar something like Isaac's sacrifice and Abraham's circumcision, something of an embodied reminder, a sealing with unmistakable certainty? It was to confirm that this night was not a dream, not an illusion, and that the blessing did not miss its target; this limping body, no other, is its bearer.

We receive our faces, our identities, not by facing the mirror or inventing ourselves. We can make ourselves up, true, we can create travesties, give us ourselves new names, and even force others to use them. All that seems to me to be a waste of time at best, and at worst – a destructive illusion. We are who we are because we face other faces, human and Divine. It is a true encounter, not passive, and not simply receptive. Often, and maybe even always, it happens also through opposition, resistance, struggle or conflict with both a friend and an enemy.

Think of it for a moment: this new name of Jacob, *Israel*, which will become the name of the chosen people, does not sound pious at all! It is rather quite subversive. The Lord preferred and shaped Jacob into 'one who struggles with God', or into 'God's struggle' (which sounds like the two sides of the same coin). Let me note that we are truly far away from the word 'Muslim', which is derived from the one who 'submits' to God, an obedient one. Where there is no wrestling, neither are there arms to embrace. The God of Abraham and Isaac wanted to be the God of Israel to have someone to wrestle with or wrestle for. How else could love even be possible? A contention, resistance between brothers or wrestling with God is a sign that these relationships are real, that there is something to be grasped. My beloved is not just a reflection mirroring my ideas or preferences. Neither am I of his. If something resists you, it is a good premise that it is something real!

Timothy: Łukasz, my first reaction was to think that what you have said is so beautiful and rich that I was tempted to add nothing. This is why I have not interrupted for once, but just let you speak. But, hey, we are friends and that means that there should be a bit of wrestling between us! Difference is beautiful and fruitful, and in friendship difference is to be cherished. But in this case, much as I want to disagree, all that I can do is to complement your fascinating analysis.

First of all, I love the idea that *God* is the consummate trickster! Our Japanese Dominican brother Shigeto Oshida loved to say that God tricked him into becoming a Christian and a Dominican. He met a Catholic priest who deeply impressed him by his spiritual depth. But when he became a Catholic, he found that not all Christians were like this priest. He laughingly said that God tricked him into baptism! Then he met a wonderful, prayerful Dominican and thought we would all be like that. Tricked again!

Back to Jacob. Jonathan Sacks, the former British chief rabbi, wrote that Jacob's mistake was that he wanted to *be* Esau.[1] His life was dominated by trying to become his older twin. He claims Esau's birthright, his blessing, but perhaps most of all he wants to take his place as the one whom his father loves: 'I am Esau, your firstborn.' So he is trapped in a struggle which never lets him be himself. Sibling rivalry is the great theme of Genesis from Cain and Abel to Joseph and his brothers. One might say that much of the tension in the world today is riven by the sibling rivalry of Judaism, Christianity and Islam, the younger always seeking to supplant the one that went before.

On that dark night, alone, Jacob is just himself, as you said. He struggles to become free of a relationship that has stifled his life. Now his identity is bound up with his God, his new wrestling partner, and so liberated from constriction. Because he is free to be Jacob, he can be more than Jacob, Israel. He asks the stranger his name, and is answered with another question: 'Why this? You are asking my name?' The revelation of God's name and identity, and so of the identity of the one who wrestles with him, always lies in the future. The God of Abraham, Isaac and *Jacob* will reveal his name to Moses. And I shall be interested to see how you translate that, Łukasz! And even that is just one step on the way towards the revelation of the one whose 'name is above every other name, that at the name of Jesus every knee should bow' (Phil. 2.9) and whom one day we shall see as He is.

So Jacob is freed from a sterile rivalry with his twin, who came before him, into an identity whose fullness always lies in the future, as it does for every one of us. Who we are is yet to be revealed (1 Jn 3.2). We do not fully know who we are called to be. This is a liberation for our society, which is so obsessed by questions of identity: identity politics, ethnic identity, even gender identity. Of course, we need to be recognized for who we claim to be, but who we are most deeply is rich beyond our imaginings!

Jacob tried to steal Esau's blessing, 'the dew of heaven and the fatness of the earth'. But in the end Esau gets his blessing. When the brothers meet after the wrestling match, Esau tells Jacob that he has enough. The stolen blessing promised that the blessed one would be 'lord over your brothers, and may your mother's sons bow down to you'. That is exactly what happens when Jacob and his vast family draw near to Esau, prostrate themselves and call him Lord, *adoni*. So Jacob never succeeds in stealing the blessing. Instead he has his own, given to him by Isaac before he leaves to seek his wife. It is a different blessing: 'May he give the blessing of Abraham to you and your descendants' (Gen. 28.3). And that is why he too can say to Esau at the moment of their reconciliation, 'I have enough' (Gen. 33.1), which is sometimes translated as 'I am complete.' He is completely himself in being freed from rivalry and bound up with the unknowable God.

So there is no need for any sibling rivalry since each receives the blessing that is rightly his. Sacks writes: 'Sibling rivalry is defeated the moment we discover that we are loved by God for what we are, not for what someone else is.'[2]

I remain puzzled by Jacob's limp. It is, as you say, a reminder that the struggle was not a dream. The journey to the Promised Land will be slow and hard, limping all the way. The history of salvation is wrought through wounded and vulnerable people, like Abraham, who was a bit of trickster himself, passing off his wife as his sister to the Pharaoh, and David, the murderer and adulterer, and Solomon, both wise and foolish.

More generally, we can say that the Divine love always wounds us in some way. St John of the Cross dwells on this in his poetry:

O living flame of love
that tenderly wounds my soul
in its deepest centre![3]

Does the Divine love wound by breaking open our hearts, piercing our self-centredness, undoing our narcissism? We are wounded and so no longer self-contained; the all-enveloping skin is pierced. The French Dominican novelist Jacques Laval gave me a copy of his novel *Les Cicatrices*. He inscribed it with the words, 'For you Timothy, who in your heart know that our scars can become the gates of the sun.'

In our risk-averse society, we fear to be wounded, even by those whom we love. But unless we take the risk of getting hurt, keeping our skins unpierced, we shall be whole but alone, empty shells. To be bodily is to be vulnerable; to be invulnerable is to become no-body.

'And if they ask "What is His name?"', what shall I say?' (Exod. 3.1–14)

And God heard their groaning, and God remembered of his covenant with Abraham, with Isaac and with Jacob. God saw the sons of Israel and He knew.

Meanwhile, Moses was a shepherd of the flock of Jethro, his father-in-law, a priest of Midian. He led the flock beyond the desert and he came to the mountain of God, to Horeb. And the angel of YHWH appeared to him in a flame of fire out of a thorn bush. He looked, and behold: the thorn bush was burning with fire, but the thorn bush was not being consumed. And Moses said, –

'Let me turn aside to see this great sight. Why won't the thorn bush burn up?'

And YHWH saw that he had turned aside to see, and God called to him from the thorn bush and said, –

'Moses! Moses!'

He answered, –

'Here I am.'

And He said, –

'Do not approach hither! Slip off your sandals from your feet, for the place on which you are standing is holy ground.'

And He said, –

'I am the God of your father, the God of Abraham, the God of Isaac, and the God of Jacob.'

And Moses hid his face, for he was afraid to look towards God. And YHWH said, –

'I have clearly seen the humiliation of my people, who are in Egypt, and have heard their cry before their oppressors so I know their sufferings. I have descended to snatch them from the hand of Egypt and lead them up from that land into a good and broad land, a land flowing with milk and honey, the place of the Canaanite, and the Hittite, and the Amorite, and the Perizzite, and the Hivite, and the Jebusite.

'Therefore, behold, the outcry of the sons of Israel has come to me, and I have also seen the affliction with which the Egyptians afflict them. Therefore, go! I will send you to Pharaoh to bring my people, the sons of Israel, out of Egypt.'

And Moses said to God, –

'Who am I that I would go to Pharaoh to bring the sons of Israel out of Egypt?'

And he said, –

'For I am with you, and this will be your sign that it was I who sent you; when you bring the people out of Egypt, you will serve God at this mountain.'

And Moses said to God, –

'Look: I will go to the sons of Israel and I will say to them, – "The God of your fathers has sent me to you". Then they will tell me, – "What is his name?" What am I to tell them?'

And God said to Moses, –

'I am that I am.' And he said, – 'This is what you will tell the sons of Israel: I am has sent me to you.'

And again God said to Moses, –

'Thus you will say to the sons of Israel, – 'YHWH, God of your fathers ...'

Łukasz: Moses has one of the longest conversations with God in the whole of the Old Testament. It fills almost two chapters, and the passage cited above is just its opening. We do not know what Moses knew of his own story at that stage. We know he was rescued from certain death on the waters of the Nile. From Moses' perspective, this encounter with God at the foot of Mount Horeb was a great surprise, and yet the readers of the Bible get some glimpse of the Divine perspective. The meeting at Horeb was planned and is anything but accidental. It surprises Moses *in medias res* of his uneventful life of an outsider; the history of Israel catches up with the unsuspecting man and makes of him a leader of his nation, a hero within the story, a hero *tout court*.

Let us remember that at this stage Moses is not a young man. He has already had two lives! The first one was in Egypt, a life of conflicting identities, of strife, of a self-proclaimed judge, of an unwelcomed vigilante, of a murderer. The second life was in the faraway Midian: a second chance of life as a runaway renegade who managed to settle down as a husband, father and shepherd of not his own sheep …

Timothy: Until now, Moses' life has been rather purposeless, shapeless. Saved from the destruction of the Hebrew male babies, raised in the Pharaoh's own house, a life filled apparently with promise, and yet here he is, an old man of no importance, shepherding someone else's sheep in a place which seemed to be totally without significance. But it is at this moment, when his life seems to be at a dead end, that he encounters the Lord and discovers who he is called to be and what he has to do.

So many people have that feeling that they must be called to do something but have not discovered what it is. None of the 'vocations' on offer seems to match what they are searching for. Their lives do not seem to be going anywhere. But around the corner, in the most unexpected place – it could even be a supermarket car park! – and when one might seem to be past doing anything new, the Lord awaits.

And the Lord is there, waiting for Moses in his meanderings, because He has heard the cry of the Israelites and seen their affliction. Moses, this man, as you say, of conflicting identities who had had a bad relationship with his own people, does not look like an answer to their pleading for help, but we cannot tell God how He is to answer our prayers.

Łukasz: The burning-bush scene is like a theophany that God prepared just for one man, and truly any vocational experience has something of it. What impresses me most at the onset of this carefully described scene is the circumstance that Moses, being already mature, or even advanced in years, kept something as youthful as curiosity. We do not know why he went 'beyond the desert'. Was it necessary for the sheep or because of some spirit of adventure? Something inside or outside of him joined forces to push him beyond his usual paths: indeed, his third life was about to begin. It is a vocation narrative, and every vocation has something of this mysterious and incalculable push towards the unknown. It will lead to the ultimate Unknown!

Moses has the readiness and openness to face the unknown God whose ways are beyond human ways. This is what St Augustine called *docta ignorantia*, 'learned ignorance' – this paradoxical type of ignorance that seems to know something.[1] It does not know the precise shape of its aim, but it seems to know the way! It is almost like a second nature, a force of gravity, or the capacity to adjust to the magnetic field. *Docta ignorantia* unknowingly but constantly directs us towards the fulfilment of our dreams, happiness, the Kingdom of God, heaven, the aim of life – you name it – all these fundamental and imprecise realities that differentiate us from other animals.

This unease, inner desire and openness is the most precious and beautiful trait of youth. For sure, youth is more a spiritual than a biological state! For me as an academic teacher, it is fascinating to work with people who know that they do not know, people with questions and curiosity. Not having answers is not a problem. One will find the way towards the truth like water finds its way through the invisible pores and impossible channels to get out of a rock. It is only a matter of time before it gushes out in a spring, be it miles away. On the other hand, when I meet a question-less student, I feel helpless. They have eyes and they do not see, have ears and do not hear!

A question-less state results in a quest-less, immobile state. Someone may continue in this vegetative state for years, passing by the burning bushes, trampling holy grounds and failing to hear that their very name is being called upon again and again. Hopefully, some drama of joy or sadness will shake them and make their steps more cautious and watchful! Moses seems to be unaware of the existence of this Divine mountain; he clearly did not know that it was a particular place.

Timothy: God is like someone fishing who knows the bait to catch the fish he wants. For some fish it is a fat, wriggling worm or a fly or a sparkling lure that excites the curiosity of the fish.

Meister Eckhart, the fourteenth-century Dominican mystic, maintained that love is God's favourite bait. But here it is curiosity that will reel in Moses. Yes, curiosity is deeply attractive in another person. My good friend and brother David Sanders, who joined the Order the same day that I did, was endlessly curious about people, trying to understand what made them tick, and about almost everything.[2] When he got cancer, not long before he died, typically he bought a book on cancer, to try to understand what was happening in his life! This is quite different from the idle *curiositas* that Aquinas condemned,[3] which is an intemperate, ill-directed curiosity, which often goes with trying to show off and pretend that you are more learned than other people!

What provokes Moses' curiosity is the bush that burns and is not consumed! There is a mosaic in the monastery of St Catherine on Sinai, which shows Moses taking off his shoes and looking at the burning bush, which is covered with flowers. It burns and flowers at the same time! I expect that, when you went there, you saw what is claimed to have been the original burning bush, still staggering on. I was delighted to see beside it a fire extinguisher. If you see a burning bush, put out the fire! This is often our reaction to meeting God.

But what is so significant, so Divine, about the fire that burns and does not consume? The encounter with God is often seen in terms of meeting fire. John the Baptist warns the people that 'He shall baptise with the Holy Spirit and with fire' (Mt. 3.11). At Pentecost the Holy Spirit comes down upon the people in tongues of fire for, as Moses noted by the end of his life, 'our God is a consuming fire' (Deut. 4.24; repeated also in Hebr. 12.29).

Might it be that ordinary fire turns everything into itself? A burning bush ceases to be a bush and becomes just a fire and then ashes. But the Divine fire, the infinite vast, burning life that is God, transforms us into ourselves, like the fire in the kiln of the potter which creates the pot. The fire of the one who says I AM, gives us to be! The disciples on the way to Emmaus say, 'Did not our hearts burn within us?' They are ignited and become what they are called to be, disciples of the Lord.

Łukasz: Moses was more curious than fearful, but there was something more than pure curiosity. He did not want only to see a sight; he wanted to know 'Why?' While we are writing these words, the world is shocked by the ongoing war in Ukraine. A peaceful continent proved to be a dangerous place. Why? I relearned my Russian to try to observe the painful process through which some Russians gather strength to awaken to the dreadful reality and begin asking, 'Why?' If that question is awakened and maintained, I am at ease that sooner or later a person or a society will regain some access to the truth and freedom. If not, the long slumber risks inadvertently turning into an eternal dream built of shadows: without real people, without relationships. According to Dante's vision, the deepest hell is not flaming hot, it is frozen.

Timothy: I suppose that there are two great 'Why's. The why of existence. Why is there anything rather than nothing? Why is there love? Why and what is beauty? And the terrible 'Why' of evil and destruction. This is the horrific 'why' that bubbles up inside us when we see the horrible events in Ukraine that you mention. And it penetrates our own lives too. Why do I sometimes hurt those whom I love? This is the mystery of the destructive urge. These opposite 'Why's are like matter and antimatter. This is not the place to explore these questions, which have haunted humanity since the beginning. Maybe all we can say is that the mystery of existence, of the fire that burns and does not destroy, embraces and transcends the mystery of nihilism.

Our most profound conversations are animated by the Why of the burning bush and not by the Why of the fire which burns up everything and leaves only ashes or, in Ukraine as we talk, ruined and burnt-out buildings and dead bodies.

Łukasz: Although from the very beginning what happens to Moses is inscribed into the great national history of Israel, it never ceases to be also his personal story. YHWH called him twice by name – 'Moses! Moses!' – as He called young Samuel sleeping in the sanctuary in Shiloh (1 Sam. 3.10) or like the Risen Christ calling upon Saul (Acts 9.4). In the Biblical stories we sometimes encounter anonymous people who have one task to fulfil; afterwards they disappear from the horizon, remaining unnamed. It is true that one does not need to know the name of the postman, even if the letter he or she brings is the most important letter of our lives. Yet there are also some Biblical missions that take a lifetime, and there are the tasks in which the identity of the mediator is of fundamental importance. Typically, this is the case of kings or any ruler. Finally, there are also these mysterious Divine elections that cannot be explained by one's task, one's job. Ultimately, God is not that interested in finding skilled workers; he is interested in finding friends, someone with whom He will speak face to face (Exod. 33.11).

It is not surprising that Moses asked 'Why me?' He is right in pointing to counterarguments to this Divine choice. For the Egyptians he is an outlaw; even for his own people he is nobody. Far away from Egypt, from the sons of Israel, without authority, he did not have even the power of words, the charisma of an eloquent leader. A similar experience touches many people even today. It is especially acute in the case of those who entered the religious life, like you and me, or a similarly visible change of one's life. Why me?

One can give many reasoned answers, but if our decision concerns choosing a person, unavoidably we follow also our intuition, memories and sympathies. We open all our unnamed physical and spiritual senses when we choose a companion, a friend or even a simple collaborator. Why would you prefer to have a walk with this person rather with another? Why do you choose this brother to be your prior? The more involving and deeper the relationship is, the more hidden before us are the reasons for our preferences. 'Why me?' is a question of everyone who discovers that he or she is loved, chosen. YHWH did not want just anybody to fulfil his mission. He wanted Moses.

Timothy: Why me? When Montaigne is asked why he loved Etienne de la Boétie, he replies: 'Because it was he, because it was I.'⁴ When we love someone, it is because they are who they are and I am who I am. They share a little of the mystery of our God whose name is I AM. We have a tiny glimpse of them as God sees them and delights in their being. Josef Pieper says that we say of a beloved friend, 'It is marvellous that you exist.'⁵ Our love is ignited, and if it is indeed of God, then it will not consume the other person. I suppose that one could say that with God's grace we are all little burning bushes, even if sometimes we can feel a little burnt out!

Getting back to Moses, it does seem to be typical of God to choose people who seem completely unsuitable! That is so that the fiery grace of God may shine out all the more brightly. St Peter, who wobbles all over the place, is called to be the Rock. St Paul, persecutor of Christians, and perhaps not an easy person, is chosen because 'my grace is sufficient for you, for power is made perfect in weakness' (2 Cor. 12.8).

Moses is, as you point out, the great outsider. Distrusted by the Hebrews for being a murderer and an Egyptian by adoption, and distrusted by the Egyptians for being an outlaw, he is no one's and everyone's. Outsiders summon us into the larger space, the spaciousness of the Promised Land, the wider tent. And this prophet who must announce the Lord cannot even speak without a stutter! Why me? God could have replied: because you, old man, are the most unsuitable possible!

Łukasz: One should never underestimate a stuttering preacher! There is more chance he actually ponders his words. When I was a teenager, my faith was awakened thanks to a conference given by a stuttering student. There is something unusual in the sequence of God's approaches to Moses; God first calls Moses and then immediately tells him to keep away. This dialogue sounds a bit as if Moses found himself on a minefield where he should mind each of his steps. It seems that this ground was holy, inaccessible to the people, because YHWH decided so. Yet why create distance? Does it make sense to call on someone and stop him or her from approaching?

When a person makes it clear that he or she has some boundaries – that is, that they retain some control as to whether another person is allowed to come close or is held at a distance – such behaviour is not necessarily a move excluding the relationship. On the contrary, it makes the true meeting possible. Some gates need to be opened, some thresholds to be consciously crossed. It makes possible the growth of both: the relationship and self-knowledge. The experience of a certain distance triggers our moves. A kiss or even sexual intercourse can lead the relationship further when it happens in a meaningful way, when it can be refused, when it is not taken for granted. One enters these gates only by invitation.

God deals with us in the most true and responsible way. When one states, 'We are still far away from each other', it does not mean it is hopeless. God did not intend to keep Moses away forever. Quite the opposite! When God reveals the distance, He intends to put us on the way to get closer to Him. This is exactly what happens in YHWH's message to Moses: leave now, so that you may return and climb the holy mountain! Moses cannot encroach upon this holy ground, and yet the mission he receives contains a promise for the future meeting and future closeness. Moses *will* climb the holy mountain, and he will enter the dark cloud. Following this experience, the whole people will receive the gift and means of approaching this God: the tent of meeting, the curtains of the sanctuary that will visibly manifest the fact that one is approaching the invisible.

Timothy: Yes, holy places often orchestrate the dynamic of drawing near and keeping a distance, of invitation and holding back. It makes me think of the Temple of Jerusalem, the surroundings of which you, Łukasz, showed me. A series of walls with gates which invite and exclude, progressively reducing the sort of people who can draw close, until finally there was the Holy of Holies, which only the High Priest could enter once a year. One is invited to enter a holy place such as a cathedral, but not to rush into the sanctuary and presumptuously sit on the bishop's throne!

Moses must draw close to the Divine presence slowly, beginning with the burning bush, coming near but held afar, before ascending the mountain and being wrapped in the cloud. He must become accustomed to the Divine presence, like the diver in the deep sea who must ascend into the light of the sun only slowly, otherwise he or she will suffer from decompression sickness.

This same dynamic, as you say, is there in when we love people. Aquinas wrote that: 'in love the two become one, but remain distinct'.[6] We draw close to people in love and yet let them be. We should not devour them. When we love we grow in intimacy, but also we give each other the most precious thing, which is space. I went on holiday with David Sanders for many years, and part of the pleasure was that we hardly talked to each other before 4 p.m. We let each other be.

Moses before the Burning Bush, sixth century, St Catherine's Monastery, Sinai

In that mosaic of Moses at the burning bush in St Catherine's Monastery he has one bare foot, and he looks at God's finger obediently as he unties the other, rather neat sandal. Bare feet are a sign of humility. Slaves had bare feet, and Moses will be called 'the slave of God' in the Septuagint. When the prodigal son comes home, his father says, 'put sandals on his feet' (Lk. 15.20). He is restored to his dignity as a member of the family. We come into the presence of God with humility.

Being barefoot gives one a sort of immediate contact with the soil, from which we are made. Our feet are planted on the humus from which we get the word 'humility'. We are grounded. For me, being barefoot is one of the signs of being on holiday from all pretension! Gerard Manley Hopkins's poem 'The Grandeur of God' brings together the fire of God – 'The world is charged with the grandeur of God./ It will flame out, like shining from shook foil' –but also bare and shod feet – 'All is seared with trade, bleared, smeared with toil;/ And wears man's smudge and shares man's smell: the soil/ Is bare, nor can foot feel being shod.' Alienation from the soil is also an alienation from ourselves, for we are, like Adam, earth creatures.

Łukasz: When Moses asks, 'Why me?', one expects that God would begin his answer with 'Because you …' And yet the Lord did not explain his choice by speaking of Moses' qualities. Instead, He pointed to Himself, as if saying, 'It is not just about who you are but about who me, who I am!' This answer also points to the name by which YHWH will present himself in the next phrase. 'For I AM with you.' The Hebrew verb *ehye* can be also rendered in the English future tense, 'I will be', or by some modal verb like 'I can be.' The use of this Hebrew form is interesting in itself, but here I am more impressed with the preposition *'im'*, 'with'. One can easily recognize it in the well-known name *'immanu-el*, God-with-us.'

You may laugh, Timothy, but the Church Fathers knew well that prepositions make theology! The great treaty of St Basil of Caesarea *On the Holy Spirit* is largely a study of the Greek prepositions used in the Scriptures. There is something deeply theological in the fact that God, who is beyond space and time, presents himself by the preposition 'with' – by the relationship to something as ephemeral as human beings. The full depth of this desired connectedness was revealed by the Son through his relationship with the Father and His Spirit. This 'Being-with' is the quality of the internal life of God; and, since God is love, it reveals something of the essence of love as well. When two lovers promise each other 'I will be *always* with you', it is a great intuition but also something never fully attained. Not even physical presence guarantees this intensity and effectiveness, and no human can literarily promise it!

Timothy: Łukasz, I would never laugh at a preposition! Yes, this is the greeting we repeat in the Eucharist: 'The Lord be with you.' It is the paradox of the Divine presence that God is both in us, at the very core of existence, and with us. God's intimacy is liberating because it is free of all rivalry. We cannot compete for space because God has made the space. Perhaps the ultimate challenge in our loving each other is to purify it of all rivalry and competition, except when one is playing Scrabble of course! Our closeness to our friends does not oppress them but gives them space to be.

Łukasz: Moses is very indirect in asking about God's name. He depicts a hypothetical scene in which, as he imagines, the Israelites would ask, 'What is His name?' Would it mean that they had forgotten the name of their God? Maybe they never knew the name of the God of their fathers, so – apparently – suddenly raise the question. Maybe this question is intended to check whether this strange originally Israelite, Egyptian-educated, Midian-interbred Moses even knows the proper name of their God? Maybe they presumed that this God has many names, as the Egyptian gods had?

It does look as if YHWH first avoided giving the simplest answer and gave us this cumbersome riddle: *ehye asher ehye*. I decided to translate it as 'I am *that* I am' to keep its meaning as open for interpretation as the original is. This was, by the way, also the choice of the King James Bible. The relative particle *asher* can introduce almost any relative clause: 'who', 'what', 'that' and 'because'.

There are whole books devoted to this phrase, and I am not going to list all their richness and possible meanings, but I suppose that, as often happens with the Scriptures, this self-presentation both uncovers and covers God's identity. I will give you now some examples of possible translations: 'I will be who I will be' – a tautological avoidance of the answer; 'I will be because I can be!' – an appeal to confidence; 'I am who I shall be'; 'I shall be who I was'; 'I am because I am'; 'I am who I am'; 'I will be and that means that I will be'; 'I am the one who is'; 'I am whoever I am'; 'I am, surely I am!'; 'I remain who I was to be'; and so on.

Timothy: Gosh, Łukasz, I had hoped you would give me the definitive answer as to what it means! I don't know anyone better qualified to do so. Perhaps all of those possible translations can either be seen as evasions of the question or else they point to God's simplicity. God is who God is. For Aquinas, God's essence and existence are the same. Or, as one modern scholar put it, God's whatness and His thisness are the same.

We need not exist. Our existence is a gift. God just is. And we are complex creatures, filled with unresolved tensions, desires pulling us in different direction. Victor White, an English Dominican who was a close friend and pupil of Carl Jung, talked of 'the anarchic self'.[7] Jesus said that 'a kingdom divided against itself cannot stand' (Mk 3.24). We conflicted, complex beings draw near to the burning bush, with reverence, hoping to be healed of our internal conflicts, our multiple personae, and seek a tiny bit of the simplicity of God, who simply is.

Our conversations with God in prayer, or even our conversations with each other, should be healing of our interior divisions, our self-deceptions and help us to drop our masks, and stop the silly games (but not the enjoyable ones!), so that we may be at peace in ourselves and with each other, children of the one who says I AM. Maybe it is only in the Kingdom, when we see God face to face, that we shall resolve all our internal tensions, conflicts of identity, and simply be.

Intermezzo:
What Name?

Timothy and Łukasz: It is worth casting a glance back over the two last conversations before we move on. In both, Jacob and then Moses put the question to God, 'What is your name?' Jacob puts it bluntly, as suits this fighter and trickster, Moses more tentatively: 'What shall I tell them if they ask?'

Jacob and Moses are both people whose own identity is rather confused: Jacob because he has been fighting with Esau and others all his life, defining himself against them, and Moses because he is born a Hebrew, was raised as an Egyptian but has left both identities behind and lives as a Midianite.

Both are in some sort of exile when they pose the question, but both are coming home to themselves. Jacob at last meets God as Jacob, not pretending to be anyone else. Moses returns to his own people. Both seem to be unlikely candidates for their task, the limping fighter and the stuttering prophet. Yet they both see God face to face: Jacob sees Him when wrestling with the stranger in the night – 'For I saw God face to face and my soul was preserved' – and Moses will see God face to face on the mountain. One in the darkness of the night, the other in the dark cloud.

Might it be that those who must raise the question of *God's* identity are those who have been somehow searching for their own? Rabid nationalistic or fundamentalist religion cements people sure of who they are to a God made in their own image and likeness. God does not answer Jacob's question directly, but he gives Jacob a new name, and future generations. God is disclosed indeed as the one who is the God of Abraham, Isaac and Jacob. But the name disclosed to Moses transcends any genealogy. God is not called the God of Moses. One can only respond to this new name with worship. Already implicitly God is revealed as the One to whom all nations are called to hearken.

6

'What is it for you here, Elijah?'
(1 Kgs 19.8–18)

He got up, then he ate and drank. Then he went in the strength of this food forty days and forty nights up to the Mountain of God, Horeb. There he came to the cave and he spent the night there. And behold, the Word of YHWH, – to him! And it said to him, –

'What is it for you here, Elijah?'

And he said, –

'I have been so full of zeal for YHWH, God of Hosts! For the sons of Israel abandoned your covenant! Your altars they have thrown down, and your prophets they killed with the sword! Then I was left, I alone. And they have been seeking my life to take it!'

And He said, –

'Go out and stand on the mountain before YHWH.'

And behold, YHWH was passing by and a great and strong wind was shattering the mountains and crushing the rocks before YHWH. Not in the wind was YHWH. And after the wind: an earthquake! Not in the earthquake was YHWH. And after the earthquake: a fire! Not in the fire was YHWH. And after the fire: a voice, a thin whisper, silence ... When Elijah heard *it*, he wrapped his face with his cloak. Then he went out and stood at the opening of the cave. And behold, towards him, – a voice! And it said, –

'What is it for you here, Elijah?'

And he said, –

'I have been so full of zeal for YHWH, God of Hosts. For the sons of Israel abandoned your covenant. Your altars they have thrown down, and your prophets they killed with the sword. Then I was left, I alone. And they have been seeking my life to take it.'

And YHWH said to him, –

'Go! Return to your way, to the desert of Damascus. And you shall arrive there to anoint Hazael king over Aram. And Jehu, son of Nimshi, you will anoint king over Israel; and Elisha, son of Shaphat from Abel Meholah, you shall anoint for a prophet in your stead. And it will happen that whoever escapes from the sword of Hazael, Jehu shall put to death. And whoever escapes from the sword of Jehu, Elisha will put to death. Then I will leave in Israel seven thousand, all the knees that have not bowed to Baal, and every mouth that has not kissed him.'

And he went from there and found Elisha son of Shaphat ...

Timothy: At the centre of this fascinating conversation God puts yet another question: 'What is it for you here, Elijah?' This time it is not about absence: Adam and Eve hiding from the sight of God, the absence of the murdered Abel, the absence of Sarah hidden in the tent. It is about presence.

What is it for you here, Elijah? Why are you here? Or perhaps: what is there here for you? This is not the question one might put to someone who has turned up unexpectedly: 'What brings you here?' God knows why Elijah is here and has His angel sustain Elijah with food on the way when, after his triumph over the prophets of Baal, he flees the fierce Jezebel, who seeks his life. Why has he left his home territory and come to this mountain in the wilderness, where Moses too encountered the Lord? Moses was on his way to the Promised Land, whereas Elijah has fled it. What then is his life for?

Yet this question is one that we all ask ourselves sometimes. What I am here for? I began a sabbatical in the École Biblique in February 2020, which is when I first got to know you, Łukasz. I was pondering a similar question: 'What is there for me to do?' I had written what I thought would be my last book; I did not expect many more years of fully active life. What comes next? What does the Lord want of me? Have I got a last task or two? I did not realize that I would end up by writing a book with this bright young Polish scholar! But the question persists and always will: 'What I am here for?'

Most of us pose this question several times during our lives; when one finishes one's education and wonders what is one's vocation; at some later stage, as one contemplates a new career, or at retirement; and most acutely when one loses someone whom one loves. Why am I here? What is the point of my life? Why get out of bed every morning? Like Elijah, one may feel exhausted and at the end of the road and in the wilderness, as I found myself after my massive operation for cancer. But it is in the desert that the answer is given to Elijah. And also when we find ourselves in the wilderness, unsure of the way forward, that we may hear the call of the Lord anew and discover the next stage in our lives.

Łukasz: My curiosity was rather triggered by the brazen repetition in the dialogue. Why ask the same question twice? And why twice the same answer? Was it rude or ironic? They are literally identical, word for word, and in Hebrew they are even repeated dot for dot (in the Masoretic system, dots express vowels).

I suggest that something would have changed through the repetition. Biblical Hebrew script does not have exclamation marks. I have introduced them in the translation in the first of Elijah's answers, as one usually does, rather arbitrarily. But I decided to remove them from the second one. I have an intuition that after 'a thin whisper, silence' the prophet would not have raised his voice. Once a partner in a dialogue lowers their voice, it is more than natural for the other to do the same.

We keep saying the same things, pronouncing the same phrases. It happens not only during a single discussion – we repeat them for years. Yet rarely do they mean exactly the same thing. Maybe especially with the most fundamental statements, such as 'God loves me', for example. We spend all our lives learning what these three apparently simple words mean: who is God, what is love and who I am. At the age of 15 going on 17, one pronounces this sentence enthusiastically and from the bottom of one's heart, but the progress in understanding does not end then. At the age of 45 or 75, even if we are only just alive and aware, we are still discovering the meaning of 'I' with its glories and miseries. Through this experience, we grasp more and more what a persisting and stubborn thing 'love' can be, when it connects us to always the same and yet always surprising One, whom we and others call 'God'.

Timothy: Yes, and in the same way, one will probably ask or be asked that same question 'What is it that you are here for?' several times in one's life, and the answer one arrives at may become deeper, but not necessarily clearer, as was the case with Elijah. Sometimes early in one's life one has grand plans about the part one will play in the world. A priest in the US spotted a young man who came to Mass every day and was very devout. So he asked him, 'Have you ever wondered whether you might have a vocation to be a priest?' The lad paused, thought and replied, 'No. I think I have a vocation to be a bishop!'

Elijah fled the land where he was at the centre of dramatic events, but even in the wilderness, far from home, he still remains the centre of the story that he tells. 'I have been so full of zeal for YHWH, God of Hosts! For the sons of Israel abandoned your covenant! Your altars, they thrown down, and your prophets they killed with the sword! Then I was left, I alone. And they have been seeking my life to take it!' It is all I, I, I alone. He is here to insist that the Lord plays His part in Elijah's story. Everything is about Elijah!

'What is there for you here, Elijah?' Maybe it is only after the repetition, after the encounter with the thin silence, the barely audible voice of God, that he can bear to grasp the implications of what the Lord is to tell him. Actually, in the great drama that is unfolding, he will no longer be at the centre of the narrative. His story is not ultimately about him. He is to anoint other people who will henceforth drive the action forward, Hazael and Jehu. And, most disconcerting of all, he is to be succeeded by another prophet, Elisha. Elijah must get out of the way. And it is simply untrue that he and he alone remains, because there are seven thousand who have not worshipped Baal or kissed him. Notice the contrast between the worshippers of Baal who must grovel and kiss his feet and Elijah who *stands* upright on the mountain before his God (1 Kgs 18.20 ff.). In the drama of God's plans for Israel, Elijah has never played the unique role that he thought. Soon he must get out of the way. He will disappear into the skies on his fiery chariot (2 Kgs 2.1 ff.).

He is one of the pivotal figures in the story of our salvation. People will mistake John the Baptist and even Jesus for Elijah returned. But in the end, like all of us, he must let go the centre stage and yield his place to others, as the old must always hand over to the young. Is that not so, Łukasz? Has he misunderstood his very name? It means: 'YHWH is my God.' Not '*my* God', who must be my supporter, and look after my plans, but my *God*, whom I must serve and whose plans I do not know.

St John Henry Newman famously said:

God has created me to do Him some definite service. He has committed some work to me which He has not committed to another. I have my mission. I may never know it in this life, but I shall be told it in the next.

I am a link in a chain, a bond of connection between persons. He has not created me for naught.[1]

So a deeper understanding of why I am here may go with ceasing to care too much what it is. God knows, and that is enough. In the previous conversation we saw that it was incomprehensible why the Lord chose Moses, that outsider. With Elijah there is even the loss of an understanding of why he has been chosen at all!

God's command to Elijah, as to us, is both liberating and disconcerting: Your life is not about you. One gets up each day and tries to respond to whomever one encounters, not knowing what fruit it will bear or what role it will have in God's plan. God knows, and that is enough. God is the Lord of the harvest. Terry Eagleton claims that 'the most flourishing acts are those performed as though they were one's last, and thus accomplished not for their consequences but for their own sake'.[2]

Do I want *my* God to serve me, responding to my crises with dramatic interventions on my behalf? Has my God got a useful role in my plans? Or do I serve the Lord whose plans for us all are achieved with infinite discretion, so that one might even not know what they are or that He is there at all.

Łukasz: What happened after the first exchange of words, after this, as you perceived it, slightly self-centred answer of the depressed Elijah? The Lord was passing by – and the elements of the universe announced it loudly. The earth trembled, but Elijah did not. He was all ears. His perception and judgement, that 'YHWH was not there', is described by the narrator. The man who fearfully ran for his life, one afraid of Jezebel and his brothers, concentrated on recognizing the passing Lord. Hidden in the cave, the man of God was listening to storms, earthquakes and perceiving the great fire – all that to grasp and recognize something more important – the voice. All these mighty phenomena were like an intermezzo within their dialogue.

The noisiest and loudest voices are not necessarily most important. Some of them cannot be escaped, like the stun grenades in my Jerusalem neighbourhood I can hear now, but they are not the most important voices of this city and definitely cannot become the most important voices in my life. There is something deeply glorious and wise in the image of Elijah listening to the uproar of the world and at the same time seeking to grasp the one silent and most important voice.

Wind, fire, earthquake – were they to display the power of the Lord? To reaffirm
Elijah's conviction that his God is strong enough to dispose of his enemies?
The reader is left to guess. The dire situation of Elijah did not change; there
were still people 'seeking his soul'. Yet now the Lord sends his prophet back to
this same dangerous world. The world did not change; apparently Elijah did,
invested with even greater power than the mighty of his days.

Sieger Köder, *Elijah at Horeb* (*Elija am Horeb*), Sieger-Köder-Museum, Ellwangen

I can see something similar in the vision of the Horsemen from the
Book of Apocalypse. These galloping horse riders – war, greed and death –
who make the history of the world are truly dreadful. They have been
ravaging the world for thousands of years, and even now they do not seem
to be slowing down. There is yet another horse and his rider – 'the Winner
who is set to win' (Rev. 6.2).

The Lord does not diminish the danger; he does not even try to discuss
with Elijah whether his perception of events is correct or not. The prophet

heard these stark words, 'Return to your way!' Instead of discussing with Elijah, God sent him on a new mission. Elijah was afraid of one queen, now he is to change two ruling dynasties! Elijah sent on his way is more dangerous than the kings of Israel and Aram together. Elijah does not need protection, any more than an unsheathed sword or a flying arrow. At the moment of departure from this world, his disciple Elisha will acclaim him as 'the cavalry of Israel and its rider!' (1 Kgs 2.12). Elijah proves to be a one-person army!

I cannot help but see in the dialogue on Mount Horeb the same demanding master that we see in the parables of Jesus. He gives great authority to his servants and demands great things. The seemingly depressed, or at least frustrated, Elijah finds here not much of a consolation but new force and a new mission, maybe even more important than the missions before.

Timothy: Elijah's drama has hitherto been all thunder and explosions. His God has intervened to burn up the sacrifices on Mount Carmel with consuming fire. This is what Divine action seems to look like. Indeed, when we looked at the conversation of God with Moses, the Divine seemed to be intimately connected with fire. But God is not in the storm or the earthquake or the fire, but in the infinite discretion of a gentle whisper, a voice that keeps on questioning us. Even a silence that speaks most penetratingly.

Does this mean that it is the beginning of a conversion, a transformation in how he sees God? Just a beginning, since the dialogue is repeated, even if without the exclamation marks. Not yet a conversion from violence, since the voice will initiate events that will lead to a lot of people falling by the sword. But a small step towards the belief that the Divine power is a voice that speaks a word, a Word that would eventually become flesh in a man who refused all violence and who some thought was Elijah returned.

You, Łukasz, are living in a world blasted often by blind forces, rockets and air strikes. Not far away is Iraq, a country almost destroyed by violent Western intervention, 'Shock and Awe'.[3] Yet I have heard the quiet gentle voices of our Dominican brothers and sisters there speak with more power than all the guns in the country. Whose are the quiet voices 'of thin silence' who are speaking in our world, probably despised as unimportant but who are God's agents in bringing in the Kingdom?

Łukasz: Maybe it is a matter of measure or comparison. We do believe that God is omnipresent. A small but meaningful voice is more effective and therefore more powerful than the forces that lay waste to the earth. The narrator said at first that 'the Lord was passing by'. Wind, earthquake and fire process by as if God's expected manifestations. The thrice-repeated 'not there' actually presumes that He could have been there. He was seen as fire on the same mountain when meeting with Moses a few centuries before. This 'thin voice' arrives as something of a surprise. It seems to me that this sequence of the ever-growing power of His messengers – wind, then earthquake, then fire – suggests that the last manifestation, even though the most discreet, is also the most potent.

To be clear, the Bible never speaks of God as a source of violence, that is, of unfair oppression. It does present Him as a source of agency, even in its most vehement, irruptive forms. God has no trouble reshaping the material world; it is easier and simpler for Him than for my will to move my fingers writing these words. And yet, in dealing with humans, God needs something more effective, more powerful than earthquakes, storms or pandemics. For a while we can be impressed by them, but we can get accustomed to pretty much everything.

You mentioned the conflicts in and around Jerusalem, where I live now. It is becoming all the clearer to me that violence is a spiritual matter and that is why it can be overcome only when the human spirit is won over. No 'successful' bombing of Gaza, of Tel Aviv, of Baghdad, will achieve that. This cannot be accomplished by any military success, or just by killing 'the bad guy'. Military success can lead to temporary ceasefires but not to the end of violence. People claiming that they ultimately ended violence with violence are either liars or stupid, or both. War will continue as long as some people think of others as their enemy. Wars begin before the first explosion and end long after the physical violence ceases. Violence originates in human heads, not in explosions; therefore, it is now – as it has always been – a spiritual matter.

I cannot but think of the first chapter of Isaiah, where God speaks like an old-school desperate teacher who realizes that his chastisement is ineffective: 'Why do you seek further beatings? Why do you continue to rebel? The whole head is sick, and the whole heart faint' (Isa. 1.5). Indeed, no punishment makes sense unless the offender accepts it together with his guilt. Physical strength is a kind of power, but it is too weak to deal with our spirits. What changes us are ideas, words and voices. Words, and not only these Divine words, are in this domain more powerful. It should not be surprising, since we have in common with the very omnipotent Creator not muscles but language! That should make us think and weigh our words …

We may pretend that we do not believe in the power of words and voices; it does not matter. In the human and therefore spiritual realm, words are mightier than a voiceless storm, quakes and fire. For good and bad, as with any power. We target with words another's brain and heart with more precision than any sniper could dream of. Meaningful voices can end or begin violence. They are the power to be reckoned with. Politicians know it. Some preachers seem to forget about it, unfortunately. Yet any human being is given this power, greater than storm, earthquake and fire.

Timothy: That is why the Revelation of God is not just an account of the marvellous things that He has done, as Mary proclaims in the Magnificat. It is our patient education in how to listen to God and how to speak. God makes us his strong friends by engaging us in conversation, most powerfully in the thin, small voice of silence. This is why we are writing this book!

'I am young. I do not know how to speak'
(Jer. 1.4–10)

There was the word of YHWH to me, saying, –
'Before I formed you in the belly, I knew you. And before you came out of the womb, I consecrated you. I appointed you a prophet for the nations.'
Then I said, –
'*Ahah*! Lord YHWH, look, I do not know to speak, for I am a youth.'
And YHWH said to me, –
'Do not say, I am a youth, for to all to whom I will send you, shall you go, and all that I will command you, shall you speak. Do not be afraid in face of them, for with you [it is] I to deliver you' – the utterance of YHWH.
Then YHWH sent his hand and touched my mouth. And YHWH said to me, –
'Look, I have given my words to your mouth. See, I have today appointed you over the nations and over the kingdoms, to uproot, and to tear down, and to destroy, and to demolish, to build, and to plant.'

Łukasz: Is it relevant that, as I write this, the night in Jerusalem is hot and noisy? Does it matter that I am writing just a few miles south from Anathoth, the village of Jeremiah? The question of what to skip in a story is as important as of what should be included. As often happens in Biblical narratives, Chapter 1 of Jeremiah gives us only the essence, the bare bones, of the event. Nothing more, nothing less. Maybe it is better so, because our mammalian curiosity – for apparently, all mammals are curious – could lead us astray. I would bet that simply nothing else mattered when Jeremiah exchanged words with the Word.

Everything is told from Jeremiah's perspective, for it is he who tells this story. The dialogue was so intimate that no one else could have heard it. There is no lightning, there are no shimmering angels, trumpets or any preparatory signs. No winds or earthquakes, or fire as for Elijah on Mount Horeb. Instead of those awesome displays, there is the great intimacy of a tête-à-tête encounter.

Jeremiah does not say simply, 'The Lord came to me.' He describes what happened to many a prophet through a peculiar phrase: in the Hebrew literal wording it is 'And the Word of the Lord happened to [or "became towards"] me.' There is no verb of coming, approaching or movement. The Word of the Lord just appears, 'to be' there with a preposition 'to', at the door of Jeremiah, without any sign of weariness caused by a long journey from heaven, not unlike the three men who appeared suddenly before Abraham in the heat of the day.

There was no greeting, presentation or introduction. No hesitation on Jeremiah's side, such as, for example, 'Are you talking to me?' No doubts about the identity of the speaker or the person addressed. Nor does Jeremiah mention the mediation of some external or internal voice. Was it a voiceless Word?

There is at least one more striking detail. Although Jeremiah will hear many words of the Lord, he speaks of the appearing *Word* of the Lord, in the singular. Is this grammatical singularity significant? It is repeated so often elsewhere that I bet it is not accidental. Jeremiah must have had, already at this first encounter, the impression of a completeness, the wholeness of the message, and maybe an experience that the Lord has said everything.

In the first sentence, the Word says to Jeremiah, 'I have known you.' It almost sounds like a phrase from some thriller: 'I/we have been watching you.' If a human being began a conversation in this manner, the one addressed would shiver, be angry or laugh.

Yet 'I knew you before I shaped you' sounds more intimate. It is like some knowledge reserved to a parent or a hidden identity of a hero revealed by an old wet nurse. Indeed, the first revelation given to Jeremiah concerns his very person. God presents Jeremiah the prophet to Jeremiah the youth. It is something that Jeremiah did not choose, did not decide upon. He learns that he was thought of, planned, shaped to be 'a prophet to the nations', whatever that might mean ...

Timothy: I agree with you completely about the utter focus of this encounter, with no extraneous detail. But I must confess that I envy you living not far from Jeremiah's village. Marie-Dominique Lagrange OP, the founder of the École Biblique, where you are teaching, wanted it to be in the Holy Land, for the land itself teaches us, its geological formation, its seasons and even its heat.

This first meeting of young Jeremiah with the Lord is wonderfully intimate, as you say. It has all the intensity of the relationship of a parent addressing a child. How do we live that two and half thousand miles away and two and half thousand years later? Are we listening to a scene which somehow excludes us, an unrepeatable encounter? After Pentecost all the baptized are prophets. St Peter quotes the prophet Joel: 'In the last days it will be, God declares, that I will pour out my Spirit upon all flesh, and your sons and your daughters shall prophesy' (Acts 2.17).

Most of us would hesitate to say that we have heard the Lord speak face to face with us as Jeremiah did. Saints like St Teresa of Avila did, and St Catherine of Siena wrote the *Dialogue* of her conversations with God, but I have never heard an audible word from the Word. But this does not mean that we are not addressed. For me to live is to be spoken into existence by a word of love addressed only to me.

God says to Jeremiah: 'Before I formed you in the womb I knew you, and before you were born I consecrated you.' The word from which I spring is a 'voiceless word', as you say. So my deepest identity, the source of my being, lies in being addressed by God even if I never hear an audible word. God speaks each of us into being, one might say, with a single word, that should overflow in all the multiple good and creative words that we speak during our lives. St Catherine said: 'In holy self-knowledge ... we see that we were loved before we came into existence, For God's love for us compelled Him to create us.'[1]

Sometimes when I hear the gospel during the liturgy or reading in my room, it feels as if it is directed to me. This was St Francis of Assisi's experience when he heard the gospel commanding him to sell all that he had and give to the poor and felt impelled to do so. This is not because Jesus had Francis in mind when he spoke these words to the rich man but because we are all shaped by the one Word which is uttered to us, the Word that was 'to' Jeremiah, as you point out, and is 'to' each of us. Each of us is, one might say, a word uttered by the Word.

So we all listen to the Scriptures with what Ben Quash called 'a kind of expectant attention'.[2] Listening to God's Word is not accidental to my humanity, like listening to some wise person whom I might or might not have encountered. I am most deeply someone who is addressed by God. If someone whom I love addresses me tenderly, it is as if I am suddenly enriched. Yes, this is who I am. And so to be addressed by the One who is Love Incarnate is to be touched at the core of my being. I am made to receive this living bread as cows and sheep are formed to eat grass. That is the foundation of the prophetic vocation of each of us.

Łukasz: Jeremiah first spoke in response just '*Ahah*'. It is not even a word that would refer to anything, a meaningful noun or a verb. It is just an exclamation, like a voice devoid of words. It is curious that St Jerome in his translation (the Vulgate) added another syllable to this reaction of Jeremiah and wrote: 'A, A, A'. Thus the youngster becomes even more like the stuttering Moses.

After this interjection, as if echoing the Word's 'I know', Jeremiah said, 'I do not know.' I don't think that he meant, 'I cannot speak', since he was pronouncing this very phrase; rather, he meant something like 'I cannot speak well enough.' In answer, the Word, like a professional speech therapist, corrected him: 'Do not say, I am a youth.' It is not exactly polite to dictate to one's interlocutor what they should say. And yet this is not some small talk. It is impossible to have that with the One who knows more about you than you do yourself. The Lord knows not only Jeremiah's past, but he also informs him of the future: 'You will go, you will speak.'

When the Lord says 'Do not be afraid', He makes clear the cause of Jeremiah's hesitation; it is not simply his young age but his fear of being faced by other people. Jeremiah excused himself saying '*because I am* a youth'; in a significant development, God echoed this phrase but changed the perspective: '*because I am* with you'. The cure for Jeremiah's fear is God's presence, and not the suggestion that the obstacles were not real. The success of the mission is warranted by the Lord, not by Jeremiah's qualities. A coach or a certain type of well-intended parent would say in every situation, 'You can make it!', or something similarly vaguely encouraging like 'Everything will be all right!' Since no human being can promise such things with lasting credibility, people want to become more convincing, and that is why they raise their voices or repeat the phrase. The Lord does not need it. We do not know if this argument was enough to convince Jeremiah. Maybe the Word of the Lord never intended to convince but rather wanted to inform or even to perform something more profound?

Timothy: I had never before noticed that Jeremiah's first word is this inarticulate *'Ahah'*. This prophet who will proclaim powerful words that build and destroy, begins with a sort of groan, a sigh. And he goes on repeating the exclamation time and again, as does Ezekiel. It is as if the underlying signature tune of these two great speakers is a struggle to find for words. The prophets stutter, as you say. You mentioned that you owe your vocation to a stuttering preacher. This is immensely reassuring when so many Christians are searching for a voice in the Church and finding it difficult to find one. This is especially so if one feels ignorant of the complexities of theology, unable to tell the difference between a homoousios and a hypostasis!

Yet the Word gives powerful words to people who are not formally theologically educated, such as St Catherine of Siena, who addressed popes and the Roman Curia without fear! Or the Curé d'Ars, St Jean Vianney, who struggled to complete his studies for the priesthood and whose Latin was even worse than mine!

Perhaps being inarticulate, struggling to find words that do not come easily, is the burden of the true prophet. In the Old Testament the great prophets are often those who do not feel up to the task, such as Jeremiah or Amos, who even said, 'I am not a prophet nor the son of a prophet' (Amos 7.14). The false prophets speak with too easy a facility! No one can say anything of depth without becoming silenced at least for a while. One of the great British poets of the twentieth century, David Jones, a Dominican layman, gave to one of his poems the first words of Jeremiah, 'A, a, a, Domine Deus'. We must stutter before we speak; we must be empty before we are full.

We may be born inarticulate, like the peasant Platon in Tolstoy's *War and Peace*, whose simple words finally give Pierre, the agonized hero of the story, repose since 'he felt that the world that had been shattered was once more stirring in his soul with a new beauty and on new unshakeable foundations'.[3] Or some of us become inarticulate as we dwell at the edge of what can be said or are rendered inarticulate by illness. One of my Scottish brethren, Anthony Ross, who was a great preacher and Provincial, was felled by a stroke and was reduced almost to silence. I went to see him before I moved to Rome in 1992 as Master of the Order, and he said just one word to me, 'Courage', which was bread for my soul for a long time.

Pope Francis summons the whole Church to embark on the synodal path, in which we listen attentively to all the baptized, on whom the Spirit of the Lord is poured. This must include those who initially only manage to say '*Ahah*'. Will we have the patience and the humility to do so?

Łukasz: At this point in the narrative, we learn from Jeremiah: 'the Lord sent his hand and touched my mouth'. Something similar happened to Isaiah in Isaiah, Chapter 6; maybe there the gesture was more dramatic because the seraph touched Isaiah's lips with a fiery charcoal. Indeed, during a significant meeting often something happens to our bodies as well. Can a peace deal be valid and carry weight without the former enemies shaking hands? What else can better express 'I am with you' than touch? No words can replace seizing someone's hand.

Yet what about someone's lips? This goes beyond psychological reassurance. I can think of very few things which the hand of the Lord touched that did not melt! See Amos 9.5: 'He who touches the earth and it melts'! There are the famous two stone tablets written with the finger of God (Exod. 31.18). It seems that God usually wrote with his finger, as the hand wrote on the wall of Balthasar's palace (Dan. 4), or in the person of Jesus writing on the sand.

Why wouldn't He turn Jeremiah and his body into a tablet, scroll, book with his finger? Further in his book, Jeremiah will speak of the broken covenant and promise a new one written on the hearts (Jer. 31.33). There is something very intimate in touching one's lips, in moving the *devarim* – in Hebrew this means both 'words' and 'things' – from one mouth to another. Touching one's mouth is like feeding, or a sort of kiss, a profound unity: your lips are my lips. How can one be surprised that Jeremiah's words become fiery and of Divine might, destructive and creative, ripping to pieces and bringing life?

We do not hear Jeremiah's *fiat*. His fearfulness, hesitation, his sense of not being ready, his ignorance of himself, of the enemies, of God – all

that must have faded when the Lord's hand touched him. I know you, I
am with you. What more is needed to go on? If this is true, everything is
possible, even being a prophet for the nations.

The scene seems to end at this point. Or does it? Jeremiah never said
that the Word left or that it was not any more. We will keep reading again
and again in the Book of Jeremiah that 'The Word of the Lord was.' Like
constant arrivals without departures, one high tide after another. Isn't that
what the Word said: 'I am with you'?

Detail of the Incipit of the Book of Jeremiah in the Winchester Bible, 1150–75

Timothy: You point to the intimate touch on the prophet's lips and
mouth. Another very bodily acceptance of the prophetic task is to eat
the word God gives us. Ezekiel is commanded to eat the scroll which is
covered with 'words of lamentation and mourning and woe' (Ezek. 2.1)
and it is sweet in his mouth. In the Book of Revelation John in turn is
told to take the scroll and eat it (Rev. 10.8). The word of the Lord is not
just addressed to our minds, but is food to be devoured and savoured, to
be internalized, part of our bodily being. We speak God's word not just
in what we say, or struggle to say, but in how we are, our bodily existence.

The Word becomes flesh, our flesh, our lips, our mouths, our faces. A story of the Desert Fathers recounts that

> three Fathers used to go and visit blessed Anthony every year and two of them used to discuss their thoughts and the salvation of their souls with him, but the third always remained silent and did not ask him anything. After a long time, Abba Anthony said to him, 'You often come here to see me, but you never ask me anything,' and the other replied, 'It is enough for me to see you, Father.'[4]

You commented when we Zoomed last Sunday on that terrible scene (Jer. 36) when the king slowly cuts up Jeremiah's scroll, made of skin, of course, and tosses the bits in the fire. It is as if Jeremiah is being dismembered himself. Maybe some of us bear in our bodies, on our skin and in our mouths the signs of a word coming painfully to birth. Martyrs speak their word through their suffering. St Damien of Molokai, canonized in 2009, ministered to lepers in Hawaii until he contracted the illness and died of it in 1889. His body, scarred by leprosy, became in itself a word of prophesy, reaching out to those marginalized and abhorred because of their illness, a Word made flesh in his body.

Łukasz: I began by talking of the personal encounter of Jeremiah and the Word which was 'to' him. You have been very attentive to what is universal and 'for all' in Jeremiah's dialogue. Let me now direct your attention back to my original perspective. I dare to say that this dialogue makes central the experience of uniqueness, election and something 'not for everyone'. This is precisely an essential quality of meeting with God – it is and it must be unique.

Jeremiah never asked the question 'Why me? Why not my brother, my neighbour?' I must admit I have never asked this question. I have always believed, maybe too naively, that they have their dialogues with the Lord, their vocation, their mission, their intimacy with God. God is for all, but not in the same way that a landscape or a superstar could be accessible for a whole crowd of people. There is something in the Word that was only for Jeremiah, and maybe only Jeremiah could hear it. And the particularity of this address is universal. It is the case for everyone.

There is another important consequence of this exclusivity. There is nobody and nothing that could relieve me from meeting the Word within

me. When the Gospel is read, I can wish that the others listen to it as
well. But this is a simple distraction if I consider that their listening could
replace my listening. The Word, whenever it appears, is always directed to
me. It is never an accident, an overhearing.

There is something else very particular in this dialogue. Jeremiah
presents himself as *na'ar* a youth, a young man old enough to marry.
There's something unique in Jeremiah's biography – he is the only Old
Testament person explicitly asked by God to remain celibate. You and I,
we both live this kind of life – as Jesus and Paul also did later – it is not
for everybody.

The young listen differently from older people. You, who seem to have
kept much of the youthful spirit, will surely agree with me! A youth will
admit more easily to some ignorance and be more open, ready to learn
and discover. Youth is also the time of decision-making, of discovering
and choosing one's path. Facing the unknown, the world, embarking on
an adventure, a journey – to set forth one needs magnanimity, even the
risk of a little naivety!

I do not think I am just ingeniously cheering up both of us when I
write that, when one meets the Eternal, everyone is objectively in the
position of a young person. And maybe more, such a meeting can restore
one's youth. Talking to God makes us young and ever younger. Not in a
sense of immaturity but rather in the sense of giving us back our freedom
to be young. Talking to the true God liberates me from the temptation
and illusion of being a little god myself: a bit of an omniscient figure,
enthroned among other similarly ridiculous little gods who just know
how to run and fix the world. A caricature of an old bore who, unlike
Jeremiah, knows very well how to speak but hasn't a clue how to listen.
Unfortunately, my experience tells me that young biological age does not
save one from this vice of elderliness.

I am deeply convinced that we deal with our fellow humans in the same
way we deal with God. What else could we do? The elements of surprise,
revelation, discovery, disagreement, self-discovery and the search to create
some unity – all of them can be found in our true dialogues.

Timothy: Yes, I agree that each of us has our personal encounter with
the Lord, the word spoken to us and heard in the privacy of my heart.
But sometimes our friends help us to hear it. I love Caravaggio's *Call of
St Matthew* in the church of St Louis des Français, in Rome. Matthew
is bent over his money, absorbed by the dead coins. He does not hear

the Lord who is summoning him, his finger pointing at the tax collector from the other side of the canvas. But nearly all the other figures do see, and they seem to be telling Matthew, 'Listen, he is calling you!' The word is addressed to Matthew, but his friends are opening his ears. And this is my experience of these conversations. We are helping each other to listen to the Word.

'Is it good for you to be angry?'
(Jon. 4.1–13)

And [this] great evil displeased Jonah and he was enraged. And he prayed to the Lord and said, –

'Please, O Lord! Was this not my thought while I was still in my land? This is why I first fled to Tarshish, for I know that you are a gracious and compassionate God, slow to anger, and abounding in love, and relenting from evil. And now, O Lord, please take, I ask, my life from me, for my death is better than my life.'

And the Lord said, –

'Is it good for you to be angry?'

So Jonah went out of the city and sat down to the east of the city and he made for himself there a booth and sat beneath it in the shade until [such time] that he might see what might become of the city. And the Lord God appointed a *qiqayon* plant and it went up over Jonah to be a shade over his head to protect him from his evil. And Jonah was greatly delighted on account of the *qiqayon*. And God appointed a worm when dawn arose the next day, and it struck the *qiqayon* and it withered. And it happened, as the sun rose, that God appointed a scorching east wind and the sun struck upon Jonah's head. And he became faint and he wished for his life to end and he said, –

'My death is better than my life.'

And God said to Jonah, –

'Is it good for you to be angry over the *qiqayon* plant?'

And he said, –

'It is good for me to be angered to death.'

And the Lord said, –

'You have shown pity on the *qiqayon* for which you did not labour and which you did not grow, which came to be overnight and perished overnight. But I, should I not show pity on Nineveh, the great city, in which there are more than a hundred and twenty thousand humans who do not know their right from their left and many animals?'[1]

Łukasz: The story of Jonah is very peculiar. It reminds me of some good animated films for families: there is a plot for children and another plot for adults. Parents and children laugh but not necessarily at the same moments or for the same reasons. I cannot make up my mind whether the Jonah story is ridiculous and funny or is dramatic and maybe even tragic. A parody makes us laugh but it touches on some not very laughable attitudes or problems. The Book of Jonah is a serious joke or a funny philosophical parable.

This final scene is also the first true conversation between Jonah and his God. At the beginning, God gave Jonah a very straightforward task: go to Nineveh. Nineveh was not just any sinful city: it was the capital of the bloody Assyrian empire. In the Biblical canon, we can find the Book of Nahum, another of the Twelve Minor Prophets, where the dreadful demise of Nineveh is announced. Jonah would love to have got that mission! In the first chapter, after God's 'Rise and go!' Jonah did not say a word, he rose … and fled in the opposite direction from Nineveh!

Jonah delayed his mission as long as possible, and even when he made it to Nineveh he did as little as possible in his preaching: no rhetorical arguments, no attempts to convince, no miracles, no promises of forgiveness, just a plain announcement of doom. It would take three days to cross this great city, and Jonah had only been gone for one when God's message worked. Honestly, Jonah seems to be the worst prophet ever. If he succeeded, anyone would. It makes me think that God could have sent just anybody if He had only the salvation of Nineveh in mind. It is quite clear to me that God did not need Jonah for this mission. The mission to Nineveh was aimed at Jonah as much as it was aimed at the city.

Timothy: This is indeed a ridiculous and comical story. Jonah is an absurd figure. Perhaps it holds up a mirror so that we can see that we ourselves are rather ridiculous figures, especially when we are being indignant about the sins of others and climbing on our high horses.

He is the worst of prophets but also the best. He converts a whole city, as you say, in a day! Maybe this was because he is preaching to the inhabitants of Nineveh about his own worst failing. The crime of Nineveh is 'the violence that is in their hands' (Jon. 3.8). But the prophet of non-violence is himself filled with violence. He longs to see the city consumed by God's wrath. It is beautifully ironical that his name, *Yonah,* means in Hebrew 'dove', the symbol of peace after the Flood, but he is anything but dove-like! Perhaps he is a powerful preacher because he understands in the depths of his own heart the violence which he denounces. Indeed religion often seems to be deeply tempted by violence. All over the world today we see Jonahs, religious prophets demanding the destruction of their enemies. We need to examine our words of faith for any traces of violence.

I suspect that we are most eloquent when we talk about what we are worst at. On one level we understand the traps, the seduction, of some failing: in this case, violence. But at the same time we do not know it, and so continue to be aggressive. When I was a young friar, I was bowled over when one of the senior brethren preached a brilliant homily on community life. He had never struck me as being very good at it. When I raised this with him, diplomatically of course, he replied, 'Of course I can preach about it precisely because I know that I fail so badly.' So if you want to know the secret failings of a preacher, ask what they talk about best! Every half-decent homily is a word of hope which the preacher needs as much as anyone else. There is an early Dominican prayer: 'Give me the grace to be a preacher for my own salvation and that of others.'[2]

Yes, as you say Łukasz, 'the mission to Nineveh was aimed at Jonah as much as it was aimed at the city'. When we speak of our faith or the life of virtue, we always, in a sense, first address ourselves as the people who most need to change. Otherwise we will come across as repulsively patronizing! Vincent McNabb, a Dominican of my Province over a hundred years ago, said: 'Love those to whom you preach. If you do not, don't preach. Preach to yourself.'

With the grace of God, our failings and sins may bear fruit in words that offer help to others who find themselves where we have been. In an episode of *The West Wing*, a brilliant TV series about American politics, the Chief of Staff of the White House tells the story of a man who falls down into a hole.[3] A doctor walks by, and he cries out, 'Help', and the doctor drops down a prescription. A priest walks by, and he shouts 'Help', and the priest throws down a prayer. And then when he calls for help to the third person, he drops down into the hole beside him. 'But now there are two of us in the hole.' 'Yes, but I have been here before and I know the way out.'

Łukasz: Yes, Jonah claims to know God all too well. On the raging sea, when the sailors had no idea what was the cause of their trouble, Jonah was the only one who knew. He also knew how to calm the storm. He knew what to say to the Ninevites. He knew that the Divine forgiveness was as real as God's wrath, suspended above the despicable Nineveh and the beloved city of Jerusalem. He knew the Divine name, the same that YHWH revealed to Moses when Israel sinned venerating the golden calf:

> YHWH, YHWH, God of compassion and of favour,
> slow to anger, great in faithfulness and love,
> keeping faith for thousands, bearing iniquity and transgression and sin.
> (Exod. 34.6–7a)

Jonah knew all that, and indeed his worst expectations were fulfilled: the enemy city made penance and the doom he announced came to nought! His mission succeeded as expected. What a shame!

Jonah definitely knows something, in the sense that he has some true knowledge of his God. Yet he definitely disapproves of God's plans. There is something very essential that Jonah does not know.

Timothy: Isn't it true that, when we speak of God's love and mercy, we touch on truths that always exceed our understanding? According to Aquinas, we can truly say that God is beautiful, one and loving, but these are statements that exceed our understanding, since we cannot grasp what it means for God to be God. Jonah really does know that God is merciful, but he cannot grasp fully what that means, and never could have imagined that it would take the form of a man dead on a cross having endured all the violence of the world. And nor do we when we stand in easy condemnation of others, blustering with absurd anger.

Łukasz: Would Jonah oppose the Divine mercy shown to himself or his people? Was he simply a small man with a small heart, a chauvinist? Or maybe the source of his anger is more profound because Samaria and

Jerusalem were not spared: his cities were destroyed, their women raped, children slaughtered, the survivors enslaved. Why did the Ninevites convert, together with their king, whereas the Israelites with their kings did not, even though so many prophets shouted out on their streets? Yes, there can be some deep bitterness when grace touches the children of strangers and your own people remain doomed.

We should take Jonah's anger seriously. It reveals something that he sees as unjust. Jonah is not the only one who thinks that mercy and forgiveness have something of unfairness and absurdity. Should not the right to forgive belong to the wronged? Who besides our victims has the right to say 'I forgive you'? And if they are dead? Indeed, without God, who gave them life, there is no one to take this burden away. Sometimes the guilt is so great that one needs heroic faith in God to accept forgiveness, even in the sacrament of reconciliation. Jonah was scandalized with God's mercy, and he is not alone.

Timothy: Yes, Jonah's anger is entirely understandable. Why should these foreigners, who have caused so much suffering to God's chosen people, be pardoned after just one day of repentance whereas Israel must endure defeat, destruction and exile? 'It's not fair', the cry of children through the ages, who have an acute sense of justice. Indeed, I remember with embarrassment often crying out as a child, 'It's not fair, Mummy', when my younger brothers got away with something!

Yet surely the readers of Jonah's book knew something that Jonah did not, which is that Nineveh did not escape the destruction for which the prophet longed, demolished by the Medes in 612 BC. One of our brethren, Richard Ounsworth, suggested to me that the *qiqayon* plant may be an image of Jonah's preaching. Like his preaching, it lasts but a day. His words protected Nineveh from the evil that was to come, just as the plant protected Jonah from his evil, the same word in Hebrew. But the relief of the Ninevites was short-lived. Maybe their repentance was like the seed sown on rocky ground (Mk 4.5), which springs up and is then burnt by the heat of the sun, as Jonah was when the plant died. How one reads this depends on what you think is the end of the story. The sparing of Nineveh in Jonah's time? It's later destruction? But for us, the only end of all stories is the victory of mercy.

What does this little book say about our conversations with God? For one, it should make us question what it means to say that God 'chose us in Christ' (Eph. 1.4). The Israelites too are God's chosen people, and for Jonah this means that God has chosen to dwell in their midst in the Temple. Jonah thinks that he can flee from God by running away from Jerusalem. When he is in the belly of the fish, he prays: 'Shall I look again upon your holy Temple?' Israel belongs to God, but also, it seems, God belongs to Israel! Jonah is the son of Amittai, which means 'My Truth'. It is as if God's people claim the fullness of God's truth. Those unchosen Ninevites deserve to get it in the neck!

This narrow, exclusive understanding of being chosen is subverted by the Book of Jonah. The choice of Jacob did not mean the rejection of Esau, who had his own blessing. God's wide compassion and love reach out even to the animals of Nineveh, who charmingly call upon him and put on sackcloth. God's compassion is beyond the compassion of 'My Truth'. Holy places do not render other places unholy. We worship the God who gives 'life to all things and makes them holy' (Third Eucharistic Prayer).

Being God's chosen is, according to the Bible, very uncomfortable and humbling, because it means living with the Holy One who demolishes our illusions and invites us into the truth. There is no sacred text that is as self-critical as the Bible, the Old and New Testaments. Being chosen does not mean being lifted above everyone else in glorious superiority but means constantly letting one's understanding of God and his ways be put into question. Jonah finds his elitist sense of superiority demolished. Being chosen does not mean that we are especially protected. James Finley wrote: 'As a person ripens in unsayable intimacies in God, they ripen in a paradoxical wisdom. They come to understand God as a presence that protects us from nothing, even as it unexplainably sustains us in all things.'[4]

Often it means the opposite of protection, that we must share God's own vulnerability. Do we in the Church dare to let the light of God's truth shine on our self-deception, arrogance and complacency? Throughout history, peoples and nations have justified violence against others by claiming to be chosen. I grew up as a child believing the British Empire was God's gift to humanity. We were a chosen people! As a Pole you may find that hard to believe! I came to realize very slowly that this justified so much cruelty and injustice. The United States of America then inherited this same claimed identity as God's chosen. Hundreds of millions died in the last century in the name of the 'chosen destinies' of Nazism, Communism and some forms of unbridled Capitalism. Yes, I believe that we are 'chosen in Christ', but this gives us no easy superiority.

Election does not protect us from getting hurt. It is not a Divine insurance policy. Rather, like Jonah, it should call the Church to self-scrutiny and transparency. A city set on a hilltop cannot be hidden, as we discovered so painfully in the sexual abuse crisis.

Łukasz: Jonah's plea for death reminds me of the similar scene with Elijah in 1 Kings 19. First, he had this smashing success when he brought fire from heaven on Mount Carmel. Instead of the expected final victory, it enraged his enemies and Elijah had to flee, helpless, exhausted and convinced that he was the last just man on this earth. It sounds both dramatic and ridiculous, like the suffering of a hypochondriac: it has the seriousness of true suffering, but it is also as absurd as it is egocentric.

God asks Jonah a great question: 'Is it good for you to be angry?' It is a good question for an egocentric: let each of us begin with him- or herself. Does this attitude of self-righteousness and sulking bring you any good? Why would you inflict pain on yourself? How will this change the general situation? It is almost like a cautious friend or a parent who does not want to infuriate the 'righteous sufferer' by shedding some doubts on his perception of the world. God simply wants Jonah to begin to think about his anger, suffering, frustration and, ultimately, about his perception of the world.

God makes Jonah live through a series of small, actually quite insignificant events that may allow him to experience even just a bit of God's compassion and love for all living things. Jonah took pity on the plant that protected him for a day. He could compare the world with this plant to the world without it. Jonah felt the heat of the sun and suffered this inconvenience. Indeed, compassion has necessarily something of a passion, a kind of suffering because of the pain borne by someone close.

In the case of the Creator, the compassion is almost the reverse of His omnipresence: He is close to all beings and therefore, close to their suffering. As He chose their existence when He made them, in the very same moment, He chose also His compassion, His passion. Your pain pains me – this is a source of God's justice and justification which is deeper than simply keeping an account of trespasses. This is what Jonah did not know.

Timothy: Yes, God gives Jonah time, lots, to come to accept that Nineveh, this boiling pot of violence, should be spared after just one day of repentance, the absurd generosity of God's love for the great city. God does not force the pace. He gives Jonah time and a plant to shelter him. When we have been hurt by someone, maybe a spouse who has been unfaithful, or people who have committed sexual abuse, we may be so hurt and angry, like Jonah, that we cannot even imagine the possibility of forgiveness. One is lost in what Stephen Cherry calls 'the wilderness of hurt'.[5] It takes time for forgiveness to emerge, while we are torn between the necessity and impossibility of forgiveness.

Łukasz: The dialogue with Jonah, and with it the whole Book of Jonah, has no closure. It finishes with the question addressed to Jonah and therefore to us as well. 'But I, should I not show pity on Nineveh, the great city, in which there are more than a hundred and twenty thousand humans who do not know their right from their left and many animals?' God allows us to question Him and His actions in the world.

I cannot but think about another similar story about forgiveness and how unobvious this act is. Jesus' parable about the father and his two sons (Lk. 15) also ends with an implicit question directed to the apparently righteous son. Is it not right to rejoice at the return of your brother? We have no idea if his father succeeded in convincing him to join the party! There too the righteous person was angry because of the mercy shown to the sinful. He stayed outside the celebration as does Jonah, who still looked at the saved Nineveh with disgust.

Timothy: It is fascinating how many of the conversations we talk about in this book pivot around God's questions. The answer is never a simple statement, for example: 'Yes, it is not good for me to be angry.' Rather, we are invited to leave the cramped confines of a narrow way of looking at the world and enter into the spaciousness of God's mind. But, as you say, it is a spaciousness that opens up when we see the particular: in this case, the particular plant under which Jonah has sheltered.

I can identify with the elder son sulking on the edge of the party celebrating the return of his prodigal brother. We can imagine a circle of dancers, everyone losing themselves in the common joy. Will he dare let go of his indignation and join in the shared happiness? Will he have the courage to lose his solitary identity and find himself in the circle of dancers? Or will he go on sulking: 'It's not fair, Daddy.' Will Jonah too leave his position on the edge of the city, and join in the joy of the Ninevites? Do we hold back too from other people's joyful celebrations? Are we wallflowers at the dance of forgiveness, hugging our indignation?

Jacob Steinhardt, *Jonah Has Pity on the Gourd*, 1965, Israel Museum, Jerusalem

Łukasz: Jacob Steinhardt, a Jewish artist, made a series of woodcuts inspired by the Book of Jonah. One of them is particularly moving for me. Although the Biblical text never says it, Steinhardt interpreted the *qiqayon* plant as a tree. One can see here Jonah with his eyes wide open, sitting on his knees and touching the dead tree as if saying goodbye to a dear friend, memorizing the texture of its bark, learning the value of life in the experience of death. His gesture reminds me of the gesture in which we approach and venerate the Cross on Good Friday. I have no idea if Steinhardt had in his mind the typical scene of the veneration of the Cross, but I do. Even more precisely, I can see that the tree is not simply the Cross but the One suspended on it:

The Rod of Jesse's root (Isa. 11.1), the One that 'grew up like a sapling like a shoot from the parched earth' (Isa. 53.2). God invites Jonah to learn compassion towards all living things in the bitterness of the casual, everyday death of an ephemeral living being. Jesus spoke of his mission in the mysterious terms of 'the sign of Jonah', and said that no other sign will be given than 'the sign of Jonah' (Mt. 12.39 and parallel texts). What could teach me more about God's compassion towards the whole of his creation?

Intermezzo:
Four Prophets

Łukasz and Timothy: Just as when we pondered on the three absences – of Adam, Abel and Sarah – let us pause to digest a little these conversations with the four prophets Moses, Elijah, Jeremiah and Jonah. We chose these four texts just because we enjoyed them and not to illustrate a theory about prophetic discourse or draw general conclusions, but it would be good to take our bearings. Every baptized Christian is called to be a prophet. How do these four stories cast light on my call to be a prophet?

Every prophetic vocation begins with an encounter with God which is unique to that person. None of us will encounter a burning bush in the wilderness, or be Elijah sheltering from the storm on Mount Horeb, or be the young Jeremiah who encounters the Word being 'to' him. But these accounts are part of Revelation, and so speak to our experience. Do they engage us differently? Each of us has had or will have our personal encounter with the Lord, which may be so discreet as hardly to be noticed. Moses had to wait until he was 80!

Every encounter of a prophet with the Word that we have looked at is disconcerting. Moses is on the edge, in the wilderness, far from the dramas of his people, when he is summoned back to the centre. 'Who am I that I would go to Pharaoh to bring the sons of Israel out of Egypt?' Similarly, Jeremiah feels inadequate for his role: '*Ahah*! Lord YHWH, look, I do not know to speak, for I am a youth.' A stuttering old man and the youth who says '*Ahah*' are both invited to take centre stage!

With the other two, it is the other way around. Elijah has been immersed in the dramas of his people, defeating the prophets of Ba'al and fighting with the fearsome Jezebel. But he finds himself fleeing to the edge, to the wilderness where Moses saw the burning bush. He still has a part to play in the rise and fall of dynasties, but he now discovers that he never was the only player; there were the seven thousand who never kissed Ba'al, and shortly he will be succeeded by another, Elisha. Elijah will have to surrender his pivotal role. He is caught up in a drama which is not his own, as soon he will be taken up into heaven.

Jonah has the even more disconcerting experience of finding that the God who he believed to be centred in Jerusalem, the Holy City, reaches out in mercy even to the enemies of Israel: 'Should I not show pity on Nineveh, the great city, in which there are more than a hundred and twenty thousand humans who do not know their right from their left and many animals?'

These four stories of prophetic vocation – and there are so many more and such different ones – make us ask whether the prophets are not always people summoned to take their part in the action of God in the world, but they might not be important in the way they think. They think that they are on the edge but are summoned to the centre, or the other way around. When people talk about the Church, often it is in terms of edge and centre: for example, that the hierarchy are at the centre but we can do nothing because we are merely marginal. Or the other way around.

But these prophetic stories all throw into the air conceptions of edge and centre. When Thomas Merton became a committed Christian, he wrote: 'Now I had entered into the everlasting movement of that gravitation which is the very life and spirit of God. God's own gravitation towards the depths of His own infinite nature. His goodness without end. And God, that centre Who is everywhere, and whose circumference is nowhere, finding me.'[1] What is striking are the words quoted from Allan of Lille: 'the God whose centre is everywhere and whose circumference is nowhere'.[2] None of us can run away from our prophetic role, however small it is, just because we think we are marginal. Think of St Catherine of Siena, an illiterate, uneducated young woman who found herself propelled to the centre. Other people exercise their prophetic role by the opposite movement, such as St Charles de Foucauld losing and finding himself in the Sahara.

Being found by God, as each of us is, will disconcert us and give us roles more important than we could ever imagine, but as participants in a drama in which each of us has a small walk-on part, for it is God's drama. Thus we shall find ourselves at the centre which is everywhere, confident, otherwise we shall have nothing to say, and humble, otherwise nothing that we say shall be of any worth.

'Have you not seen him whom my heart loves?' (Song 1.12–2.7)

'So long as the king was in his chamber, my nard gave *forth* its fragrance.

A sachet of myrrh, my beloved is to me, between my breasts passes the night.

A cluster of henna, my beloved is to me, in the vineyards of En-gedi.'

'Behold you are beautiful, my friend!

Behold you are beautiful: your eyes are doves.'

'Behold, you are beautiful, my beloved! How delightful, how our couch is fresh green.

The beams of our house are cedars, our rafters are cypresses.

I am a crocus of Sharon, a lily of the valleys.'

'As a lily among brambles, so is my friend among the daughters.'

'As an apple tree among the trees of the wood, so is my beloved among young sons.

In his shadow I delight to sit, and his fruit was sweet for my palate.

He brought me to the house of wine, and his banner above me: love.

Sustain me with raisin-cakes. Support me with apples; for I am sick with love.

His left hand ~ under my head, and his right hand will embrace me ...'

'I adjure you, daughters of Jerusalem, by the gazelles or the does of the field: Ah, if you stirred up or awakened love before she desired ...!'

Timothy: It never occurred to me to choose a dialogue from the Song of Songs for our book until you suggested it. After all, we are looking at conversations between God and humanity, and this is the only Biblical book in which God is never mentioned. But the moment you proposed it, immediately I was hooked. It is a book of erotic poetry. Erotic desire is one of the most powerful human experiences, and God has embraced all of our humanity in Jesus, and so that must include our capacity for the erotic. How is it made holy and part of our journey to the Kingdom? How is it part of our spiritual life? This is a preliminary question before looking at the conversation itself.

In our European culture, going right back to classical culture, the erotic is both feted and feared. It releases powerful forces that can blow our lives to pieces. Think of Tolstoy's Anna Karenina, whose passion drives her to throw herself under the wheels of a train (spoiler alert!). Erotic desire can make a fool of anyone, even, according to the legend, of that most rational man, Aristotle. So the erotic is wonderful and dangerous. In the Song of Songs we are warned not to awaken it until she wishes! The woman says, 'I am sick with love' (Song 5.8). Later she will say that she is slain by it.

Theologians often give the impression that these erotic songs are really about something else. As if they are an allegory of our love of God and that we must see through the surface meaning to their hidden 'spiritual' sense. This seems to me to duck their challenge and trivialize their meaning.

Łukasz: Since the beginning of the existence of the Song of Songs, this poem has been always interpreted in a theological manner. The purely erotic interpretation, as exclusively a relationship between a man and a woman, is a recent invention of our modern age. When sex was invented, as you say! In so many Biblical pages the Divine name does not appear, but does it mean they have nothing to do with God? To put it bluntly: removing the relationship with God from the interpretation is a historically unjustified exegesis. It reveals rather our modern prejudice, which places sexual life 'beyond good and evil', outside of theology or religious phenomena.

I have tried hard to find some 'purely erotic' poems from the Ancient Near East and, believe me, it is difficult to find such compositions without any religious elements! It is simply so because in the Biblical world, as in antiquity in general, everything is religious. The more important a given reality is, the more religious meaning it has. It is not an accident that Eros was a god for the Greeks. The opposition between body and soul, between religious and erotic life, results from the deplorable state of our modern disembodied beings. For the ancients, the erotic is also religious and must be so. It is a holy ground which is revered and protected by taboos, calendars, purity laws and rules of access analogous to those of the temples and holy rituals!

We do not have to choose in the interpretation of the Song of Songs between human and Divine love. The Song is about love *tout court*, about fascination with the other person, his or her beauty, about one's desire for unity etc. We love God with our human heart, for we have only one heart. That is why I do believe that the Canticle is 'about something more', because human love is always about something more than you and me. Don't you agree that also the experience of human love leads to something transcendent? It is like getting a glimpse beyond our human world. Since God is love and because the unique source of love springs in any human love, why shouldn't the Song of Songs speak also about Divine love and about how God looks at us? St Catherine of Siena said famously that it was not the nails but his love for us that kept Jesus on the Cross.[1] What a Passion!

Timothy: I agree totally. When a friend of mine, John Rae, a famous head-teacher, wrestled with whether he believed in the existence of God or not, the question to which we always returned was this: was the love that he had for his family and friends merely an emotion without ultimate significance in a tale 'told by an idiot, full of sound and fury, signifying nothing'?[2] Or was it a door into eternity, the touch of the transcendent? When I saw him shortly before he died in 2006, I had the impression that for him the answer was not yet decided. Love is for us personal, both in the sense that we love people and that we believe the mystery of love to be a person.

In the Song of Songs this love is deeply physical, bodily. It sings of the eyes, the lips, the breasts, the arms and legs of the beloved. Jews and Christians believe in the goodness of the body. We are not souls trapped in bags of flesh awaiting escape. The Dominican Order was founded to preach the good news that our bodily existence is God's gift. Aquinas famously proclaimed, '*non sum anima mea*', I am not my soul.[3]

God draws near to us in the sacraments, which consecrate all that is bodily: birth and death, eating and drinking, health and sex. The pinnacle of our relationship with God is the gift of a body: 'This is my body, given for you.' The Eucharist could be the basis of a beautiful sexual ethics, the Lord's gift of his body given freely, generously, without domination or violence.

So our bodily desires are fundamentally good. They can become corrupted, misdirected and destructive, but at its deepest, erotic desire is for the good, even for God. 'My body pines for you like a dry weary land without water' (Ps. 62). Pope Benedict, in *Deus Caritas Est*, defends the goodness of the erotic. It requires the discipline and purification of other forms of love – for all love is one, as you say – to attain its grandeur, its nobility. The problem, as the English novelist D. H. Lawrence said, is that we get trapped in small desires.[4] Our faith summons us to desire more deeply, boundlessly!

We listen in to the conversation between the man and the woman about their mutual erotic desire. Isn't there something odd about this eavesdropping, even verging on the improper? Erotic talk is essentially private. Anyway, what does talking have to do with eroticism, which can be wordless, almost pre-verbal. How does it enter into our conversations with God and each other?

Łukasz: Yes, one can read the Canticle or imagine the scene from a voyeuristic perspective. What made me change this perspective was a painting inspired by this book: *The Beloved*, by Dante Gabriel Rossetti (see FIGURE 2).

At first I was surprised that the couple is not depicted: it seems to lack the beloved man. Then I realized that Rossetti hit the mark, so to speak. He places me, the viewer of the painting, in the position of the young man. It is not only I who looks at the women; they also gaze at me. A similar composition is commonly applied in the icons: the figures there represented always keep an eye on anyone appearing in front of them. I once visited the small museum of icons in the Mount Sinai monastery. When a crowd of noisy visitors entered the little room with the famous icon of Christ, everyone went silent because of his piercing look. When we were leaving, we even felt uncomfortable turning our backs on the icon. More than looking at it, I felt as though I was being looked upon.

The Song of Songs, like the Book of Psalms, pushes us readers to pass from the third person to the second. It is a very different thing to say 'she/ he is beautiful' and 'you are beautiful'!

Timothy Yes, indeed, when we love someone, whether passionately or even in friendship, we are impelled to say so. 'You are beautiful.' The word that is the other's bodily presence – their being speaks – demands a word from us. We just have to say, 'I love you.' This is not communicating information! It is a sort of consummation.

> Behold you are beautiful, my friend!
> Behold you are beautiful: your eyes are doves.

The erotic can drive us to words that are possessive, even destructive. So we need to learn good words that are tender, reverential, which honour the other. As Pope Benedict wrote, this realizes the nobility, the grandeur of the erotic and heals it. St Augustine claimed that we cannot love other people the way gourmands say 'I love thrushes', a delicacy of the time.[5] So the passionate erotic language of the Song is intensified by the selflessness of agape. Desire is deepened by reverence for the other. As we saw when we looked at the conversation with Moses, sometimes holding back, not grabbing the other, deepens desire rather than diminishes it. Veiling the body can make it more desirable!

Łukasz: The Song teaches us to see beauty and to speak of it. There is something unique in beauty: it is both objective and subjective. On the one hand, there is some objectivity to it because we can make a judgement, discuss it and even verify it: 'I thought she or he was very average but when I approached I noted these beautiful eyes and the calm smile' and so on. On the other hand, beauty is not a simple quality, like weight or height, that can be unequivocally measured or compared. Some will explain away the beauty of the human body by its biological or sexual aspect and reduce it flatly to the reproductive preferences of the Selfish Gene. Yet we can also recognize the beauty of children, old people, of the same sex, without any erotic connotations. We even admire the beautiful things that we will never possess, the things that are 'useless' like sunsets, rainbows, stars and deserts. They are beautiful, awe-inspiring. Beauty is beyond potentially utilitarian perspectives. The universe, macro- and micro-, is beautiful and we do not know why! It does not need to be, and yet it is beautiful. All these innumerable beautiful galaxies that we can see today point to the landscapes beyond our horizon, the beautiful galaxies that humans will never see! Why are they beautiful? What for? For whom?

I find it very revealing that the bride and the bridegroom describe each other in terms of the landscape and nature. She is like a lily, a valley full of newborn prancing kids. He is like a tree, tall, strong, fragrant and precious. In the presence of the beloved, one discovers a similar experience of overwhelming space, a place where one lives. Here you are! In you the universe is smiling to me! You become my universe, my air. Additionally, this comparison works both ways. In you I see my hills, but also when I see the real hills around me, they speak of you. Antoine de Saint-Exupéry famously captured in his *Little Prince* the experience of the little fox speaking of his friend:

And then look: you see the grain fields down yonder? I do not eat bread. Wheat is of no use to me. The wheat fields have nothing to say to me. And that is sad. But you have hair that is the colour of gold. Think how wonderful that will be when you have tamed me! The grain, which is also golden, will bring me back the thought of you. And I shall love to listen to the wind in the wheat ...[6]

My perception of someone I love becomes the way, a model, through which I perceive and inhabit the world.

Timothy: Yes, beauty speaks because it is wonderfully useless. George Steiner called it 'sovereignly useless'.[7] All beauty speaks. It addresses us, and, as you say, the beauty of the universe I see through the prism of the beauty of those whom I love, and *vice versa*. I would like to say that there is something unique about the beauty of the human body. I am not sure how to put this well, and so forgive the necessary brevity of my words. The human body is not a lump of flesh which may be desirable. Every human body is a presence which speaks of love. It invites to communion. This is supremely true of the face, which, as you know, fascinates me. The human face evolved over millennia so that we may be present to each other.

Our features softened, the muscles became supple, so that we could smile and be intimate. The man says to his beloved: 'Let me see your face, let me hear your voice, for your voice is sweet, and your face is comely.' It is supremely human that sexual intercourse is face-to-face: 'His left hand – under my head, and his right hand will embrace me ...'

But not just the face. The whole body of the other is an invitation to love, to mutual gift. So when Love Eternal drew near to us, it was as a

Word made flesh, bodily as we are. Is it too crazy to say that the human body evolved so that infinite Love could become embodied in one of us? Maybe in a secular age, when religious faith has faded, it is not surprising that people become obsessed with sex, because it is indeed a window, for some the last one, onto the transcendent! But the window remains open only if the erotic is humanized with agape.

I cannot resist reading a passage from Rowan Williams, the former archbishop of Canterbury:

> For my body to be the cause of joy, the end of homecoming, for me, it must be there for someone else, be perceived, accepted, nurtured; and that means being given over to the creation of joy in that other, because only as directed to the enjoyment, the happiness, of the other does it become unreservedly lovable. To desire my joy is to desire the joy of the one I desire: my search for enjoyment through the bodily presence of another is a longing to be enjoyed in my body.[8]

Łukasz: I agree. The human face is a perfect symbol of a being that has the potential for the communion, a being that seems to exist for the sake of the other. Latin knows two terms for 'face'. One is *visus*, from the verb *videre*, which gave us 'visage'. It is something that is seen, a passive, objective quality. The second is *facies*, from the verb *facere*, 'to make', which gave us the English word 'face': something that one projects, an active, expressive quality.

The universe and all that is beautiful have a *visus*, but it does not look back at us, even though we can personify and see some natural events as a 'mockery of the heavens' or 'a smile of the sun'. In any case, beauty is like the door inviting us to enter; the beauty of the human body is like a door that opens towards another. The beauty of beings is like their face, like a promise of the deeper, hidden value, an invitation. Let me say it in the first person. I was lost, wandering around in the strange world, homeless but behold there are some eyes that are looking back at me. It is like the discovery of a surprising and mysterious door in the context of an unknown and seemingly uninhabited foreign land. The experience of beauty is like the doorway that is too big for me, as if saying that this entrance is not only for me. An attentive traveller should have at least a hunch that he or she is not the only admirer.

The Song of Songs seem to compensate for all other Biblical books because the others do not seem to be interested at all in the external appearances of its main characters. We have no idea how Moses, Jesus or Mary looked! In very few cases, such as David, Absalom and Rachel, we get some generic information, but only as much as is necessary for us to understand the plot. In the Bible the verb is more important than the adjective, and people's actions more important than their looks. That is why when Isaiah 52.7 speaks of 'the beautiful feet of the bearer of good news': it is really not about the particularly exciting shape of limbs but because they bear good tidings!

Timothy: Was Jesus beautiful? The words of Isaiah 53 are often applied to him: 'He had no form or comeliness that we should look at him, and no beauty that we should desire him.' Certainly, his death on the cross was utterly ugly. Perhaps here we glimpse the most profound beauty, which we only slowly learn to see, for it has gathered to itself all the ugliness of the world and transfigured it.

But what does this Song have to say about relationships that are not fundamentally erotic and sexual, about friendship and the relationships of parents and children? This Song is not just two people gazing at each other to the exclusion of all others! There is a third participant, the daughters of Jerusalem. All love overflows beyond the two beloveds, as the love of the Father and the Son overflows in the Holy Spirit.

The beauty of my beloved should teach me to see the beauty of others. Friendship should be infectious. So each love helps me to see others with loving eyes, even people whom I in no way desire. I must admit that my pastoral outreach to other people is often enhanced by a sense of their attractiveness. This does not mean that I want to have a sexual relationship with them. Rather, if we learn to see with the eyes of God, we get a glimpse of the loveliness of every human being, their hidden beauty. The old (as I increasingly appreciate!), the very young, people who have no obvious beauty, they too are delighted in by God, who takes pleasure in their existence. Seeing with God's eyes, we reach out to them spontaneously! Saints are drawn out of themselves – almost ecstatically – by others, because they see their loveliness. Thomas Merton famously had such an experience, when he went to Louisville and his eyes were opened: 'Then it was as if I suddenly saw the secret beauty of their hearts, the depths of their hearts, where neither sin nor desire nor self-knowledge can reach, the core of their being, the person that each one is in God's eyes.'[9]

Łukasz: You are right. Beauty sometimes needs a revelation. The Father spoke about Jesus: 'This is my Son, the Beloved, with whom I am pleased' (Mt. 3.17). Too easily we say that 'love is blind'. I think that the reverse is true. We are somewhat blind as long as we do not love. In God, love and omniscience are one. He knows the true beauty of all beings because He loves them, and vice versa: He loves them because he knows their beauty. That is why some philosophers and theologians considered beauty as one of the transcendentals: a quality that all beings possess to some extent.

Very often we are taught to perceive beauty by a third person: a teacher, a child, a friend. This can concern a sport that otherwise I would have never played, a country I would have never visited alone, a new dish I would have never tasted, a person I would have never loved. Without such 'tutors of beauty' my world would be much smaller, less joyful and less beautiful. We need to learn to recognize the value of complex realities like people, who are probably the most complex realities that exist!

It is also true that I cannot learn everything and that, thanks be to God, there are and always will be some beauties beyond my reach and comprehension. I need other people to tell me about them and witness to this beauty which remains beyond my perception. Even when I am not able to appreciate the beauty of mathematics, of some modern music or of my brother and sister, the prophets of beauty save me from an egocentric pride and contempt towards the world and its inhabitants. I need so much more a loving gaze that reveals my own beauty to myself. No mirror or selfies can do it. I need to hear it from someone.

Timothy: Yes, the selfie is the most popular form of self-representation today, and yet it never truly reveals the person. You never look remotely like yourself in your selfies! One final quick word. In this celebration, erotic love is constantly evoked in terms of the fruitfulness of the earth:

> How delightful, how our couch is fresh green.
> The beams of our house are cedars, our rafters are cypresses.
> I am a crocus of Sharon, a lily of the valleys.

There are endless references to leafy trees, fruit, twin newborn lambs. 'Support me with apples!' It is a song of springtime; the winter is over and the sound of the turtle dove is heard in the land (Song 2.12). Erotic love is fecund, the springtime of body and soul. Surely, every time we are carried outside ourselves in friendship and affection, we are blessed with fertility in some form. The world is renewed and there is a little springtime. This little book, after all, is the fruit of friendship.

Intermezzo: We See His Face

We gave to this last conversation the title of this poignant question: 'Have you not seen him whom my heart loves?' It is from the Song of Songs, even though not in the text we quote. Our answer will be, 'Yes'. For our beloved God is about to become visible in a human person, a human face. Although God is not mentioned in the Song of Songs, we are pointed to the consummation of the Divine love with humanity. Now the conversation of God with humanity will take a new form. No longer a voice addressed to us just in the silence of the human heart or in the mystical intimacy of Moses or Elijah on the mountain, the Word becomes flesh in the person of Jesus, in his body, acts and words addressed to his family and friends, to his disciples and enemies. He whom my heart loves became visible. Christianity is a religion of faces. Our churches are filled with the faces of saints, gazing on the faces of the faithful. Images are an intrinsic expression of our faith in the God who disclosed himself in a human face, which is why this book is filled with them. Does this mean the beginning of different sorts of conversations? We shall see.

But what about us who have never seen the Lord? The Risen Lord tells Thomas, 'Blessed are those who have not seen and yet believe' (Jn 20.29). Are we back in the situation of those who came before the Incarnation? Do we have to await the beatific vision when we shall see God face to face? The experience of the loving face of God, this immediate knowledge, is given to us in two ways. We can receive it from other human beings who love us as God intended them to do. We can also become ourselves the face of God for the others. It belongs to the priesthood of every Christian to become the face of the Lord. So a question that each of the following conversations puts to us is this: where do I find embodied the gaze of the Lord smiling on me? How may I offer that gaze to others?

But first a conversation that marks the transition. The one 'whom my heart loves' is announced, becoming invisibly present in Mary's womb, but does not yet enter into the conversation himself.

10

'How will this happen?' (Lk. 1.26–38)

In the sixth month, the angel Gabriel was sent from God to a city in Galilee, called Nazareth, to a virgin betrothed to a man called Joseph, of the House of David; and name of the virgin was Mariam. And coming in to her, he said to her, –

'Rejoice, begraced! The Lord with you!'

But she, at this word, was greatly perturbed and reasoned what kind of salutation this might be. And the angel said to her, –

'Do not be afraid, Mariam; for you have found grace with God. And behold, you will conceive, and will bear a son, and you shall call his name Jesus. He will be great, and will be called "the Son of the Most High"; and the Lord God will give Him the throne of David, his father. And He will reign over the house of Jacob forever; and His kingdom will have no end.'

And Mariam said to the angel, –

'How will this happen, since I do not know a man?'

And answering, the angel said to her, –

'The Holy Spirit will come upon you, and the power of the Most High will overshadow you; and that is why the begotten holy one shall be called "the Son of God". And behold Elizabeth, your relative! Also she conceived a son in her old age, and this is the sixth month for the one called barren. For it will not be impossible with God's every word.'

And Mariam said, –

'Behold, the Slave of the Lord. Let it happen to me according to your word.'

And the angel departed from her.

Timothy: This conversation is the turning point in the relationship between God and humanity. It also sheds light on what happens in a small way whenever we dare to talk with God or even to each other. It is the archetypal Christian conversation that turns everything upside down.

Paintings of the Annunciation usually show the archangel bursting in on a domestic scene. Mary, or Mariam in her native Aramaic, is at home reading a book, presumably the Bible. She reads the Word, preparing for the coming of the Word. For the Italian Renaissance painters it happens in their idea of the perfect home, usually with marble interiors, open windows, olive trees in the garden, a place of sun and fresh air. Northern painters, Dutch and Flemish, for example, give us cosy scenes, with panelled walls and perhaps an oven to keep Our Lady warm. But Gabriel's message will propel Mary out of any cosy domestic serenity.

The painting we have chosen, by the Canadian Dominican painter Gaston Petit, who lived in Japan for most of his life, shows Gabriel as a scary and magnificent samurai warrior (see FIGURE 3). His golden parasol and six fingers show that he is a messenger of God. Mary is a slender and lovely Japanese girl, overwhelmed by this irruption of the Divine. It is terrifying.

The conversation begins with Gabriel's salutation, which we repeat so often. 'Hail Mary', or more accurately, as you have translated it, Łukasz, 'Rejoice'. This salutation is not just a way of getting a conversation going, like 'Good morning. How are you today?' It is the essence of what happened on that day. Indeed, there was a profound devotion to the salutation of Gabriel in medieval England, I don't know about Poland. Pubs were sometimes called The Salutation, and a few survive today. The greatest shrine in England, at Walsingham, was built to commemorate a vision of Our Lady in 1061, 'in memory of the joy of my Salutation'.

Łukasz: I have always suspected that a British pub could be a *locus theologicus*! Indeed, any true meeting between people, where a good word is pronounced, is theologically interesting. Isn't it amazing that one of the proper names of the Divine person is *logos*, meaning 'word', 'reason' or 'meaning'? Our words, the closer they are to the true Word, must have something of its Divine life-giving might.

The Annunciation scene has an element that we have not seen yet in the scenes upon which we previously commented. Actually, Mariam is not speaking directly with God; Gabriel is a go-between. Does talking through a mediator matter? We love and desire immediacy, and yet in the case of God this immediacy is paradoxical. God is able to give a name to any single atom of my body and has a deeper knowledge of me than I will ever have. God has therefore a more direct access to me than I do, like a programmer to the code He wrote. Augustine made a superlative of a superlative to express this: *intimior intimo meo*, more intimate to me than I am to myself.[1]

It is difficult to perceive realities that are always present and so close, like the air or space, or time. It seems to me that God uses mediators to make His communication more explicit, visible and notable for our myopic and blurred perception. Sending an angel is like sending a visit card or waving a hand: it's me!

Looking at the Scriptures, we note that mediators of the Divine Word are no less common than an immediate contact with God. We will so often find an angel, a prophet, a wise man, a king, a judge. We should not make a fuss that these are just God's mediators. In any case, a mediator was good enough for Mary to accept the most important message in human history.

Timothy: Yes, sometimes I feel a little envious of the Biblical characters who were involved in the scenes of our salvation, whereas I only read about them. Wouldn't faith be so much easier if one had been there and seen everything? But the disciples who walked and talked with Jesus himself, the Word made flesh, seem to have sometimes been as puzzled and doubting as I am! The Risen Lord said to Thomas, 'Blessed are those who have not seen and yet believe' (Jn 20.29), and so maybe I ought not to be envious. We have multiple mediators: the evangelists, earlier theologians and each other!

Mary is addressed by name. Indeed, this scene is resonant with the names of people who have been addressed with their own salutations: Jacob, David, Joseph, Elizabeth, Mary. Luke's gospel is addressed to Theophilus. It culminates with the supreme name, Jesus, who is God's salutation to each of us in person. What does it mean to claim that God addresses me and you, Łukasz, albeit through mediators? It is not as if Jesus had us individually in mind when he spoke to the disciples! Surely it is deeper than that. As we said when we looked at Jeremiah, I am someone most profoundly who *is* addressed by God. My spiritual journey, my quest, is to hear the Word that God addresses to me, which summons me to live fully. I do not really know who I am until I have some sense of being addressed by a word that gives me life and existence in every moment and so says to me personally, 'Rejoice'. When I sit in silence in chapel every morning, it is so that I can hear even a tiny whisper of the One who always says to me, 'Rejoice', giving me life.

Even though no terrifying angel bursts into our homes, all our significant conversations are a sharing in that Divine salutation. Each of us is Gabriel to the other. Each of us is Mary, the archetypal disciple. When I was a bit discouraged recently at the prospect of this gruesome operation for cancer, you said to me, 'Do not be afraid.' At that moment you were my Gabriel, the messenger of God.

Łukasz: The traditional English rendition of the Angel's greeting 'Hail' is archaic, and some modern renditions argue for a simple 'Hello', but there is indeed something more to it. Ancient Greeks greeted each other with the imperative *chaire*, 'Rejoice!' as the Semites wished each other *shalom*, 'Peace!' There are significant parallels in the prophetic texts where God addresses the Daughter of Zion with the same invitation to rejoice as in Joel 2.21–2, Zephaniah 3.14 and, in particular, Zechariah 9.9: 'Rejoice greatly, Daughter of Zion! Shout for joy, Daughter Jerusalem! Behold: your king is coming to you, a just saviour is he!'

The reason for this joy is the coming of the king of Israel. This king announced by the prophet Zechariah is not another descendant from the Davidic dynasty but YHWH himself. It is this ultimate and direct kingship that is announced and acclaimed in these ancient prophecies.

The very imperative 'Rejoice!' begs for some comment. Usually when one experiences joy, no command or encouragement is needed. Indeed, Mary lives through some internal turmoil and the gospel never mentions that she actually *was* joyful. It seems in fact that she needed quite some time to come to terms with the event. Only after her meeting with the pregnant Elizabeth has her joy matured enough to burst forth in the words of thanksgiving in the Magnificat. Unlike simple immediate joys or cheerful moods into which one can be artificially manipulated, these joys originate in the depths of the human spirit (expressed in our existential decisions) and apparently need more time to flourish. They need sometimes even a particular revelation, as in this case!

In the Greek tradition, the profoundly biblical chant to Our Lady, Akathist, is composed of a great number of *chairetismoi*, 'rejoicings' through which the Church joins Gabriel's 'Rejoice!' Yes, deep joy needs also some thought and time.

Rejoice, You through whom joy will shine forth!
Rejoice, You through whom the curse will cease!
Rejoice, the Restoration of fallen Adam!
Rejoice, the Redemption of the tears of Eve!
Rejoice, O Height inaccessible to human thoughts!
Rejoice, O Depth undiscernible even for the eyes of angels!
Rejoice, for You are the throne of the King!
Rejoice, for You bear Him Who bears all!
Rejoice, O Star that makes the Sun appear!
Rejoice, O Womb of the Divine Incarnation!
Rejoice, You through whom creation is renewed!
Rejoice, You through whom we worship the Creator!
Rejoice, O Bride Unwedded!

Ikos I

In the Angel's mouth, the word 'Rejoice', once pronounced by the prophets of old, is followed by a very new word, which I decided to render by the unusual participle 'begraced'. It is the famous Greek *kecharitomene*, which English renders usually by a longer periphrasis, 'full of grace', just like the Latin *gratia plena*. Our short commentary is not the place to develop the fully fledged theory of grace. It is enough to remember that the Greek *charis* is not far away from 'privilege', 'election', 'preference' and a particular 'gift'.

One does not receive *charis* like an anonymous leaflet thrown down from a balloon to anyone who bothers to pick it up. It is much more like the owl letter addressed to 'Mr H. Potter, The Cupboard under the Stairs', if you'll permit me this pop-culture reference. It is a registered letter, one that one opens with a beating heart: whether good or bad, this is very important and personal news.

Timothy: You are right, Mary does not immediately rejoice. Her joy comes and goes. It overflows in the Magnificat, as you say, but soon old Simeon will tell her that her heart will be pierced as if by a sword. We too are not always joyful. It rises and falls in our hearts like the tides of the sea, but if we are blessed, the joy may always be there, even if very quietly, underneath the sorrow, because we know that the plenitude of joy lies in the future. The sorrow is always there too, even if just a hint, because we have not arrived yet. Until the Kingdom, it is almost like a test of the authenticity of our emotions, that while one may predominate, there is always the presence of the other. As the English poet William Blake wrote:

> Joy and woe are woven fine,
> A clothing for the soul Divine,
> Under every grief and pine,
> Runs a joy with silken twine.[2]

So when I am told that I must be extremely happy because Jesus loves me, almost as if it were a duty, excluding the possibility of any sadness, it sounds like a fake joy to me.

Łukasz: The angel reveals to Mariam her deepest identity, what she is in the eyes of God and also her path. Gabriel says 'the Lord with you!' In the Roman Catholic Mass we repeat four times *Dominus vobiscum*, literally 'the Lord with you', and mark thus our entrance into the important moments of the liturgy. When the Philistine king said to Isaac that 'the Lord is with him', he recognized that the visible success of this patriarch came from God (Gen. 26.28).

This phrase can also be a wish, 'The Lord be with you'. Since Luke's Gospel says nothing of any earlier success of Mary, it is actually likely that 'the Lord with you' is more of an encouragement before some serious trial or mission. Thus Joshua receives the same message in Judges 6.12 ('The Lord is with you, O brave warrior!') just before he sets out for the conquest of Canaan. In 1 Samuel 17.32, Saul sends the little, boyish David to face the giant Goliath with the same 'The Lord with you!' This is the very common message which an ancient king would receive from some prophet while facing trials or a battle against some fierce enemy (2 Kgs 6.16; Isa. 7.4, 10.24; Acts 18.9, 27.24).

Well, one can understand why Mary was not so much impressed by the appearance itself of the angel but precisely by these highly portentous greetings. They announce a particular grace as much as they suggest a major trial or mission ahead. The angel's 'do not be afraid!' does not presume that Mary was afraid of the angel, but rather that she should expect some mysterious and daunting challenge.

Timothy: St Bernard of Clairvaux imagines all the angels in heaven holding their breath as they wait to see how Mary will answer. Will she, won't she, say

'Yes'? All of creation waits, wondering what she will do. It is a wonderfully dramatic moment when everything seems to hang in the balance!

Łukasz: I must somewhat depart from that very noble tradition represented by St Bernard of Clairvaux according to which all creation waits with bated breath for Mary's *Fiat*! In the angelic message there is no hint of a question or of a proposal. There is no 'would you like?' or 'do you agree?' or 'would you consider?' It is a simple and plain future indicative as in the vocation narratives of Jeremiah and other prophets, 'You will go', and 'You will speak'. Mary does not really answer 'yes' because there has been no question. She rather asks a question to understand better the future presented to her: 'How will it be, since I do not know a man?' The angel speaks of the great future of her son, the future beyond her reach. She seems to have no problem believing that; the only problem for now is where this son comes from. Whereas sometimes we ask questions to meddle, to delay fulfilling of the Divine plans, Mary asks questions because she wants to be obedient.

I am not sure whether and what she understood of the lengthy answer that the angel gave her. It is possible that at that moment Mary simply understood that God will provide for that. Afterwards she would have all her life to ponder the meaning of these words.

Timothy: Gaston Petit's painting is filled with flowers, as if it is not just Mary who will be fertile but the whole of creation. This is a turning point not just in her life but in that of the universe. In our conversation about the Song of Songs, we saw that the language of love was filled with the promise of spring. Now the awaited fecundity has burst out, not just in a child but for creation.

But it is not the springtime she might have hoped for. Mary's domestic world is turned upside down. In the most radical way, she will be forever the mother of her son, a 'we' not just an 'I'.

Her son will cleave open her heart, puzzle her and bring her sorrow and joy. He will not grow up as expected and get married and produce grandchildren, but mix with disreputable people and die a scandalous, shameful death. This is the joy and pain shared by so many parents, forever bound up with their children, who often do not turn out as hoped. Often mothers suffer from post-natal depression. It is completely natural, for that solitary person before parenthood is gone forever; henceforth she will always be 'we'.

Whatever our home, God breaks it open and propels us beyond our little domestic world into the unimaginable kinship of Christ. During the Iraq War of 2003, many Dominicans all over the world stuck stickers on the bumpers of their cars: 'We have Family in Iraq.' Certainly, Dominican brothers and sisters, but more than that, ordinary Iraqi people who are our kin in God. Mother Teresa said: 'The problem with the world is that we draw the circle of our family too small.' The salutations that we offer each other should invite us to step out of our narrow domestic sphere into a larger family, God's own kinship, and we can never know beforehand what that will mean.

When we looked at Abraham's welcome offered to the three strangers, you pointed out that they were not total strangers. They were members of the same sort of culture as their hosts. Now we see in the child to be born of Mary, the birth of a family which is potentially as wide as humanity.

Łukasz: As the angel points to the future, he supports his words by another miraculous event to be seen. 'behold Elizabeth, your relative, [...] conceived a son.' Only at this stage does Mary give her implicit consent and a declaration, 'behold the slave of the Lord'.

I know that the usual English rendition here is 'servant', but Greek knew another word for that, *diakonos*. Whereas 'servant' can be simply a job or a transitory function, being a *doulous*, 'slave', is a matter of identity and belonging. Not something one could quit freely. The word 'slave' in English is derogatory indeed, but one should understand that that all depended on who was your master or mistress. A trusted slave of the royal household could be as important as a royal child and a significant power at a court, what the French language calls a *familier*, a familiar. 'The slave of the Lord' – that is, of God – is as much an expression of one's dignity as of one's humility. Isaiah called all people of Israel 'slaves/servants of the Lord' to console his homeless and defenceless nation and give them back their identity and hope that they would return to the land of their Lord. Mary declares that she belongs to the Lord as much as the angel does. Her final 'Let it happen' (commonly known in the Latin *fiat*) corresponds to *Amen* in Hebrew. Ultimately, Mary's answer to God's messenger becomes a prayer. Well, what else can a dialogue with God be other than a prayer?

Timothy: Yes. If Mary is the 'slave' of God, this means that she can be no one else's 'slave'. It is a declaration of her freedom from all human domination. It is the same title that Paul claims at the beginning of

Romans, a slave of the Lord (Rom. 1.1). In the Greek translation of the Bible, I think that it is the title given to all of the Patriarchs and to King David. It is to be the one who does the will of Our Father in heaven, as we pray, the God who sets us free. And so her final *fiat*, her *Amen*, as you say, is not a servile submission but her entry into freedom, embraced in her prayer.

Could it be that even our deepest conversations with each other should have something of the reverence, the mutual obedience, of prayer, if we are all to be sometimes Gabriel to each other, and sometimes Mary? Our conversations too announce the joy of the Lord coming into our lives. Our words to each other can be fertile, bringing new life and hope. Every time we say *'Amen'* it is our *fiat* to God's summons.

'Child, why have you treated us like this?' (Lk. 2.41–52)

His parents went each year to Jerusalem for the feast of Pascha.[1] When he was twelve years old, they went up according to custom of the feast. After they had completed the days, as they returned, the boy Jesus remained in Jerusalem, but his parents did not know it. Thinking that he was in the caravan, they went a day of way and were looking for him among their relatives and acquaintances, and not finding him, they returned to Jerusalem looking for him.

And it happened after three days that they found him in the temple, sitting in the midst of the teachers, listening to them and asking them questions. All who heard him were amazed at his understanding and his answers. When his parents saw him, they were struck, and his mother said to him, –

'Child, why have you done this to us! Look, your father and I have been looking for you with great grief!'

And he said to them, –

'Why were you looking for me? Did you not know that it was necessary that I was in [the matters] of my Father?'

And they did not understand the thing that he said to them.

He went down with them and came to Nazareth, and was obedient to them. And his mother kept all these things in her heart. And Jesus was advancing in wisdom, and age, and favour before God and men.

Timothy: Some of our most difficult conversations are when we or others are going through a transition in life; the delightful child becoming a sulky teenager for whom nothing is right. There is the teenager edging his or her way from adolescence into young adulthood, the single person feeling his or her way towards becoming someone who is married or a parent, the married person facing solitude when their partner has died.

It is hard to find the right words when one's sense of identity is shifting and one is no longer sure who one is. One might flip-flop between the earlier identity and the new one, as the breaking voice of a young lad entering puberty will sometimes be shrill and then deep! Then his parents may find it hard to talk to him, as do Joseph and Mary with Jesus,

In most traditional societies, initiation rituals ease the transition to a new identity and a new role in society. Even in my youth, the stages of growing up were marked by differences of clothes, or what meals you attended, to what social events you were invited. My sister belonged to the last generation of debutants who 'came out' by being presented to the Queen! I wonder about your growing up in Poland.

But today, in Western Europe anyway, those transitions are no longer marked by formal ceremonies. Instead Neil MacGregor writes, 'the young initiate each other into adult worlds of their own – with joyous baptisms of beer, song and dance'.[2] And often children find themselves thrust into adulthood without preparation, discovering sex before they are ready.

And many adults remain infantilized. So no wonder that it is often hard for people to talk to each other! Fumbled words and awkward silences afflict even the Holy Family in this scene!

Łukasz: You forgot the latest type of attempts at initiation via the Internet! We learn how to cook by watching the instructions on YouTube, so it is not surprising that in the same place one seeks to learn how to be a man, a woman, a student and so on. Nevertheless, reproducing the gestures is not enough. We need a living contact with guides, teachers, someone able to tell if one is wielding the sword correctly, or even if the dish tastes the way it should.

Thinking about it, if we look at the scene at the Jerusalem temple as a kind of rite of passage, the lack of human guides is striking. Jesus has found his way to the house of His Father without guides and it is he who is teaching the teachers! He is the one who amazes them with his answers. I see this scene not as a stage in the development of Jesus but as a sign that his path is different from that of any other child.

During the first class in my secondary school our teacher addressed us as 'ladies and gentlemen', and that impressed us 15-year-olds as something significant. You need an adult to tell you that you are an adult. Apart from that, I do not remember any formal initiation. If I were to point at a significant moment in my life of 'growing' up, it would have to be my decision to enter the Dominican noviciate when I was 19. I remember the heavy atmosphere at that Sunday lunch just after I informed my parents of my decision. Together with the food, my family were chewing their thoughts. When my mother finally pressed my father to give his opinion, he simply said, 'He has the years. He knows what he is doing.' That was it. Brief as usual, but at that stage I did not need anything else. He did not cheer me up, saying that all will be all right, or promising the impossible 'We will be always with you.' I do not think he even understood my choice because there is always something mysterious in Divine and human choices. He simply admitted that the choice was a serious one and gave me the freedom to take the risk, to pay the price.

The trust of the father is something that a son longs for. Colleagues, even older friends, cannot replace it. Each person that we meet has a specific and irreplaceable gift for us. Maybe the silence of Joseph can be also interpreted as a gift of trust to Jesus. I wonder whether these three days that Jesus spent without his parents was a transition experience for him, or maybe it forced the transformation of his parents instead.

The phrase about Jesus growing 'in wisdom, and age' appears only in the conclusion of this passage. It has been an important point in the theological discussion about the human nature of Jesus. Whereas all people grow up, God cannot because He is already perfect. We blame children for being impatient, but for so many adults it is also a major challenge. The naive expectation of immediate perfection is indeed childish. Even the incarnate God in the person of Jesus learned how to walk, how to use the toilet, how to express emotions and so on. Why do we not give ourselves the right and time to grow up? This means also to give oneself some time for learning, time for immaturity, for regress, for repeated mistakes. These are all part of our human path and our learning process. I think that people are more paralysed in their passage from one stage of life to another by unforgiving perfectionism than by laziness or malevolence.

You describe adolescence as a time of shifting identity; I prefer to see it more as a rapidly expanding identity or broadening horizons. Thank God, even within adults this potential for growth remains, and now and then our inner child can still show again its trusting and carefree face. And I love to see it. One needs a lot of energy to change! The wisdom of childhood enables us to learn, to admit with ease that we do not know, to dare make ourselves ridiculous while learning a new language, to recognize and approach the unknown.

Timothy: Maybe the journey of the 12-year-old Jesus to Jerusalem for the Passover might have been, either formally or in practice, truly a transition. The Passover, after all, is the great moment of transition for Israel, from bondage into freedom. For Israel, it is a moment of growing up as they enter into a mature relationship with God on the mountain and receive the ten commandments of how to live in friendship with God and with each other.

In the later tradition of the Talmud, 13 seems to have been the age of manhood, but even earlier, at the age of 12, people were considered mature enough to take vows. The difficult and hurtful conversation between Jesus and his parents – 'Child, why have you done this to us?' – must echo in the hearts of so many parents struggling to understand how their once docile child has become opaque to them. And how might Mary and Joseph talk to this young chap, who seems to be slowly awakening to his identity as 'the begotten holy one [who] shall be called "the Son of God"' (Lk. 1.35). Interestingly, the boy Jesus is described as asking questions. He is teaching and learning! It is a moment of exploration. Could they have had any conception of the mystery at the heart of his being? And who did he think he was?

Łukasz: In the Bible, I found that little Manasseh was 12 when he took the throne of Judah (2 Kings 21.1). Philo of Alexandria thought that at about the age of 14 a man is fully perfected because he is able to beget a similar being (*Legum allegoriae* 1.10). In any case, the parents of Jesus were convinced that 12 was too early for their child to roam freely through Jerusalem.

The very fact that they started seeking him only after a day seems to show how careless they were. Yet it can also show how trustworthy Jesus was and how trusting his parents were. Today parents have more means to control their children than ever; potentially, they have their children always under the electronic surveillance of their mobile phones. On the other hand, I can imagine the thoughts of parents seeking their child for two days in Jerusalem overrun by pilgrims. There must have been even more human traffickers than now! Maybe the boy had been crushed in the crowd? Maybe he was sick? Maybe he had fallen and broken his leg?

Where is he, alone and hungry?! So many horrible scenarios explode in the heads of the parents seeking their child. So many thoughts reiterate the speculations, accusations, and remorse: 'Last time I saw him there ... Had I known! I could have ... I should have ... Why didn't I ...?!' Sleepless are the nights of the one who has lost his most precious treasure. Now and then we still hear about similar cases. Sometimes these terrible questions, hopes and despair remain unanswered forever because the child is not found, not even its body ...

We see the Holy Family in a moment of crisis. It is anything but the peaceful image that we usually find in the icons of the Holy Family. St Luke gives us the image of the family torn apart. The parents are in ignorance and deep pain. The child lets himself be found, but he also points to something greater than the family itself. Maybe this image by Simone Martini is therefore the best image of the Holy Family (see FIGURE 4); its identity is revealed when they seek Jesus, not when they are content and at peace.

Timothy: It seems odd for us that Mary and Joseph might have travelled for a whole day without checking up on whether their son is with them! The famous philosopher Elizabeth Anscombe is known to have mistakenly left one of her babies in the luggage compartment and taken the luggage with her into the carriage instead of the other way around. But you know what philosophers are like! My parents would not have gone two minutes without checking where we were as children. Perhaps this suggests a radically different understanding of 'family'. I suspect that our image of the Holy Family as this nuclear threesome dates from the early days of modernity. Mary and Joseph may have had a much wider understanding of the family, a great crowd travelling together.

Yet clearly this losing of Jesus is painful and highly distressing. How could he have done this to them? These three days of his absence foreshadow that more radical loss of Jesus for three days in the tomb. They are not just losing the youngster. They are losing an image of who he is. He becomes incomprehensible to them. He is not as they thought. Drawing near to God will involve loss. It is the same with the images we have of the Son of God. We lose the image of the Big Man with a white beard. Joining the Order and studying theology, I had to lose the image of God as a really powerful being – even without the beard! – controlling everything. The closer you get to the mystery of the Divine, the less you know in a way.

I like to compare it to seeing someone on the other side of the room. You see the whole person. As you draw near, you see just his or her face. When you kiss them, they disappear. Not because they are far away but because they are so close. We have to lose the images that we have of the people whom we love too, for they too are made in the image and likeness of God and share his mystery. But this loss is always painful, as it was for Mary and Joseph.

Łukasz: Images are mediators. On the one hand, images are necessary because this is how our mind works. Out of accessible data we compose in our heads images, theories and reconstructions of the world, of other people and of ourselves as well. We need to update them constantly by modifying, replacing or adding new images to the pre-existing set. And most important of all, one should not submit to the folly of replacing reality with one of its images! In the religious sphere, this is the essence of idolatry, and the best way to kill living relationships.

We will never comprehend God completely with our images, ideas, words and theologies. The only things that pierce the skies and the clouds of the unknown are love, faith and hope. That is why there is the necessary space for surprises and discoveries. It does not mean that our God is an amorphous, shape-shifting, contradictory being, or some borderline personality. On the contrary. He presents Himself as the Rock and somebody more stable than the whole universe. The change in our perception and the numerous images of God are the consequences of the richness of His person.

The physical absence of Jesus may correspond, as you suggest, to the image of the child Jesus that Mary and Joseph lost forever. I am thinking especially about how difficult it could be for the taciturn Joseph. He is present at the scene but, as usual, silent. They knew Jesus was not an ordinary child – if an ordinary child exists! Mary had her personal revelation, but Joseph too had some share of the Divine plans. He had seen the angels and the shepherds. He was the child's protector, and it is not surprising that he too looked for the child with great grief. Now in the temple, this boy Jesus speaks in Joseph's face about 'His Father' – that is, another father! That could have been tough to swallow. Could it be an indirect reminder, 'You are not my true father'!? Yet otherwise Luke does not hesitate to call Joseph the father of the child (for example, Lk. 2.33). All Nazareth will think the same (Lk. 4.22). Yet here – as if by the way – Joseph is reminded that Jesus' deepest identity goes further, beyond being the son of Joseph, beyond even what his kinfolk could have thought of him. I find it wonderfully discreet that Luke does not mention any reaction of Joseph to these tough words. He took them in.

This dialogue with Jesus is unique. It hints at his mysterious relationship with the Father in the Temple, the relationship more fundamental than anything else. We are not the sons of God in the same way as Jesus was, and our fathers are usually our biological fathers, and yet, at some life stage, one should go through some analogous experience and discovery. We are something more than the children of our parents, more than the expectations of the society, and all that goes with it: our innate social class, nationality, race, family inheritance, national debt and so on. We are indeed potentially something more than just the children of men and women.

Timothy: Mary and Joseph's loss of Jesus evokes a similar process of losing the beloved that happens in our relationships with each other, especially when we go through these moments of transition from one stage of life to another. This is most painfully obvious sometimes when the lovely child becomes the sulky teenager! Where is this son or daughter that I loved so much? He or she once had such an easy affection for me but now seems to find me an embarrassment. You have to let the past image of the person go if you are to become close to them again.

Cecil Day-Lewis wrote a lovely poem about how loving his son meant letting him go:

> I have had worse partings, but none that so
> Gnaws at my mind still. Perhaps it is roughly
> Saying what God alone could perfectly show –
> How selfhood begins with a walking away,
> And love is proved in the letting go.[3]

Łukasz: What you 'let go' is not the person you love. True love is true, forever. Even a betrayal and rejection of the beloved do not automatically nullify it. It remains for the one who loves to make this decision. Jesus, faithful up to the Cross to those who rejected him, proves this point most luminously. Rather, we let go of control of the people we love. Love does not presume nor should serve to control anybody. This would be a caricature of love, a devilish imitation, or its yet undeveloped and uncanny foetus.

Years later Mary and Joseph will let Jesus go to the Jordan, to the desert and further, to Jerusalem. Their child will face a friendly and unfriendly world. Eventually, this world will kill him. This is also the price of letting go – of your child, friend, sister or brother. Ultimately, though, what we let go of is the *illusion* of control. Because it is an illusion that I will be there always to help and protect you. It is simply not possible; it is not true. This letting go is a great liberation for everyone. I love you but I cannot protect you against every danger. Most importantly, I cannot protect you against love, against being wounded by it, against being vulnerable. How could I?! Even the Heavenly Father did not protect his Son against this most serious 'threat'.

Timothy: Now we get to the heart of the tension between the young Jesus and Mary and Joseph. He answers their reproach with his own, 'Why were you looking for me? Did you not know that it was necessary that I was in [the matters] of my Father?' This is often translated as 'Didn't you know that I would be in the house of my Heavenly Father', the Temple. This is where you should have looked for me! It could mean this, though the word 'house' does not occur in the text.

But the whole of this story is about the obedience that will shape Jesus' life, a true son of his mother, 'the slave of the Lord'. I have no idea how that young Jesus would have described his own identity at that stage. But surely there must have been a growing discernment that at the heart of his life was this obedience to his Heavenly Father. It rings true that this would have happened in his teens. Peter Tyler, an English theologian, has argued that it is often in their teens or even early twenties that young people have a first glimpse of transcendence, an awareness of a relationship with the transcendent God. So it sounds absolutely right that the teenage Jesus, truly human and truly Divine, would have entered into a deeper understanding of himself as being called to do his Father's will at just that age. And so of course he goes to the teachers of the law, the specialists in discerning the will of God, to explore what this means. At the beginning, it all sounds amicable; we see no sign of the tensions that will arise later.

We all need to find those teachers who can help us to make sense of who we are as human beings whose freedom is obedience to God. I had such an experience, when I was in my mid-teens, of being touched by a moment of ecstasy. I found these teachers in my family and with the Benedictines, whose humanity showed that obedience to the Father is not a brutal discipline but a liberation. Doing the things of the Father will probably bring us all into conflict with others at some stage. Martin Luther King described his fellow activists against racism as children going about their Father's business, whereas their opponents saw them as rebels to be suppressed.

Łukasz: Why care about the business of God? Why care about anyone's business beyond one's own? Minding one's own business is just a caricature created by an individualistic society. By definition, a society cannot be composed of people who mind only their own business. At the beginning of its awareness, the only worldview the child knows is the view of the parents. Later there comes a discovery that there are other views. A young person must know them, evaluate, maybe even test them, recalibrate and then make his own choices. Even when one returns to the views of the parents, it will be because of one's own conviction and not just because of their authority.

It is also the time when a child tests with an uncompromising eye whether the values declared by the parents are real. If the parents have no living faith – that is, the faith that influences their life choices – they are mercilessly condemned as superficial bigots. And this judgement by the child is partially correct. I say 'partially' because the same child is usually ignorant of the parents' spiritual history. They too had moments of contemplation, miracles, visitations and trials. On the other hand, children have the gift of asking simple questions that bring us back to the core. It is no accident that the description of the personalized Wisdom in the Book of Proverbs is suggestive of a little girl. If I remember well, in the Rule of St Benedict it is said that the abbot should always consult and take seriously the opinion of the youngest as well.[4]

Speaking of Jesus and his Father, you used the word 'obedience'. It does not appear in this Biblical passage, but your intuition is correct. This noun may today sound very unattractive because it seems to contradict freedom and can be applied both to dogs and humans. We rightly spot here the potential for humiliation or the danger of losing one's soul. One should not play down the possible danger of obedience.

The problem is that since we are social beings, obedience in some measure is unavoidable. Imagining oneself as an individual free from any bonds and even arbitrary rules is, of course, an illusion. One may disobey the rules of grammar, but the result of this 'freedom' would be incomprehensible speech and broken communication. What we may and should do is to choose wisely our obedience, our allegiance. I am not sure if English-speakers can still recognize that the word 'obedience' comes from the Latin *audire*, 'to listen to'. The same intuition appears in Hebrew and Greek, and Polish too. Obedience presumes, therefore, some intellectual effort, understanding, agreement and, ideally, recognizing that the task I am to do is also my own.

Timothy: You are right, Łukasz, that there is no explicit reference to Jesus' obedience to the Father, but it is there, I think, in implicit contrast to his obedience, literally his 'submission', to his parents. Now he goes home and finds a new integration of obedience to Mary and Joseph within obedience to the Father. There is a pattern of childlike harmony, then dissonance and then a new, more adult harmony of the different obediences that shape his life.

I suppose that every one of us hopes to find that new harmony between one's obedience to some deeper identity, even to God, and what one owes to the family that gave one life. When I became a Dominican, I went through a moment of dissonance with my family. My new understanding of my faith and politics was at odds with my parents' conservative views, and it took a long time to find that new grown-up harmony in which belonging to God and belonging to my family chimed together. But I was always a slow learner!

The families of some of our brethren never understand why their children have become Dominicans or even Catholics. Some have to live with a permanent reproach: why are you treating us like this? Why will you not give us grandchildren? After all we spent on your education, why are you throwing it all away? I was blessed in that my family never reproached me, even though they seem to have wondered for a while why I had come to have such strange views! But peace came in due course.

Łukasz: It is said that Mary 'kept all these things in her heart', and it means she kept them in her mind. A very similar phrase appears in the story of the patriarch Joseph. When as a child he shared with his family his unusual dreams, his brothers were outraged and jealous, but his father, Jacob, 'kept the thing' (Gen. 37.11). It looks as if, even for Mary, Jesus and his doings remained unfathomable. She accepted this mystery as a mystery: that is, not something to be easily answered or explained as one would explain a riddle or a simple secret. A mystery is to be experienced and lived. I would even add that there is no end to this discovery. Realizing that one is taking care of a God-given child – and it is truly the case with any child! – invites one to look at this gift with the attentiveness of the keen astronomer scrutinizing the skies.

'How can you, being a Jew, ask from me "to drink", while I am a Samaritan woman?' (Jn 4.4–42)

Now, it was necessary for him to go through Samaria. He comes, therefore, to a city of Samaria, called Sychar, near to the place that Jacob gave to Joseph, his son. There was the spring of Jacob. Jesus, tired out by the journey, was sitting thus by the spring. It was about the sixth hour. A woman comes from Samaria to draw water. Jesus says to her, –

'Give me to drink', because his disciples had gone off into town to buy food.

Then the Samaritan woman says to him, –

'How can you, being a Jew, ask from me "to drink", while I am a Samaritan woman?'

Because Jews do not associate with Samaritans. Jesus answered and said to her, –

'If you knew the gift of God, and who it is who is saying to you, "Give me to drink," it would be for you to ask him, and he would have given you living water.'

She says to him, –

'Lord, you don't even have a bucket, and the well is deep. From where do you have the living water? Are you greater than our father Jacob, who gave us the well and he drank of it, and his sons and his flocks?'

Jesus answers and says to her, –

'Everyone who drinks of this water will become thirsty again. But who would drink of the water that I myself will give him will not thirst for eternity but the water that I will give him will become in him a fountain of water springing up to eternal life.'

The woman tells him, –

'Lord, give me this water, so that I won't get thirsty or come here to draw.'

He says to her, –

'Go. Call your man and come here.'

The woman answers him and says, –

'I don't have a man.'

Jesus says to her, –

'You said well, – "I don't have a man." For five men, you have had. And now, the one you have is no man of yours. This you have said truly.'

The woman says to him, –

'Lord, I see that you are a prophet. Our ancestors worshipped on this mountain. But you, you say that it is in Jerusalem, the place where it is necessary to worship.'

Jesus says to her, –

'Believe me, woman, that the hour comes when neither on this mountain nor in Jerusalem will you worship the Father. You worship what you don't know. We, we worship what we know because salvation is from the Jews. Yet the hour comes, and is now, when true worshippers will worship the Father in spirit and truth. For also the Father is looking for such worshippers of him. God is spirit, and for his worshippers there is need to worship in spirit and truth.'

The woman says to him, –

'I know that the Messiah is coming, the one called Anointed. When that one comes, he will announce us everything.'

Says to her Jesus, –

'I AM, the one speaking to you.'

At this his disciples came and they were astonished that he was talking to a woman. Yet no one said, – 'What are you seeking for?' or, – 'Why are you talking to her?' The woman left then her water jar and went to town and she told people, –

'Come, see a man who told me everything I've done! Is not this [one] the Anointed?'

The people went out of the town and were coming to him. Meanwhile, the disciples were asking him, saying, –

'Rabbi, eat.'

But he told them, –

'I, I have food to eat that you know not.'

So the disciples were saying to one another, –

'Have someone brought him [anything] to eat?'

Jesus says to them, –

'My food is doing the will of the One-who-sent me and accomplishing his work.[1] Isn't it you who say, – "It is four months more and the harvest comes?" Look, I tell you, open your eyes and see the fields that are white [ready] for harvesting now! The harvester receives his wages and gathers a crop for eternal life, so that the sower rejoices alike and the harvester. In this [respect] the word is true, – "Different is the sower, and different the harvester." I have sent you to harvest what you have not toiled for. Others have toiled, and you, into their toil you have entered.'

Now many of that town believed in Him, from the Samaritans, because the word of the woman that had testified, – 'He told me all I have done.' So when the Samaritans came to him they asked him to stay with them, and he stayed there for two days. And many more believed because of her word. And to the woman they kept saying, –

'It is no longer because of your speaking that we believe, because we have heard ourselves, and we have known that this is truly the Saviour of the world.'

Timothy: The first conversation of the New Testament that we looked at, between Mary and Gabriel, is prior to Jesus saying anything. In the second, when he is lost, his family is torn apart by Jesus' emerging sense that obedience to his Heavenly Father is at the heart of his identity. Now, in this conversation, this same obedience has become the very core of his being: 'My food is doing the will of the One-who-sent me and accomplishing his work.'

This conversation by the well is one that should not have happened, an impossible conversation! 'How can you, being a Jew, ask from me "to drink", while I am a Samaritan woman? Because Jews do not associate with Samaritans.' It is a conversation that crosses the boundaries which in that society should silence all communication: differences of sex, of ethnicity and of religion. Both Jesus and the woman would surely have regarded it as rendering them both contaminated. This transgression is heightened by the fact that it initially revolves around water, which is symbolic of purification.

This conversation clearly invites us too to engage in impossible conversations with people from whom we are separated by divisions of belief, ancient quarrels and old silences. Imagine a conversation in Israel today between a Zionist Jew and a Palestinian! Even within the Catholic

Church some conversations seem doomed to be mere shouting matches, especially where the 'culture wars' rage. How can a liberation theologian and a fervent supporter of the Tridentine Mass be at ease in conversation with each other? Yet, as Pope Francis encourages the Church to embark on the synodal path, these awkward, painful, challenging conversations must happen if the Church is to be renewed! So how is it that Jesus and the woman at the well manage to talk?

Łukasz: You are right to stress the hostile context of this encounter. There were not just 'culture wars' but actual wars between Judaeans and Samaritans, and blood was spilt. According to the Book of Nehemiah, the Samaritan elite were Nehemiah's main adversary during the reconstruction of Jerusalem after the exile. The conflict between the two groups, both claiming to be the true Israel, escalated under the Jewish king John Hyrcanus, who destroyed the Samaritan temple on the Mount of Gerazim about 111 BC. And later, in Roman times, Flavius Josephus (*Antiquities of the Jews*, 18, 28–9) describes how some Samaritans dumped a dead body in the Jerusalem Temple during the Passover to render it impure. Similar provocative actions were experienced by both sides. Unlike the newcomers, the Romans, Samaritans were well-established enemies, over against whom one's identity was constructed, a rival nation whose wickedness was confirmed by the Bible, tradition, history and recent experience. Rivals before the same God, with a rival holy site, not unlike the two altars of Cain and Abel – built for the same God, fuming not only with the religious zeal but also with quite unreligious jealousy.

As Dominicans, because of our association with the Inquisition, we do not get a good press as practitioners of religious 'dialogue'. Indeed, there are meetings called 'dialogues' that aren't at all. I mean here those wearisome shows in which well-intended participants keep exchanging smiles, nods, handshakes, and at the same time tiptoe around any issue that is worth talking about. Indeed, such social gatherings should lead to true dialogue and not replace it. Jesus started like that. The first gesture was his simple presence and the fact that he asked for the woman's jar.

Dialogue with an enemy appears to be, therefore, quite a holy place, where one's God can be met surreptitiously. We who at times have difficulty in engaging even with our friends are challenged by this only seemingly bucolic scene. Can a meeting with a heretic be theologically fruitful and lead to a deeper truth? Much good theology has been born of those tense encounters. Our thoughts and arguments remain half-shaped and ill-articulated as long as we are not challenged to arrive at clarity.

Timothy: Yes, the dialogue with an enemy can be a place of revelation, of new truth, and not just because we arrive at a new clarity about what we think. Also there may be some precious truth concealed in their assertions, if only we are open to receive it. Rather than saying, weakly, 'Well everyone has a right to their own opinion', we have to wrestle with them, like Jacob wrestling with the stranger in the night to get his blessing! In our Catholic tradition, a heretic is not someone who has got everything wrong but, usually, someone who has got one thing right at the expense of other truths, like the third-century theologians who so loved the humanity of Christ that they denied his Divinity or the other way around. A heretic is someone who bangs on about something true to the exclusion of other aspects of the mystery.

Łukasz: At the outset, Jesus recognizes that he needs something from the woman. She is needed. She has something to give. It is quite a good tactic with which to woo a partner but, as is usually the case with Jesus' dialogues, something deeper is at stake. Further, Jesus will also present himself as the one who can offer something even more precious.

To appreciate this little-great gesture of asking for water one should remember that the rules that prohibited even touching impure objects were very strict, and went so far as to prohibit using them, or worse, even sharing drink! They kept the foreigner and the enemy at a distance. This 'trifling' custom enraged Paul against Peter more than any theological divergence. In practice, the strictly applied ritual purity rules make it impossible for a Jew to share a meal with non-Jews. The stranger's wife is impure, his plates, food and everything he touches. How can people have a conversation if they cannot even share a table?

The enlightened contemporary reader can laugh at this as at some outdated superstition but the behaviour of some vegetarians I know produces quite similar effects of isolation. Jesus decided that meeting with this woman was important enough to enter her 'impure' territory, to be there on her conditions, and even ask to drink from her 'impure' jar.

Timothy: She meets her Saviour as someone who needs what she can give. Our impossible conversations begin when we dare to let ourselves be seen as needy, people who thirst for what another has to offer. In the battles of the culture wars, do I dare to admit that I long for what someone, from whom I am separated by profound differences and incomprehension, can offer me? Even our conversations, though we are friends, evolve in the hope of receiving something from the other for which we thirst. I do!

With every provocative, mischievous response, the thirst deepens. First, his need for water from the well, but then her need for the living water he will give, which will flow up from the depth of her being. Finally, the deepest thirst of all emerges, which is the Father's thirst for her: 'For also the Father is looking for such worshippers of Him.' God thirsts for her, this woman whom others regard as soiled and compromised by her many love affairs. Jesus' human thirst has been the first moment in the revelation of the Divine thirst, for the Father longs for her!

So improbable conversations, even within the Church, happen if we let ourselves be touched by an ever-deepening thirst. How many arguments begin with a thirst for something small, like smashing your opponent! But can we transcend the destructive urge by deepening our thirsts, so that we thirst for the other, even the heretical other, and ultimately for God who sustains them in being?

This thirst will climax for Jesus on the cross, when he cries out: 'I thirst.' Indeed the meeting with the woman is at the sixth hour, the hour of crucifixion. Their meeting prefigures the wedding of God and humanity on the cross. So let us become thirsty people. Thirst is not to be quenched immediately, but cultivated. The gospel of John leads us on a journey of deepening thirst, from the thirst for wine at the marriage of Cana, to the thirst at the well, to the thirst on the cross. As we journey deeper into the mystery of our faith, we become ever thirstier. The more we glimpse the mystery, the more we are thirsty.

In a novel called *Soif* ('Thirst'), by Amélie Nothomb, Jesus shares his innermost thoughts as he nears death on the cross, inviting us to live with thirst:

> I advise you to prolong your thirst. That the thirsty person delays the moment of drinking. Not indefinitely, of course. It is not a question of putting one's health in danger. I am not asking you to meditate on your thirst, I ask that one feels it to the full, body and soul, before quenching it.[2]

We thirst on all sorts of levels of our being. Jesus ratchets up the conversation by addressing a need in her which is deeper than for water:

'Go, call your man and come here.' But she does not go. She has no need to. Those successive love affairs, those passing passions, are left behind now she is meeting the one whom her soul truly desires. When she does finally go, it is to call not her lover but the citizens of the town. She leaves the water jar behind for she has transcended that level of desire too. So let us cultivate deep thirsts and hungers so that we may be drawn to the one who alone has what we seek most passionately and more!

Łukasz: Initially it is an encounter between a Jew and a Samaritan. Admittedly, the behaviour of both of them was a bit irregular, and they both knew it. Their group identity was therefore immediately toned down but not excluded: a marginal Jew and a marginal Samaritan. There they meet with the burden of history, conflict, with the rights and wrongs known by both sides. It is telling that this complexity and their national identities were not simply rejected or forgotten.

To have done that would be not a short cut but a dangerous illusion. Some ideologies have promised that and discarded the 'old' identities. Let us forget that you are a Jew, a Palestinian, a woman, a man, who your father was, what your brother did to my sister and so on … It will not work for long. International political ideologies (communism or Islamism) promised that, but instead they created some new form of chauvinism. The weaker renounced his or her national identity whereas the stronger kept it, for we need to speak some language, don't we? Denying the importance of group identities does not help. Rather, it imposes some newly made-up group identity, a false one and a strange one too. In consequence, a meeting with a real person, with his or her multiple and complex identities, becomes very difficult.

Jesus lets the Samaritan woman be a Samaritan. He does not say that his being Jewish 'is not a big deal' either. She claimed to be a descendant of Jacob and Joseph, something that the Jews generally disagree with. Most Jews called the Samaritans 'Kutheans': the non-Israelite foreigners who were settled in Samaria by the Assyrians, according to 2 Kings 17. As often, the history is more complicated, because the same chapter of 2 Kings clearly explained that the Samaritan priests were of Israelite origin.

Jesus does not deny the Samaritan woman her version of history or her self-understanding. I would say that he goes along with it. Jesus and the Samaritan woman seem to share even some popular legends about the patriarch Jacob and his well. According to these non-Biblical but popular stories (like our donkey and ox in the Nativity scene), when Jacob removed the stone from the well (Gen. 29), the water 'came up to its mouth and was overflowing' (*Jerusalem Targum*[3]). This explains why, in John 4, the well becomes a spring and why in the end Jesus does not seem to need a bucket. Indirectly, he claims to be someone greater than Jacob. He supplants Jacob, the Supplanter of old (Gen. 27.36).

Timothy: It is fascinating how, as you say, their identities, as a Samaritan woman and a Jewish man, are not denied. That is who, in a sense, they are. But slowly they edge beyond allowing such identities to confine or limit them.

How does this happen? Initially they say very little. Jesus' opening words are brief, 'Give me to drink' – just three words in the Greek. Every time he talks, he says a little more. The conversation slowly catches fire, until at last Jesus bursts forth into a long speech about the nature of true worship. And what seems to set it alight are her goading, teasing, provocative remarks. You should not be talking to me at all! So you are going to provide living water. Who do you think you are? Greater than our father Jacob? OK, so you know about my private life! Come on, so you think you are a prophet? So this unnamed woman gets ever ruder, needling Jesus into talking all the more!

Maybe when we engage with the stranger, the 'enemy', we do not launch immediately into long speeches. We feel our way like fencers, testing reactions, seeking a way through to the other, not to pierce them with a sword but to touch their hearts and minds.

Or is she being flirtatious? In the Bible when men and women meet at wells, romance often follows, and even betrothal. Isaac and Rebecca, Jacob and Rachel, Moses and Zipporah, all meet at wells. It is a classic scene. Like people meeting today in a pub? In English it is often called 'a watering hole'! When the disciples reappear, they seem shocked. What has Jesus been getting up to? Unlike this talkative pair, getting on like a house on fire, they do not know what to say and are reduced to silence until they can change the subject and ask him to eat something. There follows a parallel conversation, but this time beginning from food rather than water. They too break the silence with minimal words, 'Rabbi, eat', also just two words in the Greek.

Let's get back to the conversation of Jesus and the woman. Don't we in the Church need to learn the art of teasing, flirtatious conversation? Theodore Zeldin lamented: 'Unfortunately, though humans ruminate, cogitate, brood, play with ideas, dream and make inspired guesses about the thoughts of other people all the time, there has been no *Kamasutra* of the mind to reveal the sensuous pleasures of thinking, to show how ideas can flirt with each other and learn to embrace.'[4] Just imagine how liberating it would be if opposing groups in the Church – feminists and patriarchal dinosaurs, for example (I have been accused of being both!) – could engage in teasing and affectionate debate rather than dry point-scoring! Some matters are too serious for us not to joke and tease!

Łukasz: The thorny question of being Jewish or Samaritan took the form of an honest and playful dialogue. Now they are just a man and a woman, both thirsty at the same well. It was now time to move to something even more delicate than ethnicity. Jesus refers to her individual story.

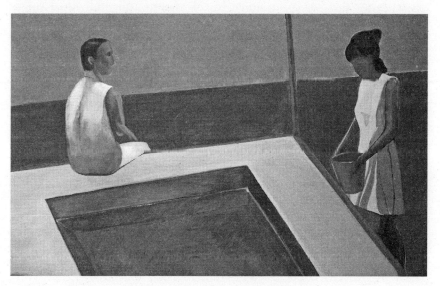

Monika Sawionek, *Meeting at the Well*, 2010, private collection

Unlike Jesus, we do not have insight into the private life of our interlocutors. People might be offended if a stranger were to ask or speak of it. And yet it is unavoidable; to develop a true conversation, one needs to go beyond group identities. There is an art of small talk and there is a danger to it. With all respect to this difficult art, I once listened admiringly to the president of a certain country who spoke for ten minutes and did not say anything. The great art of hot-air production. My old Jewish friend laughs at me saying that we would both die of hunger if we had to make our living in diplomacy! Well, thank God I am not a diplomat but a

Dominican priest, and one's personal world is something that interests me most. I must confess that I am often very relieved when I wear my habit for official meetings because it rapidly says so many things, and among them some most intimate things too. A lot about my faith, my lifestyle, moral convictions, even about my sex life! It is almost like having a big banner. The advantage for me is that I do not need to retell all that to the people I meet. Actually, judging from my experience, many people tend to respond with a similar openness.

Saying something personal creates a kind of bond. That can be scary but also precious. When Jesus revealed his knowledge about the woman's private life, it created the trust for them to speak further about God, the future, worship and all those complex things that touch not only her and her faith but also her community. In this manner this individual and at times even intimate encounter proves to be transformative not only for her but also for the people from her town. The most intimate but meaningful conversations with Christ also have some very public consequences!

Timothy: Fascinating! The more personal it gets, the more it touches other people. The Word became flesh in a particular Jewish man, with his very personal story which becomes universal, the story in which we can all find ourselves.

She makes this movement from the personal to the public in the most startling and unexpected words which she addresses to her fellow citizens: 'Come, see a man who told me everything I've done! Is not this [one] the Anointed?' She is a woman who has surely been judged by her fellow citizens for her erratic love life. She comes alone to the well at midday, when the sun is hottest, because no one else will be there. The judgements passed on her have condemned her to loneliness, to be an object of scorn. Yet here she delights in the one who told her everything that she had ever done! Jesus sees her, knows her, in all the mess and confusion of her life, and for the first time she delights in being known fully! His judgement is liberating, and liberates her to share herself with her town people.

Another friend of mine, Carmody Grey, said:

Often I feel that the prospect of judgement is disincentivizing for people, in their experience of Christianity. Why would anyone want to be, volunteer to be, judged in that way? Jesus' encounter with the woman at the well shows something of Jesus' tenderness for the actual reality of people's lives: the muddle of confused desires, the partially followed-through choices, the compromises of a wandering heart.[5]

He embodies the Father's tender desire for us as we really are. His judgement sheds a light which shows how this stupid, fallible, weak person is lovable! The Last Judgement, utterly truthful, will disclose our weakness and how lovable we are!

So impossible conversations, carrying us across boundaries that seem to condemn us to mutual incomprehension, are possible if we learn to be thirsty, longing to meet someone who will offer us water at the well, especially the person who we never dreamed might have anything to offer us.

Once a woman came to see me who had always seemed to me alarmingly moral and superior. I had not really liked her. But when she confessed the utter mess of her life, suddenly I saw her as lovable and even, paradoxically, as good in a way. Like Sebastian Flyte in Evelyn Waugh's *Brideshead Revisited*, the person whose life is a disaster, who is weak and apparently with nothing to give and yet in whom we already see signs of holiness.[6] That is a book I would love you to read!

Let us thirst for what the other can give us, as we ascend to the unquenchable thirst for God who thirsts for us and who calls us to worship him not on this ideological mountain or another one, but in spirit and in truth. And may we dare to let ourselves be seen, vulnerable and naked to the other's gaze, confident that the only judge who really matters is the Lord, whose eyes see with unfailing compassion.

13

'Who do you say that I am?'
(Mt. 16.13–28)

When Jesus entered the parts of Caesarea Philippi, he asked his disciples, –

'Who do people say that the Son of Man is?'
They said, –
'Some say, – "John the Baptist", others, – "Elijah", still others, – "Jeremiah", or, – "one of the prophets".'
He said to them, –
'And you, who do you say that I am?'
Then in reply Simon Peter said, –
'You are the Christ, the Son of the living God.'
Then in reply Jesus said to him, –
'Blessed are you, Simon Bariona, for flesh and blood has not revealed *this* to you, but my Father who is in heaven. Also I, therefore, I say to you that you are *Petros* ('the rock'), and upon this rock I will build my church, and the gates of hell shall not prevail against it. I will give you the keys of the kingdom of heaven and whatever you bind on earth shall be bound in heaven; and whatever you loose on earth shall be loosed in heaven.'

Then he expressly ordered the disciples to tell no one that he was the Christ. From then on, Jesus began to show his disciples that it was necessary that he go away to Jerusalem and suffer greatly from the elders, the chief priests and the scribes, and be killed and on the third day be raised. Then Peter took him aside and began to rebuke him by saying, –
'Mercy on you, Lord! No such thing shall happen to you.'
But he turned and said to Peter, –
'Go after me, *Satan*! You are a stumbling stone to me because you are not thinking about the things of God but about human *things*.'

Then Jesus said to his disciples, –

'Whoever wants to come after me, let him deny himself and take up his cross, and follow me! For whoever wants to save his life will lose it, but whoever loses his life for my sake will find it. What would profit a human being even if he gained the whole world and forfeited his life? Or what will anyone give in exchange for their life? For the Son of Man will come in the glory of his Father, with his angels, and then he will give back everyone according to his conduct. Amen, I say to you, there are some standing here who will not taste death until they see the Son of Man coming in his kingdom.'

Łukasz: I think it is the only scene in which Jesus seems to care about public opinion, and even this seems to be contextual. His survey of partially correct opinions may have simply served to encourage the disciples to formulate their answers. All these identifications are flattering. Indeed Jesus did have something in common with John the Baptist, with Elijah and with Jeremiah. All very well, but to be compared to someone else was not good enough. Jesus hoped that his closest men would have some more precise answers as to who he was!

'Who am I?' What an extraordinary question in the mouth of the One who bears the Divine name of 'I AM'. Would the Creator of heaven and earth really care what these few simple Galileans think about him? Surprising as it is, he does care. Jesus wanted to be known. We also want to be known. Would you not wish that there would be at least one person in the world knowing what it means to be you? There is no personal relationship without ever-growing and reciprocal knowledge. The more one loves, the more one desires to know the other; the more one knows, the more one desires. Knowing and loving are like two sides of the same coin. Jesus wanted to be known and recognized by his followers.

Timothy: You ask whether we would not all wish that there is at least one person in the world who knows what it means for me to be 'me'. Yes, that is the heart of all friendship surely, the desire to really know and be known by this person who stands before me. It belongs to friendship that we honour in some way the identity that they claim or reveal. Today, so much of politics and social life and the culture wars revolves around the question of identity, claimed and contested, from Ukrainian national identity to transgender identity. This question is always in the air: 'Who do people say that I am?' Above all today, 'Who do I say that I am?' Of course, it is with one's closest friends that one discovers who one is! Every close friend both accepts who I claim to be and discloses who I am. I see who I am in their eyes, in their gaze.

Łukasz: When God speaks about Himself, the theologians call it *revelation*. There is no other way we can learn about some essential truths about God without revelation. By analogy, there is also revelation concerning human beings, when we reveal our interior world. We do not have access to another person's world from the outside. One can do as much psychological testing as possible, squeeze one's brain for neural oscillations, use serum, or torture – nothing will replace the revelation of one's heart. The door opens from the inside only. This is a precious discovery that we are in charge of this door with its locks and have the freedom to decide to whom to open, and how far.

Timothy: This makes me think of the famous painting by William Holman Hunt of Jesus as *The Light of the World*, in Keble College Chapel, Oxford, two minutes' walk from Blackfriars. It illustrates Revelation 3.20, 'Listen, I am standing at the door, knocking; if you hear my voice and open the door, I will come in to you and eat with you, and you with me.' In the painting there is no knob on the outside, as you say. We have to choose to open the door to let the Lord into the sanctuary of our deepest identity, and we do so to our closest friends too.

Łukasz: Peter's answer was correct. In fact, it was too perfect for Peter to understand! Peter identified Jesus properly but did not grasp the full meaning of his own words. Ultimately, Jesus attributes them to his heavenly Father as a kind of internal revelation.

When God reveals something of his Divine person, it is a supernatural revelation. Jesus' blessing pronounced on Peter is immediately followed by the shocking rebuke in which the very same Peter is called *Satan*. The cause of this shift is clear. Peter was happy with the first part of revelation, the truth about Jesus as the expected anointed saviour. Yet Peter did not want to hear about his Passion. The disciple rejected Jesus' further self-revelation to this extent that he did not even register the mention of the Resurrection! Don't we fall into the same trap? We so easily listen to the truths about our family and friends that suit us and strongly reject the difficult points. In Hebrew *Satan* means 'enemy'. Partial truth can be as bad as a lie. That is why by the end of this scene Jesus forbade them to speak of his messianic identity at all. When even his disciples did not grasp the identity of 'Christ', such partial identification would be misleading. He had to hide when the people wanted to make him a king!

If I do not want to know my loved one more deeply, there is a growing risk that I love some non-existent person, a figment of my imagination, a comfortable and amenable idol. Making a mistake is not a great impediment to love, as long as one's knowledge is increasing and he or she has a true desire to know and meet the true other. On the contrary, at the moment when I refuse to know, to progress, and reject some elements of this natural revelation, then the movement stops. I have preferred to love my ideas about someone more than the mysterious and maybe more difficult person in front of me.

I believe that the loving and attentive ear will be tuned to the minuscule dissonances between the internal image of the beloved and the perceived reality. These can be difficult to grasp, but they are expected and precious: 'I want to know you, more deeply, better, closer.'

Timothy: Jesus poses this question 'Who do you say that I am?' – at just the same moment that he reveals the journey on which he is embarking, to Jerusalem, to suffer, die and rise. Yes, it is disclosed to Peter who Jesus is – the Christ, the Son of the Living God. What this means is only discovered in the journey, and most beautifully perhaps on the beach when they see this stranger inviting them to breakfast. We shall look at that later.

Maybe this is true of every one of us. To know and love someone is more than to grasp facts about them, or recognize their qualities. It is more than assenting to the identity that they claim, their self-image. It is to have some glimpse of the journey on which they are embarking, the hunger and thirst that are in their heart, how they are on the pilgrimage towards the fullness of being in God. We are all touched surely, implicitly or explicitly, by some yearning for infinity and who we *are* is disclosed most deeply in how we seek it, whether through marriage or art or writing poetry, our job or just loving the people we bump into day by day. In that sense our vocation *is* our identity, our response to the one who says, 'I AM', and summons us to follow him on the way. So knowing you is inseparable from seeing you as a fellow pilgrim, intuiting the journey on which you are embarked, the thirst at the core of your being. Remember the Samaritan woman at the well!

So Simon's identity now as Peter – the Rock – is interesting in two ways. Because he recognizes who Jesus is, Jesus recognizes that he is the Rock. His own identity is founded on that glimpse of who Jesus is. Who Peter is is inseparable from who Jesus is. And isn't it true of each of us too in some way? Each of us is created to encounter the Lord and recognize Him. We may do this implicitly, even unconsciously, but unless we glimpse, in however a foggy and even distorted way, that we are addressed by the Lord, we don't know who we are!

Second, Simon's identity as the Rock lies in the future. He is only a wobbling rock at the moment, a stone that people trip over. His name is a sort of summons! As St John said, in one of my favourite texts, 'Who we are is yet to be revealed.' That means that I only know a little bit who you are, my friend Łukasz, if I get some tiny glimpse of you as more than I can know. I can only know you if I have some sense of you as unknowable, more than I can grasp, whose mystery is hidden in Christ, awaiting full discovery. Once I think that I have someone nailed down, sorted, put in a box, at that very moment they escape my knowledge and love. One only knows another in seeing how they transcend one's knowledge.

That is the essence of a Christian friendship, perhaps of all friendship, that you recognize in each other the pilgrim and you help each other to be unburdened of the superficial claims to identity – machismo, or based on celebrity or beauty or intellectual elitism or ethnic superiority – because each has seen in the other a hint of the unknowable mystery.

This radiates especially from the eyes of another person. As icon painters know, the eyes disclose the Divinity which inhabits each of us. I am reading *This Is Happiness*, by the Irish novelist Niall Williams, and I was bowled over by these words: 'It seems to me the true and individual nature of a human being's eyes defy description, or at least my capabilities. They're not like anything else, or anyone else's, and may be the most perfect proof of the existence of a Creator.'[1]

'Who do you say that I am?' The answer to that question is also shown in a very odd way, by instituting Simon Barłona (*bar* is an Aramaic word for 'son', as you told me, which carries us right back to the earliest days of Jesus' relationship with Peter) as the rock on which the Church is built. Who Jesus is is revealed in the foundation of an institution. From the beginning, it is revealed to be an ambiguous institution, just as Peter the rock is also the stumbling stone, a source of scandal. Christ's body, the Church, is always, and always will be, the community of saints and sinners, a light that shines in the darkness and a place of betrayal. Only God could have so daringly chosen that ambiguous figure Peter, the denier and the martyr, to be the foundation of his community.

Our society is deeply suspicious of all institutions: the law and the police, government, the army but also, above all, the Church, which has been so shamed by the sexual abuse scandal. People will say, 'I love Jesus but I want nothing to do with the Church.' Many treasure a personal relationship with the Lord but not an institutional one.

In a way this is illusory since without institutions there can be no communities, just mobs. Without institutions there can be no football or symphonies, no families or nations. But more than this, at the heart of Jesus' identity is this mad generosity. He entrusts himself to this community of the good, the bad and the ugly – humanity. He embodies himself in this Church which has been rocklike through the ages, and the source of scandal in every generation. To refuse this is to try to shove Jesus back into heaven, into a remote and impossible purity.

It would be to deny that the Christ, the Son of God, is this person who now takes the road to Jerusalem with his band of uneducated and foolish friends, who quarrel on the way about who is the greatest (as they will throughout history, loving bizarre titles), who will deny him and run away in his hour of need, but who will all die for him in the end. Who is he? The one who outrageously entrusted himself to them and to us.

Annibale Carracci, *Domine, quo vadis?*, 1602, National Gallery, London

Łukasz: Indeed, accepting the full mystery of Jesus leads us to accept our own mystery. Jesus calls us not only to accept his words about the cross of the Messiah but also to accept one's own cross. Well, to understand the meaning of the word 'cross' is one thing, but to know the cross is something else. I can list the components of a dish, provide details of its preparation and inform you about the nutrients in the final product. Yet no data and no definitions will replace the experience of tasting it. We understand better our own parents when we become parents ourselves. How to understand the loving Jesus without loving and living like him? Ultimately, we interpret his words not by providing some other set of words but more like musicians who interpret the sheet music by playing it. This performative interpretation is probably the best manner to grasp his words, his teaching and the depth of Jesus' heart. That is why Jesus' love even until death on the cross is constantly on the horizon of his disciples. Turning away from it is like turning away from the chance of getting closer to the Lord and learning what it means to be Him. Do you want to know what it means to be me?

Timothy: When I was young, I was always a little uneasy with this stress on the cross. It sounded grim and masochistic. 'If you want to share the glory, you have got to suffer.' That would make Christianity a depressing religion indeed. Now I have grown up a little, I look at the cross differently, as a way into that infinite vulnerability which is Lord's love. In the sacristy before we process into the chapel for Mass each day, we bow to the cross. We look at it as if to say, 'Yes. That is what love looks like!'

Intermezzo: Who Is He? Who Am I?

Łukasz and Timothy: The first three conversations from the Old Testament focused on absence: Where are you? Where is your brother? Where is your wife? The first four conversations we look at from the New Testament ask with growing insistence: Who is He? So it is good to pause and ask how this question engages each of us. How does this question challenge our sense of our own identity?

In each conversation, the question is raised with increasing tension. When Gabriel bursts into Mary's life, the identity of her child-to-be is announced. 'He will be great, and will be called "the Son of the Most High"; and the Lord God will give Him the throne of David, his father. And He will reign over the house of Jacob forever; and His kingdom will have no end.' It is proclaimed who he is, but this cannot have made much sense to Mary yet. Yet she accepts her vocation without reserve: 'Behold, the Slave of the Lord. Let it happen to me according to your word.'

Then we move to the uncomfortable conversation of the child Jesus with Mary and Joseph after he had been found in the Temple. In the Annunciation he had been identified by being placed within the genealogy of his family, but in this fraught exchange it becomes unclear what this means: 'Did you not know that it was necessary that I was in [the matters] of my Father?' Who then is He?

The conversation with the woman at the well ups the tension. It moves between flirtation and confrontation. It pushes them both beyond their initial tribal identities, as Jew and Samaritan: 'Believe me, woman, that the hour comes when neither on this mountain nor in Jerusalem will you worship the Father.' The question of his identity becomes urgent: 'Come, see a man who told me everything I've done! Is not this [one] the Anointed?' What does that mean for her own identity?

At Caesarea Philippi, the question becomes central: 'Who do people say that I am?' And the tensions become explosive: 'Go after me, Satan! You are a stumbling stone to me because you are not thinking about the things of God but about human *things*.' For now, any proclamation of his messianic identity must be silenced until his trial. Conversations will often be with his enemies. We shall look at just one example. Who he is cannot be understood until the moment of his death. Then the High Priest will ask openly: 'Are you the Messiah, the Son of the Blessed One?' (Mk 14.61). Pilate too will wonder whether he is a king.

So at every stage, as the conversations become more tense, the question of his identity becomes more urgent and in consequence the identity of his interlocuters is more radically put into question. What about us? Who do we say that he is? How does the answer challenge our own sense of identity? His parents, the Samaritan woman and Peter have all been challenged to understand themselves anew. For it is not a theoretical and theological question but one that makes each of us ask: who do I say that I am? Our identities prove to be provisional until we know fully who he is: 'Beloved, we are God's children now; what we will be has not yet been revealed. What we do now is this: when he is revealed, we will be like him, for we shall see him as he is' (1 Jn 3.2).

14

'Whose wife will she be?' (Mk 12.18–28)

And the Sadducees come to him, those who say that there is no resurrection, and they were interrogating him, saying, –

'Teacher, Moses wrote for us that if one's brother dies, and leaves a wife behind him, and leaves no child, let his brother take the wife, and raise up seed to his brother. There were seven brothers. Now, the first took a wife and when dying left no children. And the second took her and died, leaving no children; and the third likewise. And the seven did not leave seed. Last of all also the wife died. In the resurrection, when they arise, whose wife will she be? For the seven took her for wife.'

Jesus said to them, –

'Is it not that you err because you know neither the scriptures nor the power of God? For when they rise from the dead, they neither marry nor are given in marriage, but are like angels in heaven. And as for the dead, that they rise up, did you not read in the Book of Moses, in the story about the bush, how God said to him, "I am the God of Abraham, the God of Isaac, and the God of Jacob"? He is not God of the dead, but God of the living. You err greatly.'

One of the scribes came near and heard them disputing with one another, and, having seen that he answered them well, he asked him, –

'Which commandment is the first of all?'

Timothy: This is one of the most bizarre conversations in the Bible. The Sadducees recount this ridiculous story about the woman who marries seven brothers. Jesus replies that the risen will be like angels, in whom the Sadducees did not believe. Then Jesus offers a bizarre proof of the resurrection, referring to God's words to Moses: 'I am the God of Abraham, the God of Isaac and the God of Jacob.' Surely no Biblical scholar would accept this as evidence of the Resurrection? And then the conversation collapses entirely when Jesus brings it to an abrupt end: 'You err greatly.' So why bother with this non-conversation? Because it holds up a mirror by which we can understand why there are so many non-conversations in our Church and in our society and how we may learn how to dialogue better.

The Sadducees are deliberately recounting an absurd story about the woman because they think that belief in the Resurrection is ridiculous. We should imagine them slapping their thighs and keeling over with laughter! It is a typical ploy in bad argument, the *reductio ad absurdum*; they call him 'teacher', but they have no intention of being taught.

Łukasz: A question! A question! A kingdom for a fair question! Formulating a true question presumes several important shared views between the discussing parties. One should not take fair questions for granted. Think of little children when they ask all sorts of questions: why is the sky blue? Did Adam and Eve have navels? Why didn't God save Jesus on the cross? Why are you crying, mummy? These questions deserve to be answered with all due seriousness. Children expect to get the answers because they trust us and believe that the adults will answer; when their expectations are not met, they stop asking …

Our mothers and fathers were not able to answer many of our questions. Yet I think it is good to keep this childlike attitude towards God and keep asking Him our everyday questions and life-and-death questions. I am asking you because I believe you will make some good use even of my confused words. By asking truly, I reveal my ignorance, my limits, my incompetence and so on.

Since you, Timothy, were a teacher, you know that the best students have the most questions. It is not because they are unprepared but the opposite: they ask because they are informed, they care about the subject and they trust you can engage in seeking the truth together with them. At your numerous public meetings you must have also met people who asked long questions that were actually a self-presentation rather than a chance to meet and listen. Such participants do not have true questions because they think they already know all that they need. Their inquiry has only the grammatical form of a question; it seeks a simple confirmation, no challenges. There is nothing wrong with a rhetorical question in a rhetorical monologue. In a dialogue, though, rhetorical questions rather preclude the answer. Not only journalists but also lawyers and politicians do it. Commonly, in personal quarrels, one encounters accusation questions, insinuation questions, manipulation questions, mockery questions …

Timothy: Indeed, in the New Testament mockery is frequently the reaction to belief in the Resurrection of the dead. When Jesus hangs on the cross, 'they derided him, wagging their heads and saying "Aha, You who would destroy the Temple and rebuild it in three days, save yourself and come down from the cross"' (Mk 15.29–31). When Paul preached the resurrection of Jesus in Athens, 'some mocked' (Acts 17.32). In 1 Corinthians, Paul acknowledges that the cross is folly to the Gentiles.

At the heart of our faith is an apparently absurd claim: Jesus was not just a teacher who told us that we should be nicer to each other. He died and was raised from the dead. One cannot get around this shocking claim, which still today many people, like the Sadducees, will just dismiss as mad.

How then are we to respond to those who dismiss it as absurd? One approach is to glory in its absurdity. Tertullian, the third-century theologian from North Africa, is supposed to have said: *Credo quia absurdum (est)* – I believe because it is absurd. Come on: Christianity is absurd and that is fantastic! Let's glory in its absurdity. But scholars claim that this was not what Tertullian actually wrote. It was a caricature of Christianity created by the Enlightenment's false opposition between faith and reason. Voltaire had a hand in the invention of this quotation.[1] Tertullian believed in reason and virtually quotes Aristotle! What he actually wrote was: *certum est, quia impossibile.*[2] It is certain because it is impossible. It was only the encounter with the Risen Lord that could have convinced the early disciples of this apparent impossibility.

Jesus accuses the Sadducees of not knowing 'the power of God'. Only encountering the Risen Lord could have transformed this bunch of disappointed, fearful disciples, who fled the scene and some of whom denied Jesus, into the preachers of the gospel. They witnessed the power of God, defeating death. The Big Bang of the New Creation! Nothing less could explain the birth of the Church.

So when people accuse us of holding to a faith that is absurd, I myself would not glory in this accusation. It is entirely rational to believe that the very origin of the Church must lie in an event which is not irrational but beyond reason. But I have gone on for too long. I must shut up and give you a chance to say something!

Łukasz: Is the belief in the resurrection absurd? Modern religious studies as well as the Church Fathers pointed to the conviction present in so many traditions and cultures that death cannot be the end of human fate. Gilgamesh, the hero of the most ancient Mesopotamian epic, mourning

a friend, sought the source of eternal life. It is difficult to find a culture
that does not deal with the question of the afterlife. Is it absurd to state
this question seriously? Is it truly more rational to believe that a human
being is nothing more than a rational animal and that its ashes can be
simply dumped under some tree? Since we experience that human life is
something more than biological life, is it absurd to hope, to believe, to
seek life beyond its biological termination?

Mockery and laughter do not answer any question; they are an avoidance
of answering. Whereas self-mockery can be sometimes funny and even
spiritually useful, mockery of others is dangerously close to contempt.
It is true that in this world there are some spiteful people and contempt
towards them should be a right attitude, yet one should know when and
why to express it. Laughter can be a very serious thing, and dangerous too.
Try to laugh at a dictator in his own country! Well, we learn that 'God
laughs at the wicked' (Ps. 37.13).

Tell me what makes you laugh and I will tell you who you are! Laughing
at the things one does not understand or disagrees with is the least good
reason to laugh.

Timothy: Yes, I agree that the idea of eternal life, that death is not the
end, is found in almost every culture. Nearly everywhere one finds some
sort of belief that life is eternal. I suppose it is one thing to believe in
theory, but imagine actually encountering someone alive and glorious
whom one had seen die a horrible death on a cross three days earlier!
That would be surely astonishing and transformative. I think that it is
only such an awe-filled event that can explain the transformation of the
weak and frightened disciples into confident preachers of the Risen Lord,
who dare to leave the upper room where they were locked in for fear of
their enemies.

But why did the Sadducees find the whole idea of the resurrection
from the dead absurd, whereas the Pharisees did not? I think that it
is because of their understanding of what it means to be alive in the
first place. The story that they tell about raising up children for the
dead brothers – levirate marriage – shows they think being alive means
belonging to a family whose name must be kept alive. The Greek word
sperma, 'seed', occurs four times in this text. In this context it means
'offspring', 'child'. To be a human being is to be the seed of a parent,
and the source of another generation, part of a genealogy. The Sadducees
belonged to the wealthy priestly caste whose priority was to perpetuate

FIGURE 1 Rembrandt van Rijn, *Jacob Wrestling with the Angel*, 1659, Gemäldegalerie, Berlin

FIGURE 2 Dante Gabriel Rossetti, *The Beloved*, 1865, Tate Britain, London

FIGURE 3 Gaston Petit OP, *L'Etonnant Message*, 1990, priory of St Sabina, Rome

FIGURE 4 Simone Martini, *Christ Discovered in the Temple*,
1342, Walker Art Gallery, Liverpool

their families and wealth, and so good relations with the Romans was the only reasonable policy.

This is true surely of all wealthy elites. Think of *Downton Abbey*, the immensely popular TV series about a rich aristocratic British family. The great question is: who will bear an heir to carry on the family name? The crises of the family are about being childless or, God forbid, marrying outside their own circle, rather like the Sadducees! So after the fall of Jerusalem, when that network of rich priestly families was destroyed, the Sadducees disappear from history. The family names are no longer passed on.

Jesus' reply is founded on a fundamentally different idea of what it means to be alive. To live is to be in relationship with the God of life! The angelic life is not about being liberated from something physical like sex; it is about being more than just part of a genealogy. Angels have neither parents nor children. The angelic existence is to be turned towards God, to the giver of life. Jesus says: 'See that you do not despise one of these little ones; for I tell you that in heaven their angels always behold the face of my Father who is in heaven' (Mt. 18.10). And the angels are also turned to us, bearing God's face, as when Gabriel comes as the bearer of the Annunciation. The angelic life is not fundamentally ethereal – for example, transcending sex – but exists in direct relationship with God, regardless of who was your father. The angelic existence is then about turning one's face to the one whose face shines on us, now and for all of eternity.

This is why Jesus makes this seemingly unconvincing use of the quotation from Exodus, that God is the God of Abraham and of Isaac and of Jacob. The existence of each patriarch is founded on this abiding personal relationship with the Lord. The covenant is renewed with each one, chosen and accepted, rather than just inherited.

So each of us is faced with the individual decision of choosing to turn towards God's face and finding there our life and hope or turning away. Christianity implies a certain individualism. Of course, we are not *just* solitary individuals. We are the fruit of families and friendship. But a true family forms us to be people who individually choose to love and live, and the fruition of individuality is to choose each other and the vast family of God. That is why, I think, the conversation with the Sadducees flows naturally into the question of the scribe, about the greatest commandment, the love of God and neighbour. Because love is the foundation of a truly human existence, and love never dies. Love is an individual choice and the foundation of community.

Łukasz: I think it is wonderful to know one's family history, and this is one of the advantages of coming from a family with a long and well-documented history like yours. I suppose that to know that there in one's lineage are saints and the wicked, the noble and the less honourable, makes one more aware of the importance of one's life decisions and how different paths lead to heaven or hell. These family stories are also often very enjoyable. Biblical stories about the patriarchs, their wives, concubines and children, their deaths and births, have all this seriousness and entertainment just as our family stories do.

There is a potential problem with a noble origin and a long ancestry, similar to the case of the identity of the first Christian Israelites, as tackled by St Paul. A young prince can become a passive, self-satisfied person; the treasure of his inherited family identity can replace his personal identity; he can remain just an ennobled reproducer and his family history stagnates. On the other hand, the same rich history can challenge a young prince to seek in earnest his ways and his vocation, through his choices; thus also the family history will go further. As a Dominican, I can say it is good to know the ups and downs of our 800-year history, not to enshrine it and celebrate ourselves but to be challenged and inspired by it.

Three Patriarchs, tenth century, church of Deir al-Surian, Egypt

The verse quoted by Jesus gives something deeper than a 'scriptural proof' for the resurrection. It comes from the famous scene in which Moses encounters YHWH for the first time (Exod. 3.6). He receives in an answer the mysterious name 'I AM' and then the God of the burning bush identifies himself via his relationship with his forefathers.

God does not present Himself as 'I keep the heavens above you' or 'I am the one who makes the sun rise' or 'I am the one who sends the rain.' He points not to any of these visible, perennial and cosmic realities but to the relationship with ephemeral human beings! Jesus is right that if Abraham, Isaac and Jacob make part of God's name, they are as if inscribed in His identity – their existence is more stable than the foundations of the earth!

Timothy: This conversation ends abruptly. 'You err greatly.' But can we ever let a conversation finish forever? Mustn't we always go on trying to talk? It may happen that, for a time, conversation becomes impossible. The anger is too intense, or the lack of a common language too radical, to be bridged. Or we personally may find that the conversation is too threatening or painful. A few times I have had to stop an email exchange because the other person appears to have no desire to engage in anything other than personal attacks on me.

Alan Jacobs, a professor of the Humanities at Baylor University, read a blog post which blisteringly attacked Rowan Williams's views on sexuality. He was furious and began to write a reply but he had to pause:

> I paused because my hands were shaking so violently I couldn't type accurately. That's how angry I was. So I had to 'give it five minutes'; I didn't have a choice. And during that enforced break I *did* start to realize what I was doing – what I was becoming ... I had a problem of my own that I needed to address. So I deleted the comment I was writing and shut down the computer and walked away.[3]

The dialogue between Jesus and the Sadducean community ended abruptly. Indeed, it had never really begun. But for all their communal understanding of the human being, as begetter and begotten, the fruit and the giver of seed, they *were* individuals. No one has an identity that is entirely determined by the group. Who knows if an individual Sadducee might not have heard the summons of Jesus to follow the God of the living? They may have hung around and heard the conversation with the scribe, about the love of God and neighbour, and begun to think again.

The possibility of a new conversation is always there. When I was a young friar, I found that differences of political opinion made conversation with some members of my family really painful, and silence seemed the only option. But that was not the end. We grew beyond those silences. We have to be patient as we wait for the springtime of a new conversation.

Łukasz: Everything that Jesus has done is a fruit of His goodwill and love. The same needs to be said about these blatant words, 'You err greatly.' Although Jesus got only a rhetorical question, being a good teacher, he gave a fair answer. Maybe the Sadducees did it for fun, but Jesus made the effort to deal with them seriously. During his passion, when asked questions by the curious King Herod, Jesus did not answer any of his questions, or maybe better: he answered with his silence. Here Jesus' words, although sharp, are the sign of hope that some of the Sadducees will listen. As long as the word of the Lord reproaches us, there is plenty of hope for us!

'What is truth?' (Jn 18.28–19.16)

Then they brought Jesus from Caiaphas to the praetorium. It was morning. They themselves did not enter the praetorium lest they be defiled but so that they could eat the Pascha. Pilate then went out to them and said, –

'What accusation do you bring against this man?'

They answered and said, –

'If this one were not an evildoer, we would not have handed him over to you.'

Pilate said to them, –

'Take him yourselves and judge him according to your law.'

The Jews said to him, – 'we have no right to kill anyone' – so that the word of Jesus be fulfilled that he had said indicating what kind of death he was to die.

Then Pilate entered the praetorium again and summoned Jesus, and said to him, –

'You are the King of the Jews...'

Jesus answered, –

'On your own are you saying this or did others tell you about me?'

Pilate replied, –

'I am not a Jew, am I? Your nation and the chief priests have handed you over to me. What have you done?'

Jesus answered, –

'My kingdom is not from this world. Were my kingdom from this world, my servants would be fighting so that I would not be handed over to the Jews. Now, yet, my kingdom is not from here.'

Pilate said to him, –

'So you are a king.'

Jesus answered, –

'You say yourself that I am a king. I, for this I was born, and for this I came into the world, to witness to the truth. Everyone who is of the truth listens to my voice.'

Pilate asked him, –

'What is truth?'

And having said that, he went out to the Jews again and says to them, –

'I find no case against him. But you have a custom that I release someone for you at the Pascha. Do you want me to release for you the King of the Jews?'

They shouted again saying, –

'Not this one, but Barabbas!'

Now Barabbas was a bandit. Then Pilate took Jesus and had him flogged. And the soldiers, having woven a crown of thorns, put it on his head, and they wrapped him in a purple himation. They kept coming up to him, and said, – 'Hail, King of the Jews!', and were slapping him on the face. Pilate went out again and says to them, –

'Behold, I am bringing him out to you so that you may know that I find no case against him.'

So Jesus came out, wearing the thorny crown and the purple himation, and Pilate says to them, –

'Behold the man.'

When the chief priests and (their) servants saw him, they shouted saying, –

'Crucify him! Crucify him!'

Pilate says to them, –

'Take him yourselves and crucify him, for I myself find no case against him.'

The Jews answered him, –

'We, we have law, and according to the law he ought to die because he has made himself the Son of God.'

Now when Pilate heard this word, he became even more afraid and he entered the praetorium again and says to Jesus, –

'You, where are you from?'

But Jesus gave him no answer. Pilate therefore says to him, –

'To me, you are not talking? Do you not know that I have power to release you, and power to crucify you?'

Jesus answered him, –

'You would have no power over me unless it had been given you from above; therefore the one who handed me over to you has a greater sin.'

From then on Pilate tried to release him, but the Jews cried out, –

'If you release this one, you are no friend of Caesar! Everyone who makes himself a king opposes Caesar!'

When Pilate heard these words, he led Jesus outside and sat on the judge's seat at a place called *Lithostroton* (The Stone Pavement), or in Hebrew *Gabbatha*. Now it was the day of Preparation of the Pascha, about the sixth hour. And he says to the Jews, –

'Behold your King.'

Then these cried out, –

'Away! Away! Crucify him!'

Pilate says to them, –

'Your King, shall I crucify?'

The chief priests answered, –

'We have no king but Caesar.'

Then he handed him over to them to be crucified. So they took Jesus.

Łukasz: We have commented on the 'failed' dialogue between Cain and God. The dialogue with Pilate seems to be another such failed encounter. Yet I would not go so far as to call it hopeless. Cain killed his brother, and God came to talk to him and even protected him at the next stage of his life, even as he was sent 'away from the face of the Lord'. It is more difficult to say what happened later to Pilate. Christian traditions hesitate between legends of his conversion and even holiness and Pilate's damnation to such an extent that the earth did not want to receive his dead body and kept spitting it away from the tomb as if announcing his raising 'to reproach and everlasting disgrace' on the last day (cf. Dan. 12.2). Let us follow Pilate's failed meeting with Jesus. Hopefully, we can learn something from his mistakes.

Through the narrative of the trial of Jesus in John's gospel, we are admitted to the inner chambers of the Praetorium and witness the dialogue between the two. Most certainly, more people accompanied the procurator of Judaea: his guards, servants, a secretary or a translator. The narrator, nevertheless, gives us an impression of a personal meeting. Pilate, though, as in a theatre, continuously moves from one space to another. He walks to and fro between the inside and outside, between the dialogue with Jesus and listening to the shouts of the anonymous crowd. The two worlds are in stark opposition.

Outside, the crowd is nameless and faceless. No one is looking for the truth. They have already passed judgement. Unsurprisingly, what happens has nothing to do with reflection; everything is a power game, threats, buying and selling; the discussion concerns only legal competencies. Inside, we enter a different world. The words of Jesus are poetic. There are moments of silence. Jesus provokes Pilate to reflect by questioning his questions. Even though one should expect the fiercest argument between the accused and the judge, the rhythm slows down and this dialogue seems almost to be outside of this limited space and time and addresses even us today. A window opens onto something that is not transitory.

Timothy: Yes, the constant passage of Pilate from the inside to the outside and back again is fascinating. Inside is, as you say, the place of personal encounter with the Lord; outside is the place of impersonal power games, the faceless mob.

When Jesus is taken to Pilate, 'it was morning'. A pregnant phrase in John's gospel. The time of light and resurrection, and yet Pilate dare not step into the light. I suspect that most of us can identify with Pilate. He seems to be torn between engaging with Jesus and holding him at a distance. His questions open, real contact with the prisoner and then seems to dismiss him. If we dare to encounter the Lord personally, what alarming things might he not invite us to do? Do I really want to get involved with this strange person who may upset my life? You know the English saying: 'If you want to make God laugh, tell him your plans!' Who might I become?

So, rather than be brave and come face to face with the Lord, the temptation is to take a peek but then withdraw and keep a distance, especially if we suspect the Lord wants more from us than we want to give yet, especially if things get personal. Like Augustine: 'Make me chaste but not yet!'[1]

The invitation to a risky adventure is surely implicit in every personal encounter, and not just with God! If I really see the person begging on the street, or listen to the asylum seeker, it might turn my life upside down. If I really open myself to someone with radically different views, whether of the left or the right, might not my simplistic convictions be challenged? Loving another person is a risky adventure that will not leave me unchanged. So the temptation is to keep others mostly at bay, engage with them for a moment and then retreat. One way is to look at them as if they were not real people, 'those awful conservatives', 'those terrible liberals', 'those foreigners' (except the

Poles of course!) or those Protestants. We turn people into abstract categories and so hold them at a distance, but glance out of the side of our eyes. Pilate keeps himself apart – 'Am I a Jew?' But one senses a certain fascination with the stranger standing before him.

Łukasz: The beginning of the personal meeting with Pilate looks quite promising. It begins, as would be expected, with an interrogation of Jesus, but Pilate quickly allows Jesus to question him. Pilate seems to be hesitant, and this is also a good sign that he is seeking the truth. There are some true questions and true answers. I would even say that Jesus gives answers that are *too good*; they are beyond what Pilate expects and is ready to listen to. He just wants to solve the case, get it done and move on, and behold there is something greater in front of him. This demands reflection, time and more serious involvement than he is prepared to give.

I suppose all the answers God gives us are of this type. They are always more than we expect. How could it be otherwise? How else could the infinite Word enter our finite language? That is why in the Scriptures one can expect and find usually more meanings than elsewhere, and even possibly a deeper meaning. This Word created the Universe; it is of no surprise that It is greater than this world!

Pilate received too much in reply to his questions, and this could make him back off. It is true with God; it is true with our relationships. People think and declare that they are looking for the true love of their life and the ultimate truth, but finding anything even close to that can be scary. When you encounter something potentially so decisive, you cannot pretend to be the same afterwards. A meeting that promises everything is also capable of taking everything away.

If only Pilate had stayed there longer. Inside with Jesus. The solution could be as simple as that. Why rush away from the question of your life? Why move onwards elsewhere? I do not understand why Pilate left Jesus; I can only speculate. The Nazarene has just said: 'everyone who is from the truth listens to my voice', and in answer, Pilate asked the One who is Truth, 'What is truth?' and then left! It is one of the most dramatic and deeply sad scenes I can imagine. It was there just before you, in your hands, everything you need and desire. The answer, the meaning of your life, your goal, the treasure you are seeking! And you just left and went away. It is the nightmare of an unrecognized love, of your lost last flight. You missed it by an hour, you missed it by a minute, it does not matter, the result is the same. Now you live at the airport, nowhere.

I think it is even better to make a mistake and take falsehood for truth than to abandon any quest for it. I would rather be betrayed by a loved one than not love at all for fear of betrayal. It is almost suicidal, like surrendering before any attempt to fight. Like dying before one has even begun to live! I can even think of an even greater drama if Pilate never realized what he lost, the moment he had missed. It would be a truly zombie life: one is so dead that does not even know oneself to be dead.

Timothy: Francis Bacon, the seventeenth-century English philosopher, said, '"What is truth" said jesting Pilate, and did not wait for an answer.'[2] I imagine Pilate here having some sense that he had broken off a conversation that could have changed his life. Even if he did flee, there must always have been some nagging memory that a door had opened and he had not gone through it.

If one encounters the Lord, one embarks on a search for the truth that has no end. The people outside, the anonymous crowd, they know everything. They have nailed it. They have their certainties. But inside, with the Lord, the search goes on and it does not end. Rowan Williams said that in John's gospel, 'to be at home in the truth is to be on the way to seeing the world with God's eyes'.[3] Always on the way.

I joined the Dominican Order because I loved its motto, *Veritas*, Truth. I thought that I would be able to rest in the truths that I attained. I had it all sorted. In a sense I had. I assented to the truth of the Creed. I came to love the teaching of the Church. But all of our lives we are on a journey to discovering what they mean! As Gregory of Nyssa said, we go from beginning to beginning to beginning.[4] Every time I look at the gospels in preparation for preaching, I must let myself be surprised. To say that the Word of God is inspired does not mean that the evangelists and others made a strictly accurate record of what God whispered in their ears; it means that what we are offered is always more than we grasp. Yes, it is settled that Jesus rose from the dead. I believe! But what does it mean? I am still discovering. Or maybe it is more accurate to say that I am forever being liberated from false, narrow understandings of what it means, for the fullness of truth always lies ahead. Did it for Pilate?

Łukasz: What is truth? – it can be a good question. It is a good question if one wants to know the answer. Reality is so complex and we humans are complex, we can therefore multiply the questions *ad infinitum*. This could be a great adventure and a life-giving attitude in a relationship if one keeps the freshness, curiosity, and rightly presumes that there is something more in the truth than one has already chosen and loved.

Yet there is also Pilate's questioning. It is a rhetorical formula, this type of questioning that dismisses the answers and does not listen to the questioned person. This attitude can be also deadly dangerous because it is a way to keep the answer at bay. Yet one can play the non-involvement neutrality game only for some time. The very gesture of washing hands is so paradoxical: exactly when Pilate announced his own innocence, his non-involvement, he became guilty. Legally, it was not him who pleaded for Jesus' conviction, but putting the innocent man in the hands of his enemy makes him morally responsible for his death. Avoiding responsibility does not liberate us from guilt. It is like culpable ignorance, which is nothing other than a refusal to know. It does not matter how many people are ready to take on your responsibility. It simply does not work because ultimately nobody will live your life, love instead of you or die instead of you.

Timothy: Pilate's question – 'What is truth?' – is very pertinent today. When we lose the love of truth, society disintegrates because we have lost the common ground on which we can stand together. In the world of 'fake news', wild assertions in the social media, conspiracy theories like QAnon, the idea of seeking the truth seems problematic.[5] It is perhaps the deepest crisis of our time.

The war against Ukraine is a terrible revelation of what happens when the truth is lost. Today there is a battle within Russia, and it is over the truth. Vladimir Putin's regime has imposed classes for students on the difference between truth and falsehood. It has declared that the truth is that there is no war in Ukraine. It has decreed that anyone who asserts otherwise must be silenced and punished. The greatest conflict in Europe in my lifetime is about the possibility of truth. George Orwell foresaw this in his novel *1984*, published in 1949. He portrayed a world in which the government declares that war is peace, freedom is slavery and ignorance is strength. Some of the heroes of our time are journalists who, at risk to their safety and their lives, go on trying to tell the world what is really happening. In so many places now they are suffering persecution.

Yet in the midst of this flight from truth, this cynicism and collapse, the one who is the Truth shines out all the more strongly. Somehow, beyond 'my' truth and 'your' truth, the truth is one, in ways that we can just barely discern, and draws us into unity. It is the only basis for community. Jesus' seamless tunic (v. 24) is not torn, and at the foot of the cross Mary and the Beloved Disciple are given to each other.

Łukasz: While I am pretty optimistic that Cain's remorse made him restless but also moved him forward possibly in a good direction, it is more difficult to see it for Pilate. He insisted on keeping the title 'King of the Jews' at the top of the Cross but it may simply have been his way to nag the Jews. He allowed them to take down the body of Jesus because of the Jewish law but he also killed Jesus because of the same law. The evangelist wrote that Pilate tried to save Jesus. He wanted to make a deal, bargained to exchange for Barabbas. As the next step, he proposed a compromise: he sent Jesus for an almost deadly flagellation, probably hoping that the public would be satisfied and the death penalty could be avoided.

Yes, prudence and politicians speak about the social skill of finding a position that is acceptable to both sides, and yet truth is not always in the middle. Compromise is a part of our life but so often it is a result of an unachieved negotiation; the true needs of the disputing sides are neither made clear nor satisfied. Instead of the solution where everyone gets what they need, people get equal portions, so they are equally happy and unhappy with the division of 'the cake'.

What I personally grasp of the truth is important not only for me but for everyone. This so-called 'my truth' is indeed the truth I know and it is important also for you. Pilate should have opposed the crowd also their own sake too.

Mikhail Bulgakov wrote his *The Master and Margarita* in the years of Stalinist terror (1928–40). While millions were killed simply and without much ado, some thousands, before being killed, went through a more sophisticated, staged process. It was just another element of terror, since all the participants of those shows knew that the accused were innocent. An ultimate mockery of truth. In Bulgakov's story, Pontius Pilate appears a few times. The last one is most touching. Pilate has been sitting on the same platform, Gabbatha, for the last two thousand years. He has suffered insomnia all those years and lived over and over again the same dialogue with Jesus. In Bulgakov's book Pilate is finally freed with the words 'He's waiting for you!' Two thousand years of pondering on the dialogue that he interrupted and rushed through. If Jesus was indeed waiting, this time was not wasted.

Timothy: What wonderful words, 'He is waiting for you!' Yes, Pilate is so near to saving Jesus and doing the right thing. He is on the brink of acting for the good and engaging with the one who addresses him. The hope for Pilate and for us all is that, however much it looks as though the powers of this world are winning, they are shown to be weak and doomed. It is the lonely prisoner, the victim of their plots, who actually stands in calm majesty in the centre. Just as when the soldiers came to arrest him in the Garden of Gethsemane, he majestically declares the Divine name, I AM, and they all fall on their faces. Therein lies the hope for all of us, including Pilate and the religious authorities. He waits for them and for us. Our hope is in God's vast patience, so difficult to understand in our world of the immediate communication, instantaneous gratification.

The theme of the trial recurs all through John's gospel. Think of the woman caught in adultery. She is brought to Jesus for trial. But of course, it is Jesus they are putting on trial. If he condemns the woman, his offer of mercy is shown to be fake; if he lets her go, his claim to be a faithful, law-abiding Jew is exploded. But Jesus' extraordinary cry – 'Let the one who is without sin cast the first stone' – puts all of them on trial.

Rembrandt van Rijn, *Ecce Homo*, 1634, National Gallery, London

Rembrandt's marvellous picture *Ecce Homo* reveals a scene of chaos. Pilate is kneeling abjectly on the seat of judgement while a priest tries to force on him the rod of judgement, which was used in executions in seventeenth-century Holland. The religious leaders are on their knees. Two figures dominate: the bust of Caesar, which is high in the background, but which is just a lifeless stone, seeing and hearing nothing; and Jesus, who is impassively there, standing upright while his enemies are grovelling around him. The vast clock in the background is ticking. Death draws near but also Easter morning. You pointed out that Rembrandt's name is inscribed on the clock. It ticked for him as it does for us.

To be a Christian in the first three centuries was to risk martyrdom, to risk being put on trial for your life by the Roman authorities, but John shows that the victory is with the victim. These exercises of violent judicial power are vacuous. The martyr has the palm of victory.

We too live in a society that constantly puts people on trial and condemns them. Not just in courts, which is necessary, but in the media: trial by Twitter, condemnation on Facebook. The anonymous trolls cry out 'Crucify!' against those whom they hate. Our language is saturated with accusation. Even in universities, academics fear to say the wrong thing lest they be condemned, cancelled, no-platformed. There is something Satanic in the air! Do we dare to resist? Jesus promises the Holy Spirit, the advocate, the defence lawyer who will defend us and the truth. 'Whoever believes is not condemned' (Jn 3.18).

Pilate proclaims of Jesus: 'Behold the human being, *anthropos*'! Aren't those among the most extraordinary words in the gospels? A mocked and crucified king, crowned and bearing a sceptre, whose royal dignity is simultaneously in plain sight and concealed. Yes, this is every one of us when we are what we are called to be, God's royal children, but whose dignity is hidden even from ourselves. We saw how the question of identity – 'Who do people say that I am?' – becomes ever more insistent, and always linked to our own identity, until Caesarea Philippi, and then it stops. It is now in this final confrontation, when the question of Jesus' identity can no longer be evaded and who *we* are to be is revealed: Behold the Human Being. The revelation of God in this moment is also the revelation of who we are!

Łukasz: Pilate stopped listening to Jesus; he moved on to listen to and 'meet the crowd'. I am putting this phrase in quotation marks because I am not sure if one can really meet a crowd. A crowd is faceless. One may say that it has 'one heart' or 'one mind', but I am more inclined to say that it has none. It has emotions, for sure, and will, but not much reason. A voluntarist nightmare. I have heard from one of our Dominican lawyers that in our Constitutions some decisions are reserved to an individual, and it is so for a reason. One has to sign it with one's very own name. On the other hand, democracy, as it is anonymous, has no conscience and a very weak memory. There is some scholarly oversimplification in this characterization, but I think that it is a good mental exercise to check whether I would shout the same words alone as I would when I am part of a group. Would I publish and sign with my own name judgements I repeat so eagerly when I am not a part of a group?

Nothing will replace my personal quest for the truth. Community life has great value, but it will never replace the personal time spent alone with Jesus. There He can speak words too difficult to grasp otherwise; there He can remain silent. You can confront Him with the views of others, of his accusers, go on bringing Jesus to trial if you wish. As long as you stay with Him, you are safe. Maybe at some stage you will realize who is the ultimate judge. Indeed, the judgement you pass on Jesus will judge you. The readers feel sorry for Jesus but, make no mistake, Pilate is being judged at the very same moment!

One cannot meet Jesus and live on as if nothing happened. One cannot meet true love without consequences. If you recognize and receive it, it gives you life, makes you better. If you reject it or, worse, destroy it, it makes you worse. You go up or go down and there is no middle way. Jesus spoke of himself: 'If I had not come and spoken to them, they would not have sin; but now they have no excuse for their sin' (Jn 15.22). Our judgements judge us.

Timothy: Yes, I agree. Pilate could not really 'meet the crowd', because a crowd is impersonal. A mob baying for blood destroys the personhood of those whom it has absorbed. When Jesus confronts the lynch mob demanding the death of the woman caught in adultery, he summons each one to take his or her responsibility, and they go away one by one, starting with the oldest. I would have gone before you, Łukasz!

I like the contrast you make between a personal search for the truth and the mob shouting its empty slogans, its half-truths. There can only be a communal search for truth if the community gives space to each person for their individual reflection, because a true community consists of individuals, just as we only attain personhood in community. The beauty of Dominican life is that, at its best, which is not always the case, we are brothers and sisters who flourish together in our individual search for the truth, and who flourish individually in our common pursuit of *Veritas*.

I wonder what the people caught up in the mob demanding the blood of Jesus thought when they went home one by one that evening when he had died on the cross. Did they judge themselves? That would have been the beginning of a homecoming to the one who always waits for them! Think of Peter who had denied his friend before the charcoal. There will be a stranger waiting on the beach for him. We will look together at their conversation later.

Intermezzo: Questioning Him

Timothy and Łukasz: The context of these last two dialogues is unfriendly, to say the least. The Sadducees question Jesus to order to ridicule him. The Pharisees and the high priest accuse Jesus of being an impostor, to be distrusted. Pontius Pilate summons him for interrogation, perhaps intrigued by this strange man, but surrenders to the hostility of his accusers.

The best context for a dialogue is a friendly space, yet these cases prove that some form of it is possible even in situations of antagonism. Jesus does not refuse to engage: this is the first and impressive lesson. Jesus is not a narcissistic type who would only listen to or make compliments. How do we engage in dialogue with people who provoke us? Are we able to abandon our comfort zones? Do we have the courage to tackle difficult themes and express unpopular opinions? Are we up to having unpleasant dialogues with those who would reject us?

God revealed himself to be an open listener in the Book of the suffering Job. Although the tradition spoke of the proverbial patience of Job, it must have been at an end when for whole chapters he hurls his words at God, accusing him of injustice, of intimidation, of silence. We find a number of other conflictual dialogues with God in the Psalms, or Lamentations. 'I suffer because you betrayed me!' – Biblical authors shout to heaven, and thus they pray ... Do we seriously listen to the people who accuse us?

Clearly God does not refuse confrontations. They become opportunities to speak to his interlocutors and meet them there where they really are: in their anger, in their disbelief or in their accusation. Quarrelling with God is not against faith; on the contrary, it is another way of meeting the living, resisting-therefore-real God. If a serious matter is at issue, a serious accusation, this is even better. God gives a fair answer even to an unfair question. In fact, from the beginning God insists on engaging with us who do not play fair. We break the rules and yet he keeps answering. Do we have a similar openness, patience and, ultimately, love to respond in the same way to people who fight us?

'What are these words that you are hurling at each other while walking?' (Lk. 24.13–35)

Now behold, two of them, on the same day, were going to a village distant sixty stadia from Jerusalem. Its name was Emmaus. And they were conversing with one another about all these events. And it happened that, when they were in conversation and questioning together, Jesus himself approached and went along with them. Their eyes, yet, were 'seized' so that they could not recognize him. Then he said to them, –

'What are these words that you are hurling at each other while walking?'

Then they stopped with a dismal look. Answering, the one named Cleopas said to him, –

'Are you alone visiting Jerusalem so that you did not learn what [things] happened in it in these days?!'

And he said to them, –

'What [things]?'

So they said to him, –

'The [things] about Jesus of Nazareth, how he became a man, a prophet mighty in deed and word before God and all the people, and how the high priests and our rulers gave him away to the judgement of death and crucified him. But we, we were hoping that it was he who was to redeem Israel. And yet, in addition to that, it is the third day since it happened. And also some women from us astounded us. Having arrived early at the tomb and not finding his body, they came saying that they had also seen a vision of angels who said he was alive! Then some of us went out to the tomb and found [it] thus as also the women said but him they did not see.'

And he said to them, –

'O foolish and slow of heart to believe in all that the prophets said! Wasn't it necessary that the Christ suffer these [things] and enter his glory?'

And beginning from Moses and from all the prophets, he interpreted for them, in all the scriptures, the [things] about him. Then they approached the village where they were going and he made as though to go further. And they constrained him saying, –

'Stay with us because it is towards evening and the day has already declined.'

And he entered to stay with them. And it happened that when he was reclining with them, having taken the bread, he blessed [it] and having broken it, he was giving to them. Then their eyes were opened and they recognized him; and he 'became disappeared' in front of them. And they said to one another,

'Was not our heart aflame within us when he was speaking to us on the way, when he was opening for us the scriptures?'

And having risen, that very hour they returned to Jerusalem and found the eleven and those with them, saying, 'Indeed the Lord is risen and has made himself seen to Simon.' Also they were relating [the things that happened] on the way and how he made himself recognized by them in the breaking of bread.

Timothy: Perhaps this is the most difficult conversation we discuss, because here the Lord is talking not to his enemies, who would always be ready to do battle. Nor to his followers, who are puzzled and want clarification, nor to people who need forgiveness, and will surely long for a word to set them free. This is a conversation with people who are utterly disillusioned and who probably think that there is no point in talking anyway – 'Are you the only one visiting Jerusalem so that you did not know what [things] happened in it in these days?'

These two disciples are fleeing Jerusalem. This is not because they are setting off on a mission, as the disciples will be sent after Pentecost. They have given up. They are deserting the earliest community of the Church and heading home. They had put their hope in Jesus and feel let down: 'We were hoping that it was he who was to redeem Israel.' They have had enough. Perhaps they had hoped for an armed uprising against the Roman occupiers, but Jesus had not even struck a blow and had let himself be led away without resistance. The women claimed to have seen something, but the apostles dismissed this as 'an idle tale'. They were just women, after all.

Think of the millions of people in the West who have given up on the Church and maybe even faith in God. Perhaps they have been scandalized by the sexual abuse scandal and the failure of most Church leaders to confront it. I think of a brilliant young friend of mine, whom I met in Paddington Railway Station and who declared that the latest scandalous revelation was the last straw. She was off! Or young people who think that science has demolished any plausibility of faith. Or those whose idealism has been betrayed. How on earth can any conversation with these disillusioned ex-believers even begin?

Łukasz: Your perspective on the Emmaus meeting proves that you have been a pastor much longer than I was. My first spontaneous reaction is rather to place myself rather in the position of one of the disciples and not that of the mysterious Risen Christ. The behaviour of Cleopas and his friend reveals some precious traits of their character. There must have been some emotions because the emotions are always with us as with any other animal. These two disciples weren't just 'sharing their emotions' like some ignorant bystanders in a poor-quality TV news. They were together asking questions – that is, trying to understand not only the what but also the why of the events. They were seeking for truth.

I admire your patience in dealing with public outbursts of emotions. Even worse when it is a crowd-induced thoughtless hysteria. I would rather walk away, I suppose, waiting for some reasonable reaction. The evangelist mentions the disciples' failed hopes only *en passant*. Their main effort is to give an account of the events and make some sense of them. However one feels about some difficult or painful experience, it is good to begin by *feeling* it, yet the feeling should become an element of a broader reflected story and not all the content. Otherwise, such a meeting of frustrated disciples will be as one-sided, egocentric and fruitless as suffering can be. One can walk along with the people shouting their emotions hoping for the further deeper meeting. How to encounter a free and thinking person at a level beyond his or her emotions is a good question. Jesus seems to know how to do it. Exchanging the experience of our miseries can be, but is not always, a helpful experience. In any case, it should not stop there.

Timothy: Interesting! So you see them as searching to understand whereas I see them as having given up. Maybe there was something of both. When people leave the Church, as I see happening in Britain today, there remain unanswered questions hovering in the air. They ask: how could this have happened? Who would have believed that priests could behave in this way? Sometimes people leave as part of their search. Let us hope it ultimately brings them back too! Sometimes they just give up.

Anyway, as you say, people should not remain mired down in their misery. How can the conversation move on? Jesus does two things: he asks them what they are talking about, and he walks with them. They are 'hurling words' at each other, sharing their bottled-up anger. First of all, people must be free to let rip their anger and their disappointment. We have nothing to say until it has all poured out. There was a time when, whatever I talked about in lectures, anywhere in the world, when it came to the Q&A, almost the only topics raised were the sexual abuse scandal and the question of why women are not ordained in the Catholic Church. One just had to listen and listen and bear the pain and fury before a word could be said. 'What are you talking about as you walk?' This will mean suppressing the impulse to swat away accusations, and immediately to defend the institution. Just listen and listen and listen, entering into the pain, the hurt, of the questioner. So, the most difficult and creative conversations begin thus: 'What are you talking about? What is bubbling in your hearts, positively or negatively? What do you fear? What do you love?'

Even more extraordinarily, Jesus walks with them as they *flee* from the Church, as I see it. He does not block the way and demand that they go back. Is there anything more painful, especially for parents, than to accompany people whom one loves when they reject the faith one holds dear, and listen to them as they share new convictions which may be abhorrent or incomprehensible to those who love them? But one hangs in there, because love is eternal and no true friendship should ever end. The disciples will only return home when they can do so freely, and not because they have been told to. When we have conversations with people who have given up the faith that we treasure, we need the same patience that Jesus showed as he walked with them, going the wrong way.

'O foolish and slow of heart to believe in all that the prophets said.' Calling people stupid does not seem to be a good way to begin a fruitful conversation! But I think it means not so much stupid as blind. Even bright people can be blind! He expounds the scriptures, their hearts burn within them, but they still don't get it. Their eyes will be opened finally not by what he says but what he does. We shall get to that anon!

Łukasz: I find the context of walking along particularly significant. In such circumstances, people usually do not look at each other, or maybe just occasionally. Instead, they look in the same direction, ahead or at the same obstacles shaping their path. I have had some great experience of such discussions on the way, in particular during our walking pilgrimage to Czestochowa in Poland. I love walking pilgrimages: I have made even one from Jerusalem to Emmaus Nikopolis. One descends from the Judaean hills heading to the Mediterranean in the west; it is actually a very pleasant and picturesque route.

These unarranged meetings on the way are freer, more relaxed. They approach the accidental chat of a group of people watching or playing a game. There is plenty of freedom for everyone: to answer or not to answer, to pretend that one did not hear, to change the topic, to return to the first point, to avoid further engagements and walk away. Such freedom is extremely precious and even essential for more creative thought, similar to brainstorming, less disciplined but more open. These walking, peripatetic dialogues happen to be liberating and even fun, like a walk itself. Maybe because other muscles take on the tension and work, our brain is freer to express and receive fresh thoughts.

Cleopas and his companion are on the move; they have difficulties making head or tail of what happened but do not pretend that they know the answer! I admire that they were not offended by or dismissive of this stranger, who, as a matter of fact, called them fools. To 'be slow of heart' refers, of course, not to their heartbeat and blood pressure but to their brains. Anyone who seeks the truth would bear this challenge and even being called a fool if he sees any chance of getting a deeper glimpse into the meaning he missed. Can I become wiser without recognizing that I have been a fool?

They take the provocative words of the stranger as a chance to learn something. I would like to keep my spirits open enough not to evade people challenging my perspectives. It proves to be a truly Divine moment. Docility – in other words the capacity to confront oneself with a different perspective, recognizing one's ignorance – what a wonderful set of virtues! Many sociologists speak of the 'echo chamber effect' of our interaction with the Internet 'friends' who think as we do. Well, maybe the best point of going to Emmaus would be to listen to the people who call us fools? Not all of them, but one of them may be the Risen Lord.

Watercolour copy of *Christ as pilgrim received by two Dominicans*,
Emilio Costantini, Fra Angelico in the Museo di San Marco, Florence

Timothy: That reminds me of when I first came to Blackfriars as a young friar, knowing almost no theology. One day, on the Feast of the Assumption, I stopped the great theologian Cornelius Ernst OP on the staircase and asked him to explain what it is all about – just like that – and he said, 'Oh, silly boy.' I did feel a fool, but realized I had an awful long way to go! Have I ever called anyone else a fool? I have felt it. Maybe I should have said it!

But what opened their eyes? Here we come to the beautiful irony of this text. These restless people, who have taken to their feet, invite the Lord of the Sabbath to stay with them. They have not remained with the community in Jerusalem, but they invite the Risen Lord to remain with them! He reclines with them at table. The Son of God, who rested at the end of creation, accepts their hospitality and puts his feet up. Their flight away from him ends when they rest together.

Often our faith begins to be shared when we accept to be guests at other people's tables, enjoying their company, wasting time with them, putting our feet up, sharing a glass. When Jesus sends out the disciples to preach, they are told to take nothing with them, 'and whatever house you enter, stay there, and from there depart' (Lk. 9.4). Jesus stands at the door and knocks, and whoever opens the door and lets him in, he will stay with them (Rev. 3.20). Accepting hospitality is part of our preaching, which is my excuse for going out to dinner so often!

Even when the great Marie-Dominique Chenu OP, the grandfather of the Vatican Council, was 80 years old, he would be out most evenings, listening to lectures, eating and drinking with academics and trade unionists and artists, accepting their hospitality. When we met late in the refectory for a final beer, he would ask what we had learned that day. At whose table had we been guests? We must be at home with them if they are one day to be at home in the Church.

Now we come to that gesture which opens their eyes, the blessing, breaking and sharing of bread. This gesture, made in the face of death and repeated in the face of disillusion, cleans the scales from their eyes. They see everything anew! Any small insight that I have into the utter beauty of this breaking and sharing of the bread has been gained in situations that seemed desperate: in Rwanda at the beginning of the genocide, in Syria near the frontier with ISIS, in Burundi during the civil war. When violence seemed to be victorious, the small gestures of the Eucharist shone forth in the night.

The history of the world pivots around the still point of this gesture, as the journey of these two disciples turns around so that they go home freely! It is the moment in which freedom and necessity meet and embrace, the utter freedom of the Lord embracing the necessity of his suffering. It frees us to embrace the Church with all its failures and scandals as our home, the place of our rest, for, whatever has happened, he rests with us here.

Towards the end of the novel *The Bell*, by the Irish-born British novelist Iris Murdoch, the main character is wondering what he believes and whether anything makes any sense. He comes back to this ritual. 'The Mass remained, not consoling, not uplifting but in some way factual.' He had thought of becoming a priest, but this did not happen. 'Yet whoever celebrated it the Mass existed and Michael existed beside it.' Yes, that is so absolutely right! The primordial fact of the Eucharist, that gesture around which everything turns, including my very existence. My existence most fundamentally is to be someone to whom the Lord offers his body and blood! We squabble about who is allowed to preside, but who the priest is, is not so important. What matters is the fact of the gift! The priest disappears because the Lord is present; the Lord disappears because he is everywhere. But I have gone on too long!

Łukasz: You may have noted that in my translation I used a strange phrase: 'he "became disappeared"'. Many translations will say simply 'he disappeared' or 'he vanished', as though his presence there ceased. Yet the Greek original says that Jesus became something else, he literally 'became *aphanos*'. In the whole Bible this word appears only here and makes the reader stumble, I think, for a reason. It comes from the negation of the verb *phaino* – 'to reveal', 'to shine through' or 'to manifest'. So maybe 'he became unrevealed' could also be a good translation. In any case, I want to suggest that the ceasing of the sensual, visual perception does not mean Jesus' absence.

As in the mystery of the Incarnation and of the Blessed Sacrament, He came to stay. For God, relationship with us is not a fleeting and transient adventure. He is not like the imagined Divinities of ancient and modern mythologies that descended from their heavenly abodes because they were bored and set out for amusement with humans. Yet God's involvement with the real world, Israel, the Church, with you and me, is not like a computer game from which God would log out, stop playing and move back to his previous 'God business'.

Since St Dominic, the brothers of our Order have spent much of their time traversing the uneasy paths of the medieval Europe. It is not surprising that they easily identified themselves with the disciples of Emmaus. Fra Angelico depicted two friars constraining the Resurrected Christ to stay with them. It is a wish, a prayer, but also a suggestion to our brothers to keep our eyes open and to set off on our journeys. Christ will walk by.

'Do you love me more than these?'
(Jn 21.1–22)

After these *things* Jesus showed himself again to the disciples by the Sea of Tiberias; and he showed himself thus. There were together: Simon Peter, and Thomas called the Twin, and Nathanael, the one from Cana of Galilee, and *the sons* of Zebedee, and two others of his disciples. Simon Peter says to them, –

'I am going fishing.'

They say to him, –

'We also are going with you.'

They went out and got into the boat, but that night they caught nothing. Yet, when it was already early morning, Jesus stood on the shore, and the disciples did not know that it was Jesus. Jesus says to them, –

'Children, haven't you anything to eat?'

They answer him, –

'No.'

Then he says to them, –

'Cast to the right side of the boat, and you will find.'

So they cast, and even to haul they had not the strength, because of the abundance of fish. So that disciple whom Jesus loved says to Peter, –

'It is the Lord.'

So Simon Peter, having heard 'It is the Lord', put on some outer garment, for he was naked, and cast himself into the sea. Now the other disciples came in the boat – because they were not far from the land, only about two hundred cubits – dragging the net of fish. When they went up on the land, they saw a charcoal *fire* laid and some fish laid on it, and bread. Jesus says to them, –

'Bring some of the fish that you have caught now.'

So Simon Peter went up and hauled the net on the land, filled with 153 large fish. And even though they were so many, the net was not torn. Jesus says to them, –

'Come, have breakfast.'

Now none of the disciples dared to ask him, 'You, who are you?' because they knew it was the Lord. Jesus came and took the bread and gave to them, and similarly with the fish. This was already the third time that Jesus appeared to the disciples *as* raised from the dead.

When they had had breakfast, Jesus says to Simon Peter, –

'Simon *son* of John, do you love (*agapas*) me more than these?'

He says to him, –

'Yes, Lord. You, you know that I love (*philo*) you.'

He says to him, –

'Feed my lambs.'

He says to him again, a second time, –

'Simon *son* of John, do you love (*agapas*) me?'

He says to him, –

'Yes, Lord. You, you know that I love (*philo*) you.'

He says to him, –

'Shepherd my sheep.'

He says to him the third *time*, –

'Simon *son* of John, do you love (*phileis*) me?'

Peter was saddened because he said to him the third *time*, 'Do you love (*phileis*) me?' And he says to him, –

'Lord, you, you know everything. You know that I love (*philo*) you.'

He says to him, –

'Feed my sheep. Amen, amen, I tell you, when you were younger, you girded yourself and went wherever you wanted. But when you grow old, you will stretch out your hands, and someone else will gird you and lead you where you do not want to.'

He said this indicating by what kind of death he would glorify God. And having said that, he says to him, –

'Follow me.'

Having turned, Peter saw the disciple whom Jesus loved following them, who also had reclined at the supper on his chest and had said, – 'Lord, who is the one who gives you away?' So having seen this one, Peter said to Jesus, –

'Lord, and this one, what (*will become of him*)?'

Jesus says to him, –

'If I want him to stay until I come, what is that to you? You, follow me.'

Timothy: In the previous conversation, the disciples offer hospitality to the Lord; now he is the host and they are the guests. In the first, the turning point is when he 'became disappeared'. Here it is his appearance.

The conversation between Jesus and Peter is one of the gentlest and most healing exchanges in the Bible. But to understand what is going on, we must place it in the context of the whole drama on the beach. This begins with a conversation that is abruptly terminated. 'Children, haven't you anything to eat?' 'No.' Their answer – in Greek, *Ou* – sounds almost brutal, like a groan. It means 'No', but it sounds more like a bellow of despair. It evokes an emptiness. Their nets are empty. They are empty! They have no food for themselves or to feed their flock.

After all the glorious excitement, the ecstasy of the encounters with the Risen Christ, the gift of the Spirit, the release from the prison of the upper room, they are back in the mundane world they left when they began to follow Jesus. Peter says, 'I am going fishing.' Back to the old work. They are flat. They have worked all night, just as it was night when Judas went out to betray Jesus (Jn 13.30). The excitement is over. Cardinal Hume shared with me just before he died that, when he was told that his illness was terminal, at first he was filled with the presence of God. 'Then nothing and nothing since then.'

After moments of intense religious experience, of conversion, when one feels forever changed, the ecstasy passes, and one wonders whether anything has happened after all. One is baptized or joins a religious order, or gets married, filled with hope and joy. Then comes the night. One is empty. Nothing. One thought that one's life would never be the same again, but was one wrong? I believe that the Emmaus scene shows the disciples fleeing in disillusionment, though you are more positive about them. In this scene it is not so much disillusion as an experience of the humdrum, the loss of excitement, though I expect again that you will be more positive!

Łukasz: One can understand Peter's words 'I will go fishing' as an expression of his failure as a disciple. He simply goes back to his former life. Could be. Maybe, though, there is indeed another, more positive intuition. He lost Jesus or he felt lost himself, so he returns to the place where he met him first: to the shores of the Sea of Galilee. This is our spontaneous reaction when we are lost in a strange city: we seek for a known place. In a moment of personal crisis, we like to return to the place of our birth and childhood. When we long for someone, unknowingly even, we seek out the place where we met him or her. Well, in the case of Peter, it proved to be a right intuition.

I do not know whether having an empty net was something unusual. I would find it so. Especially if it were a drag-net. One would expect to get at least something, although just a few fish would make it still a failure. But to have absolutely nothing – this must have been strikingly abnormal. A spectacular failure is as significant as a spectacular success, and it is very likely to be a Divinely assisted failure! One would become suspicious that the Lord is surely not far away. That could explain their obedience to the stranger and their readiness to recognize in him the Risen Lord.

James Tissot, *Jesus Appears on the Shore of Lake Tiberias*, 1886–94, Brooklyn Museum, NY

The known Unknown was there ashore, waiting for them with some bread and fish already grilling on charcoal. Did they come from some heavenly rivers and paradisiacal bakery or from the lake nearby? Was Jesus jovial, casual or solemn? He behaves as if nothing particular had happened. As if he had never left. Maybe he hadn't. They lost sight of him for some time, but he has been there preparing this breakfast and taking care to share it with them. I feel it like that. Homely. The place where you enter after toiling all night, and there is someone waiting for you with breakfast – this is home. It does not matter if there is a roof or not, this person makes your home. He or she is your home. Remember the first question of the disciples when they met Jesus by the lake, right at the beginning of the gospel: 'Rabbi, teacher, where do you live? Come and see' (Jn 1.46). They are back. They are home again.

Timothy: It is true that already in the first words that Jesus speaks there are hints of hope. Jesus calls them 'children'. It sounds so odd to call grown-up fishermen children that I was tempted to suggest to you, Łukasz, that we put 'lads', as some other translations do. But they *are* children in the faith, inarticulate, unable to make sense of what they are living. The Lord's challenge to Peter will be to grow up. When he is young he goes where he wants, but when he will be old, he will be led to where he does not want to go, to a death like that of his Lord.

The shift happens when, without a word, they do what he asks, and cast the net on the right side. It may seem pointless but they do it. In these moments of flatness, when the initial fervour has passed, the only way forward is to do what the Lord asks: say one's prayers, go to Mass ('*Do this* in memory of me'), try to be kind, even when nothing seems to be achieved. That is how one grows up, hanging in there, enduring, even when it seems fruitless. Sometimes in my own life as a Dominican, especially in middle age, when some aspects of the religious life did not seem to make much sense, one went on doing things, going to prayers, meditating, preparing lectures, taking one's turn cooking and washing up and so on, until the dawn comes and the net is filled. It must be same in marriage too, when the initial passions cool, but one sticks with the practical expressions of love, until love finds a new and deeper form and it is morning again.

It is all about food! 'Haven't you anything to eat?' Jesus asks. In Emmaus, it was they who asked him that question I suppose. The nourishing food they need for their flock is hope-filled conversation, words that sustain and make strong, words of the Word made flesh, words on the beach and food for us. So let us pass from the non-conversation of the opening scene – *Ou!* – to Jesus' beautiful conversation with Peter. This is nutritious food for a starving person.

The last time Peter was at a charcoal fire was in the house of the high priest, when he denied the Lord three times. The supreme delicacy of this exchange is the way Jesus opens a space for Peter to undo his denial without ever directly alluding to it. Jesus addresses Peter as 'Simon, son of John'. It is as if he has to take him back to the infancy of his discipleship, before he received a new name: Cephas, the Rock, Peter. Through this conversation he becomes who he was called to be, rock-like, strong. He is strong enough to haul in the net which the other disciples struggle to handle. He must become grown up enough to feed the flock.

Lukasz: You make a good point noting how a charcoal fire connects the betrayal scene and this breakfast with the Risen One. It looks almost like a trademark of our Lord, his capacity for transformational reversal, of turning a terrible event into something beautiful and loving. The wounds of the crucified body – a sign of human injustice, cruelty, nonsense – become in Christ signs of His fidelity, of His love, something infinitely precious and beautiful. Analogously Peter's infidelity becomes the background for the fidelity of Christ. On the charcoal of betrayal, He prepares his meal: this is my body given up for you. Forgetting our perfidy would lead necessarily to concealment of God's faithfulness and forgiveness, right up to the cross.

That is why we should remember our treachery, pettiness and sin in general. Also, probably the only good way of remembering it is when one is encouraged by the loving presence of Christ. You say that Christ was gentle when he was giving Peter some hints about past events. I would say that it was a very precisely aimed *touché* of a painful and therefore important spot. I suppose that we need to wait and ask Peter himself how he felt this allusion!

In the Gospel of John, Jesus after his resurrection spoke to Mary Magdalene, then greeted all the disciples, 'Peace be with you', and he spoke with Thomas Didymos. He did not address Peter specifically. Peter must have felt he had had a particular relationship with Jesus; he declared it eagerly before the Passion and he wanted to be close. What were his expectations and fears when he learned that the master he disowned is, against all the odds, alive? Jesus was back and spoke some kind words to everyone but none towards Peter in particular … Could it mean that his, Peter's, desire to be close was dismissed forever? Silence is sometimes more difficult than a direct reproach. Peter deserved some words, whatever they would be.

Timothy: Yes, Peter did deserve some words from the Lord after all that silence. And now there is that extraordinary conversation with Peter. Here we come to the most disputed question, the meaning of the different words that are used for 'love'.

'Do you love me more than these?' I think that this is a gentle tease! Earlier, Peter had boasted 'I will lay down my life for you!' (Jn 13.37). In

Matthew and Mark, he even claims that he loves Jesus more than the other disciples. 'Even if they all fall away, I will not' (Mt. 26.33; Mk 14.29). One can almost imagine Jesus smiling as he makes this gentlest allusion to Peter's childish boast! This time Peter does not dare to claim so much. He sticks to his own love. I love you. No more silly claims to superiority.

How does one undo betrayal and denial? Every marriage, every friendship, every commitment, may face this supreme challenge. One can rub someone's nose in the dirt of their failure or open a new space in which the wrong is quietly acknowledged and transcended. Imagination, even humour, is needed to help the other embrace all that has happened and move on.

The passage evokes Chapter 6, the feeding of the five thousand, which leads to Jesus' command 'Gather up the fragments left over, that nothing may be lost.' In this scene, the net is hauled in, and is not broken. Again, nothing is lost. Not just of our good deeds, our kindnesses, but even of our failures and sins nothing must be lost. Peter's shameful betrayal is not forgotten; It is remembered in a way that heals and will feed us. Peter's most glorious witness – the best food he gives us – is when eventually, years later, he is able to speak of his denial of his Lord and acknowledge that it was not the end of his vocation. If Mark's gospel is, as many claim, the 'memoirs of Peter', then It Is here for the first time that Peter's betrayal is remembered, presumably because Peter told his fellow disciples about it. What an encouragement for us when we deny or betray those whom we love! Even the Rock wobbled! Nothing is consigned to oblivion. Rainer Maria Rilke described himself, in a letter to his sister, as being 'like a man gathering fungi and healing herbs among the weeds'; as a poet, his role 'is to be among what is human, to see everything and reject nothing'.[1]

Do we in the Church and in our families have conversations that gently embrace all that we have done and been, bring all to light, perhaps implicitly, like Jesus, so that our hope for all that we are and have done is recovered?

Let's look at that conversation between the Lord and Peter and ask what is going on:

When they have had breakfast, Jesus says to Simon Peter, –
'Simon *son* of John, do you love (*agapas*) me more than these?'
He says to him, –
'Yes, Lord. You, you know that I love (*philo*) you.'
He says to him, –

'Feed my lambs.'
He says to him again, a second time, –
'Simon *son* of John, do you love (*agapas*) me?'
He says to him, –
'Yes, Lord. You, you know that I love (*philo*) you.'
He says to him, –
'Shepherd my sheep.'
He says to him the third *time*, –
'Simon *son* of John, do you love (*phileis*) me?'
Peter was saddened because he says to him the third *time*, 'Do you love
    (*phileis*) me?' And he says to him, –
'Lord, you, you know everything. You know that I love (*philo*) you.'

Innumerable articles have been written on the meaning of the words
agapan and *philein*. Some have asserted that they mean the same thing,
and so the alternation is without significance. This is not plausible. In
John's gospel every word is weighed and measured as in a poem. I shall
be fascinated to see how you respond, but I think there are two beautiful
interpretations and our readers will make their choice.

The first is that *agape* is the beautiful Divine love that typifies
Christianity, the unselfish, almost disinterested love that reaches out to
strangers and even enemies. And so Jesus twice asks Peter if he loves him
in this pure and transcendent way, but all that Peter can offer is the warm
friendship of *philia*. He cannot reach as high as *agape*. Finally, Jesus asks
him for what he does offer: 'Simon *son* of John, do you love (*phileis*) me?'
Jesus contents himself with the small love of which Peter is capable. It's
as if God were to say, 'I will take whatever you can manage. If you can
only give me a little love, that will be enough.' God humbly accepts the
small portion of affection that we sometimes remember to offer him, even
though God has for us a love which is infinite. In the words of the poet
W. H. Auden, 'If equal affection cannot be,/ Let the more loving one be
me.'[2] When we love someone more than they love us, we are sharing God's
own pain and joy.

But it might be the other way around. Perhaps *philia* here implies a
warm love. Jesus asks whether Peter loves him, and he replies, 'Yes, I love
you *dearly*.' Peter is stressing the human affection of his love. After his
friend's denials, Jesus does not initially ask for so much, until Peter has
opened the way. We too, when we love someone who has betrayed us
or drifted away, may not initially dare to ask for much. We do not push

the pace and demand fulsome declarations. We respect their freedom. No pressure! Until they show that they are ready for more. The humility of the Lord is thus only to dare to ask for our warm *philia* when we have shown that we wish to give it.

I do not know which interpretation is right. Both are beautiful. But surely *agape* and *philia* need each other, and even a touch of *eros*! Our love for strangers and even enemies cannot be a bland, blanket affection. 'I suppose that I must love you even though I find you a bore because I am a Christian.' W. H. Auden, again, joked that 'we are here on earth to do good to others. What the others are here for, I don't know.'[3]

Surely a love is only human and Divine if we are open to how others are delightful and attractive. God delights in them and so they must be delightful, attractive, if only we could see. *Agape* needs to be salted with a touch of *philia* and even *eros*. And when we have *philia* for another, even *eros,* there needs to be that touch of *agape*, which leaves them be, which gives them space and does not gobble them up. There are so many other things to talk about, but I must stop since you are obviously itching to have a word.

Łukasz: Yes, something makes me itch to intervene when we talk to each other, though it is less when we correspond than when we talk face to face. I suppose simply because there is more time to reflect and digest one's words. You propose two somewhat opposite interpretations: according to the first one, *philia* is less than *agape*; here Jesus accepted the still imperfect *philia* instead of the more desired *agape*. According to the second, *philia* adds something to *agape* and Peter succeeded in convincing Jesus of his lasting warm friendship. If the same text produces two contradictory interpretations, it is likely that this ambiguity was intended, or that the contradiction is only superficial, or that our exegesis still misses some point.

Only in the first question does Jesus ask about 'more' love. It may refer to Peter's earlier boastful claims to be better than others. Let me point to a similar question asked by Jesus at the ends of the parable about two debtors from Luke 7.42: 'When they could not pay, he cancelled the debts for both of them. Now which of them will *love him more*?' Peter's debt was greater than the debt of other disciples, as his fault was greater in the flagrant rejection of Jesus. He has been forgiven a greater sin, and yes, only now because of this newly received forgiveness, Peter has a good reason to claim that he loves more than others. Not because of his own virtue but because of his greater sin and the greater forgiveness he received.

The issue of loving 'more' disappears from the two following questions. The second is about *agape* and the third about *philia*. Maybe they are not questions about *more* or *less* love but about its different aspects? The commandment of love from Deut. 6.5 is not that interested in distinguishing different types of love of God, more or less desirable, but – in a rather opposite movement – is interested in subduing *all* to the relationship with God: 'You will love with all your heart, with all your soul, with all your force.' One can try to differentiate between different aspects of love, but the God of Israel simply wants it all. Jesus is the same God and desires nothing less: intellectual love, emotional love, passionate love; all-inclusive.

Peter keeps repeating 'Lord, you know' at the beginning of his triple answer. It seems to be another key to the meaning of his answer. In the scene where the Lord shows to the prophet Ezekiel the valley of dry bones, which is a shattering image of the spiritual situation of his people, we can hear a somewhat similar answer given by Ezekiel: 'He said to me, Son of man, shall these bones live? I answered, O Lord God, you know' (Ezek. 37 3) They will live if and only then when the Lord wants them to live. There is no other way they could. Jesus' words 'Do you – still, yet, again love me?' touches the heart of every sinner, and the longer I live the louder I say 'Lord, you know' because the more I need the miracle of resurrection.

Jesus prophesied Peter's betrayal when Peter denied its possibility. Now Peter indirectly recognizes that he does not know himself any more, that his Lord knows him better. How would you answer such a question asked by the betrayed God? I think Peter's answer is as good as one can get: our own heart is only partially known to us. Our access to ourselves is limited. Through memories of our past and our resurging present desires we can forge a deeper answer, all the while remaining aware that our self-knowledge is limited. 'You know, Lord' is the best foundation one can give to the declared love.

And the Lord knew. His answer seems to be quite at odds with the question of love as well as with Peter's answer. How would the role of a shepherd be a consequence of this humble love? And yet it seems to be so. Jesus' triple answer contains both forgiveness and promotion. This was the way of Cephas Peter, and of Saul of Tarsus, known later as Paul. The last time when Peter was following Jesus, he got as far as the courtyard of the high priest and could not find the courage to go further. Now, in the twice repeated phrase 'Follow me!', he gets his second chance to go on. Did his path this time come more easily to him? I have no idea, but the gospel suggests that this time he succeeded and followed the Lord to the end.

There is one more last question asked by Peter: 'What will be with this one?' A curious question concerning the beloved disciple sounds almost like unnecessary curiosity in the context of this grand finale of the gospel. Maybe this question hides something deeper? Was it an expression of particular care for this disciple? Or a question about his mission or position within the community? In any case, Jesus deals with it as with a mere distraction. Apparently, one shepherds Jesus' sheep and lambs not by following other disciples but by following Jesus himself. That is all.

Timothy: Two post-resurrection appearances: the first, in my opinion, heals the disciples of disillusion, and the second of a certain flatness. The disciples after the resurrection struggle with just the same things that we do two thousand years later: disillusionment with the Church and boredom! Things do not change that much.

In both, the healing of the disillusionment and the heartening of the discouraged disciples pivot around recognition. The disciples who flee to Emmaus fail to accept the loving witness of the women who faithfully stayed with Jesus in his suffering and went to his tomb as a final expression of their love. These men only recognize him in the gesture of love made at the Last Supper in the face of death. In the scene we have just looked at, it is the beloved disciple who recognizes that the stranger on the beach is the Lord. He too had been there at the cross. Recognition of the Lord is always by eyes which are opened by love. Who are the loving witnesses who speak to us today, when our faith becomes tepid or faltering? Who for us are the women who went to the tomb, and the beloved disciple? Rowan Williams wrote, 'Faith has a lot to do with the simple fact that there are trustworthy lives to be seen, that we can see in some believing people a world we'd like to live in.'[4]

But we must leave further comparison of the two scenes to our readers. We must turn to the last conversation in this book.

'I opposed him to his face' (Gal. 2.1–14)

Then after fourteen years I again went up to Jerusalem with Barnabas, having taken with me also Titus. Now I went up in accord with a revelation. So I set before them the gospel that I announce among the Gentiles, in private to those of repute, lest in any way in vain I was running, or had run. But not even Titus, who was with me, being a Greek, was compelled to be circumcised, *not* even because of the secretly brought in pseudo-brothers, who slipped in to spy out our freedom that we have in Christ Jesus, so that they might enslave us. To them, not even for a moment did we yield in submission, so that the truth of the gospel might endure for you.

But from those reputed to be something – what they once were makes no difference to me; God shows no partiality – to me those of repute added nothing. But on the contrary, having seen that I had been entrusted with the gospel of the Uncircumcision, as Peter of the Circumcision – because the One who had worked in Peter for an apostolate of the Circumcision worked also in me for the Gentiles – and having known the grace given me, James and Cephas, and John, reputed to be pillars, gave their right hands of communion to me and Barnabas, so that we *should go* to the Gentiles and they to the Circumcision. Only, we should be mindful of the poor, which is also the same thing I strived to do.

Yet when Cephas came to Antioch, to his very face I was opposed because he was condemnable. For before the arrival of some *people* from James, he was eating with the Gentiles. But since they came, he was withdrawing and separating himself, being afraid of those of the Circumcision. And the rest of the Jews were play-acting together with him, so that even Barnabas was carried away by their pretence. But when

I saw that they were not walking straight towards the truth of the gospel, I said to Cephas in front of them all, – If you, being a Jew, are living in a Gentile and not in a Jewish *manner*, how can you compel the Gentiles to judaize?

Timothy: This is the first conversation we explore which is not between God and humanity. Here Paul is writing as a Christian to his brothers and sisters. We are now in our epoch, of the Church which has received the Spirit. Pentecost has transformed the conversations of the community, for now God speaks to us often through each other. The shift is not absolute. The Old Testament and the gospels are filled with conversations between human beings, kings and prophets, for example, and the New Testament shows the disciples arguing with each other and so on. And God still speaks to us directly through his Word or in the secret of our hearts. Christ appeared to Paul, as he tells us, on his way to Damascus, and God speaks to the saints throughout history: to our own Catherine of Siena, for example. Nevertheless, we are in a new world! At the beginning of Acts, lots are drawn to see who will take the place of Judas. But after Pentecost, lots are drawn no more. The Church, guided by the Spirit, meets in Acts 15 to discuss and take decisions about its life and mission.

Scholars argue – they always do! – about the dates of this letter to the Galatians and whether it is before or after the Council of Jerusalem, but whatever one decides, we see here a Church seeking its way forward in debate, and people getting thoroughly worked up, as they do today. So this is a great text to help us think about how we debate with each other, seeking to know God's will, as we embark on what Pope Francis calls 'the synodal way'. Some people groan at the Pope's introduction at this 'new' way of being Church, which will transform the Church we have known. But my old teacher, Yves Congar OP, always maintained that synodality is the archetypically Catholic way of government, which in recent centuries has lost its former prominence. Pope Francis is summoning us back to what is central in our tradition.

Here, in almost the earliest text of the New Testament, soon after Pentecost, we see the most enormous row! Peter and Paul will be celebrated together as the twin pillars of the Church in Rome – they share a feast– and yet here is Paul denouncing Peter as a coward. When I see the rows that divide the Church today, and indeed the Churches, I find it rather encouraging that this is how it was from the beginning!

Łukasz: Paul does not give us a full report on the discussions he had with other Apostles; actually, he does not quote any dialogues, but only at the end of his account he quotes himself. Unlike in the Gospels or the Old Testament stories, in the Letter to the Galatians there is no third-person narrator. Clearly, we are getting only the perspective of Paul here. Of course, it would be fascinating to hear what Peter, Cefas, would have to say or remembered of these two encounters with Paul. Actually, according to the Acts of the Apostles, he had plenty in common with Paul. It was Peter who began the mission to the Gentiles and baptized the first heathen centurion Cornelius. He even had a particular revelation in Jaffa which abolished the principles of the Old Testament kashrut (Acts 10). Whenever I am in Jaffa, I honour this freedom given to Peter by having some local shellfish!

Timothy: Yes, it is fascinating that Paul's hot anger is for someone who has been so close to him and shared a journey. He is especially upset with Peter because Peter had already opened the door for the Gentiles! Often in the Church, as in politics, the harshest disagreements are with people with whom we thought we were in close agreement. Family rows are more passionate usually than those we have with strangers!

Łukasz: Timewise, the letter to the Galatians is closer to these events than a later account in which Luke reconstructed the events in Acts 15. In Galatians we get a look at the hot-headed and passionate Paul fighting for the faith of this community. Only a chapter further on, in Galatians 3, twice he will call them *anoetoi*: 'without knowledge'. I would hesitate to call Paul a conversationalist here. He clearly is something more, maybe an impatient teacher, or a frustrated father, or even a mother! I find what he goes on to say very touching:

> My children, for whom I am again in labour until Christ be formed in you! I would like to be with you now and to change my voice, for I am at loss because of you. (Gal. 4.19–20)

He tells the Galatians about his confrontation with the other Apostles not because he wanted to boast about his personal victories. Actually, he does something theologically very profound. He speaks of the past to reveal that there has been some consistency within God's revelation and actions in the past. The Galatians are not the first to be confronted with the temptation to seek salvation through keeping the Old Testament ritual customs. Since the Jewish religion was recognized and legal in the Roman Empire, being circumcised as Jews could also have given some legal protection to the first Christians; Jews were exempt from participation in the cult of the Empire whereas Christians were not.[1] The freedom from circumcision preached by Paul came with the price of becoming an outlaw. Paul calls Galatians *anoetoi*, 'without knowledge', not 'without intelligence'. He wants them to learn something from this brief but apparently already very eventful Church history and from his own example.

Timothy: Contrast Paul's open, strong words, with the secret manoeuvres of the pseudo-brethren, who slip in, spy and no doubt institute nasty things, spread rumours, whispering behind Paul's back. Peter may have lost his nerve but he is not underhand.

Oh, if only in the Church we could breathe the fresh air of open and honest speech, free of poisonous gossip and insinuation. Paul does argue heatedly. No punches are pulled. But even so they do eventually find their way to consensus, though with a touchy person like Paul this must have been tough. How can we today argue openly, and even be in profound disagreement, without beating each other up? How can we, in a Church which is sometimes polarized, give each other 'the right hand of mission'? Does Paul give us any clues?

Łukasz: You are right that Paul is anything but a gossip or someone who would seek to solve public scandal by using secretive ways, backstage manipulation. In his reaction to Peter's inconsistency, there is something more than his temperament though. Since Peter's fault appeared in public, it is just and fair to react to it also in public.

Note, please, that Paul speaks about two different encounters with Peter: the one in Jerusalem, which ended peacefully, and the second one, in Antioch, where Peter was reproached. Paul speaks of the 'pseudo-brothers who sneaked in' for his first meeting in Jerusalem. They must have been believers in Christ, but the very fact that they should not have been there – they 'sneaked in' – suggests that this meeting was not open to the public. In a veiled way, Paul says that they were 'brought in'. I suppose that one of Paul's opponents wanted to get more weight in the meeting and brought in his groupies for support.

It was not a public event or lecture in which everybody could participate and even less, in which everybody could take decisions.

Even though Paul seemed to relativize their authority, he presented the matter of the Gentile believers 'in private, to those of repute' (Gal. 2.2). What Paul denounces so eagerly is that later, in Antioch, Peter was not consistent in his actions with his own earlier decision. If Paul was so blunt about the same issue with Peter himself, how much blunter he should be with Galatians!

Bartolomeo Cavarozzi, *Dispute between St Peter and St Paul*,
1615–16, Galerie G. Sarti, Paris

Timothy: You are right to say that Paul wants to relativize the authority of those who opposed him. In fact, much of the letter is an argument for Paul's authority in this bust-up. And he has different sorts of authority. He has his personal authority because Christ has appeared to him. He appeals throughout to the authority of the Scriptures to support his case. There is the authority of the *experience* of the Galatians, when they lived with the freedom of his preaching. There is also, one might say, the authority of his rhetoric in this powerful dramatic letter. He needs to drum up all these 'authorities' in the face of the authority of the Church in Jerusalem and his opponents.

Actually, he reminds me of St John Henry Newman who recognized that in the Church there were three authorities, or offices: roughly government, reason and experience.[2] The Church flourishes when these authorities play together in symphony, counterbalancing each other, none being silenced. These are quite similar to the authorities to which Paul appeals in this letter. Most arguments in the Church are about the relative weight we give to different authorities: 'The Church teaches this'; 'But this is my experience!'; 'But the Bible says this.'

As Pope Francis invites the Church to move forward on the synodal path, and as the Churches seek unity, it is good to ask whether we have properly understood the play of different sorts of authority in the Church. Every Christian has authority because we have all received the Holy Spirit. But the bishops have a particular sort of authority as pastors of the flock and guardians of the tradition and the unity of the whole Church. But there is also the *magisterium* of thinkers, especially theologians, in the Church, who appeal to the authority of reason. And we all have the authority of experience, as we all seek to know the Lord in prayer. Do we recognize sufficiently the authority of lay women and men who marry and bring up children and plunge themselves into the complex issues of the day?

The bishop should be the one who nurtures the conversations of the Church, ensuring that no one is left unheard, no one is silenced, and that the diverse authorities are each recognized. The bishop should be the conductor of the symphony orchestra of debate, bringing in the strings, quietening the percussion, encouraging the wind section, conjuring up the silences, making music.

Łukasz: One of the Apostolic Fathers of the early second century, St Ignatius of Antioch, used a similar musical image in his letters. He wrote of the Ephesians: 'your presbytery, being worthy of God, is fitted as exactly to the bishop as the strings are to the harp' (Eph. 4.1). Yet he did not forget about being attuned to the Lord. The bishop 'is in harmony with the commandments and ordinances of the Lord, even as the strings are with a harp' (Philadelphians 1.2). Not every harmony is desired. One should demand where the music comes from. Paul did not hesitate to break up the harmony he found contrary to the Gospel.

Paul claims that his authority and mission is directly God-given. I find it very significant that Paul says explicitly that he came to Jerusalem because of the particular 'revelation' (Gal. 2.2). A true charismatic is pushed by the Spirit to be in the Church, not to avoid it.

It is not so clear what happened in Jerusalem. When we have a look at that ancient controversy, we can see that this semi-private deal between Paul and other Apostles solved the matter for Paul but not for those brothers who wanted to keep circumcision. Their voices persisted in Antioch. Maybe by stepping back Peter wanted to save the fragile unity of the Church? The first decision of the Apostles did not stop the dissenting voices. They continued, grew and came even to Paul's beloved Galatia. Truly, I have no idea if this first conflict is to be taken as a good or a bad example of solving issues in the Church!

Maybe the Apostles should have taken the opposing voices more seriously? Taken more time explaining, arguing and teaching? Should they have said: 'Brother Paul, we know that you are right but for the sake of other voices in the Church, let us wait for the final decision. Come back, let us say, in two, three years'? This avoidance, a non-statement, would have really come close to the attitude of the Jewish authorities when Jesus asked them whether John's baptism was from heaven. They did not want to disagree with the public opinion and said, 'We do not know.' In consequence, Jesus also refused to give his answer (Mt. 21.27).

Maybe we should agree that there will be voices of dissent and still it should not stop the Church from making decisions? In any case, we can see that this first tension within the Church did not destroy her. The voices opposing Paul went on and, paradoxically thanks to them, we have now the Letter to the Galatians! Paul had to explain his Gospel to them and thus he did it also for the generations to come, for us. The opposing voices are indeed important in the quest for truth.

Timothy: I suppose that Gamaliel (Acts 5.34) embodies the 'wait and see' principle. He advised the opponents of this new Messianic movement to wait and see if it was from God or not. In the debates in the Church today, many people are impatient for change. There was frustration that after the Amazonian Synod many of their hopes were disappointed – for example, for the ordination of married men. But Pope Francis insisted that discernment of the way forward demands patient waiting, living with tensions in the Church, refusing to make quick decisions that exclude the voice of minorities. This is counter-cultural in our impatient society which demands instant solutions and instant gratification. God is patient beyond our imagination.

Does this row have anything to say to us today as Christians, and indeed Catholics, often divided and unable to speak to each other? During the Reformation, texts from Paul's letters to the Galatians and the Romans were invoked to oppose Catholicism, which the Reformers maintained was a religion of works, unlike the pure faith of Paul and themselves. But this is an old quarrel, which has been pretty well resolved.

Galatians does home in on an issue which is very alive in all of our Churches, indeed in Western society: identity politics! Paul's opponents

– and this is oversimplifying it a lot – maintained that you could not become a 'real Christian' without taking on the badges of Jewish identity, the Law and circumcision. One had to become a part of the first Chosen People if you were to belong to Christ. Paul will argue that a true Christian is freed of the law. A new identity is possible in Christ.

Much division within Christianity is about identity. Who are 'real Christians'? Or 'real Catholics?' For some, the old Latin Mass is a touchstone of true Catholic identity. Others feel rejected because they are divorced and remarried, or are gay or whatever and so are considered not 'real Catholics'. But God always invites us into a larger identity, a more spacious Church. A full Catholic identity – that is to say, one that is truly 'universal' – always lies ahead, beyond every culture. We are always on the way to understanding what it is to be Catholic. God will go on surprising us! We may draw strong lines and say, 'This is who we are. No one else is welcome.' But God may surprise us and invite us to enlarge our sense of 'we'.

One symbol of identity and unity does spring out of the letter: 'We should be mindful of the poor, which is also the same I strived to do.' In the Church today too our shared identity is also anchored in a concern with the poor. For Catholics this is above all embodied in Caritas Internationalis, one of the biggest charities in the world. Our identity is bound up with the poor, as theirs is with ours. And by 'the poor' Paul probably means the poor Christians of Jerusalem, the mother Church for whom he organized collections. For us Catholics, this 'mother Church' has become the Church which looks to Peter and Paul as its pillars, the diocese of Rome.

Łukasz: Paul wrote the letter to his Galatians out of love, because he cared. Even though he did not know exactly what to say, or 'how to change his voice', he wrote it. Out of love he rebukes, and out of love he consoles. For him, it is not an abstract academic discussion to be won. It is a struggle, a labour, through which he wants to shape the faith of the Galatians.

If conflicts become personal, it is always because of the lack of love. I know, it may sound like a too spiritual solution for a sociological problem. Yet this is the starting point which changes everything. Conflicts and discussions are not the end of the love story but part of it. They are actually signs that the two parties did not give up on each other. Silence is worse. Speaking out of love does not mean avoiding difficult themes or compromising on everything. The Catholic Church and the Lutheran World Federation signed the 'Joint Declaration on the Doctrine of

Justification' (in 1999), not because the two sides gave up their convictions but because they understood that each of them had misconstrued some of the other's beliefs. A certain step towards unity was made through the common quest for truth and not by dismissing the differences as unimportant.

Group identities will always be with us, for as long as we are social beings. Since this situation is natural, there is nothing wrong with group identities. The gospel preached by Paul intended not to remove them but to relativize them, as he famously says in the same letter: 'There is no longer Jew or Greek, there is no longer slave or free, there is no longer male and female; for all of you are one in Christ Jesus' (Gal. 3.28). The identities he speaks of are mostly innate. Paul did not incite the Galatians to remove or change their ethnicity or gender. To begin with, it is simply impossible; and second, the main point is that through faith and relationship with Christ they can personally and individually choose their deeper identity.

When one has no personality, the group identity becomes everything. On the other hand, mature faith and a personal relationship with Christ transforms a thick-headed ideological groupie into a person to whom one can relate, someone to talk to. Love has an individualizing power because we cannot love humanity, thank God, but we can truly love only particular people. Any dialogue with any person that is seeking for truth will be profitable and life-giving. Ultimately, it will lead to love and friendship. The opposite sequence of events is also true: a dialogue with a true friend or beloved will touch deepest and most difficult issues. This tandem of love and truth is ubiquitous, a truly virtuous circle.

Avoiding difficult or divisive matters may be a good temporary solution in the moment of heightened emotions, but in the long run it is definitely not a good tactic. Neglecting the matters which are important for my brothers and sisters doesn't have much to do with love and has much more to do with keeping up appearances. How to be faithful to Christ is an essential question. How to be 'a real Christian', or a better Christian, is also a fundamental question and should not be abandoned. How to ask the question 'Who is a real Christian?' with love and not to wave it like a club – that is another matter. I suppose that we will agree, though, that it is not too complicated to tell the difference between the two approaches.

Timothy: A final word on the theme of this letter and what it might mean to us: freedom! Paul talks of 'the pseudo-brothers, who slipped in to spy out our freedom that we have in Christ Jesus, so that they might enslave us'. This is obviously freedom from the precepts of the Law. But what is the freedom that we should embody today? Paul will say, 'For freedom Christ has set us free' (Gal. 5.1). What is our glorious freedom as the children of God?

I doubt that there are many Christians who need to be freed from the precepts of the Torah! From time to time groups of Christians claim to be free of any moral obligations at all and so embrace free love, unbounded liberty, antinomianism, but that makes no sense, Paul's letters are filled with moral obligations.

Perhaps for us it is primarily a 'freedom for'. The freedom to embrace Christ and belong to others. It is the freedom to give our lives away. This implies all sorts of obligations. Obligation comes from the Latin word meaning 'to bind'. Because we are bound to others, we have obligations. My friend and brother David Sanders OP always insisted that I was bound to celebrate his birthday, because that is a consequence of the bonds of friendship. Catholics have all sorts of obligations, such as 'holidays of obligation', when one should go to Mass as on a Sunday. These are not impositions or constrains, though they may feel like it when one has to struggle out of bed. They are expressions of who one is, the community to which one belongs, one's identity in Christ. They say, 'I freely belong to Christ and his brothers and sisters.'

Łukasz: When one says 'freedom', most often one thinks of something like 'You are free to go.' God gives us a slightly different freedom, of a peculiarly warm and loving type: 'You are free to stay!' Freedom to stay is much greater than freedom to leave. It can be also scarier. The first one ends the adventure of the relationship; the latter is an invitation and a promise for a new beginning. I suppose that with a similar phrase we will be invited into our heavenly abode: 'You are free to stay, forever.' Maybe that is why, whenever such an invitation is made and when indeed I am truly free to stay, it is like a foretaste of this unknown happiness that we are all moving towards. Apparently there will be plenty of singing in heaven. I am sure, though, that there will be also plenty of time for 'holy conversations'! Thank you, my dear friend, for the gift of our conversations. They make for a set of worthy appetizers!

Epilogue

'For our conversation is in heaven' (Phil. 3.20)

The Holy Spirit has been poured upon the Church at Pentecost. All around the Mediterranean, people are being baptized into the Body of Christ. And yet, as we saw in our final conversation, there is dissension and confrontation. But the same St Paul who denounces St Peter will later write to the Philippians: 'For our conversation is in heaven; from whence also we look for the Saviour, the Lord Jesus Christ.' The Greek word *politeuma*, translated here as 'conversation', usually rendered today as 'citizenship', means 'form of government' and 'way of life'. The King James Version and many other English translations follow the Vulgate.[1] The Latin word *conversatio* has a broader meaning than conversation: it means spending time with someone, conduct and way of life. Christian conversation should build our common home in Christ, putting us at ease with each other even in our differences, as the New Testament bears within itself the differences of the four gospels. Yet almost every document in the New Testament witnesses to quarrels and disunity.

God's Word invites us today to share in the Divine friendship of the Trinity. Our conversation should also be 'in heaven', and yet when we Christians talk to each other, surely there is the same mixture of loving communication and misunderstanding and antagonism that we find between Paul and his communities. Lovers exchange hurtful as well as tender words. Parents and children are distraught at finding themselves at a loss to understand each other. Think of Mary and Joseph looking for the adolescent Jesus in the Temple. Communication delights in differences; otherwise there would be nothing to communicate. It breaks down because of mistrust, failure to search for understanding, pride or ignorance.

The universal tendency of human beings both to love and to misunderstand each other is exacerbated by instant global communication. We can be in immediate contact with people on the other side of the globe and create friendships with strangers whom we shall never meet. Yet sound-bite communication, and the compressed slogans of modern politics, have stoked ideological divisions, in families, society and the Church. In our global world, there are many silos. We do not give each other the chance or the time to converse.

So the future of humanity in this perilous time surely demands that we learn the subtle art of listening and talking to each gently, with truth and transparency. How can we speak words that reach across differences of generation, cultural, ethnicity, gender, party politics and ideology? How can we speak words that heal rather than hurt, that illuminate rather than obscure?

> 'Do not let any unwholesome talk come out of your mouths, but only what is helpful for building others up according to their needs, that it may benefit those who listen.' (Eph. 4.29)

Do these 18 conversations between God and his People offer us any clues as to how we can share our joy and heal the hurts that wound our families, our society and the Body of Christ? If not, we shall be unable to speak a word of hope with authority to a world that views the future with dread.

So many conversations today revolve around the question of identity: national and ethnic identity, religious identity, gender identity, even sporting identity! In the Biblical conversations we have often seen that the quest for identity is inseparable from the encounter with God. Jacob is called to be Israel when he fights with the Divine stranger in the night. His fight with himself and with his God are two aspects of the same quest. When Peter confesses that Jesus is the Christ, he hears the call to be the Rock. Conversation with God summons us beyond small and defensive identities, as we are caught up in the mystery of the one whose name is I AM. So how we speak to God and how we speak with each other are two sides of the same coin. John said it clearly: 'If you do not love the brother you see, how can you claim to love God whom you do not see?' (1 Jn 4.20). We do not have one hemisphere of brain for 'supernatural' relationships and another for relationships with our brothers and sisters. Our faith is incarnate in the tissue of our human relationships, in our loves and hatreds, our passions and our fears.

Our friendship with God shapes our openness to friendship with others, and vice versa. If I cannot listen to God, I will not listen well to others. If I open myself to those with whom I disagree, it is more likely that, when I sit in silence in the presence of God, I shall hear a word of friendship addressed to me. If I am impatient, self-centred and unfaithful here, I will be the same there. So let us see whether these 18 conversations with God give us any clues as to how we may renew friendship in our families, the Church and society. Building a just world implies learning to talk to each other with transparency and delight. Slogans will not achieve much.

Listening requires silence. Not just the absence of words but that deep inner tranquillity in which one dares to be vulnerable to another. Silence can take many forms, and be both the plenitude of communication and its failure. It can be companionable and easy or fearful and aggressive. There is the joyful silence of those who have no need for words and the frigid silence that shrinks from communication. Think of the silences that inhabit the lives of our families and our communities: the silence of mutual incomprehension, of suspicion and fear. But also the silences of mutual presence, of the sheer delight of being with those whom we love. How can we move from silences that hermetically seal us off from each other to the blessed silence of communion, from having nothing to say to needing to say nothing?

In so many of these Biblical conversations God breaks an oppressive silence with a healing word. To Adam and Eve, who have fled his face and hide in the garden, God says: 'Where are you?' He invites them to come out of concealment so that conversation may begin again. Cain, who has silenced his brother, is wrapped in solitude. But God reaches out to protect him: 'And YHWH put a mark on Cain, so that no one who finds him would strike him.' No silence need be final. As Moses wanders in the silence of the desert, exiled from his own people, he hears a voice calling him by name. God breaks the silence of Jonah who did not wish to preach in Nineveh, perhaps the silence of Mary in her room and of the woman at the well in the heat of midday. On the cross he will bear the apparent silence of God – 'Oh God, my God, why have you abandoned me?' – and break it on Easter morning.

God's word can dissolve any silence, because silence is never primordial, nor need it be final. 'In the beginning was the Word' (Jn 1.1). The negative silences in our lives, when we feel trapped in solitude and alienation, are only pauses in the great conversation which gives us life, with God from whom everything springs and to whom all returns. The first word and final word come from God. St Paul wrote to the Corinthians:

> For the Son of God, Jesus Christ, whom we proclaimed among you, Silvanus and Timothy and I, was not 'Yes and No'; but in him it is always 'Yes'. For in him every one of God's promises is a 'Yes'. For this reason it is through him that we say the 'Amen' to the glory of God. (2 Cor. 1.19–20)

The whole of creation and recreation springs from God's great Yes in the beginning, and reaches to our final Amen. How then can we simply and without reserve say No to others, and finally close a conversation? Even Jonah, who longed to speak a No to Nineveh, finally speaks the merciful Yes.

There are moments of silence, when God does not appear to address a word to us, but these moments are within the symphony of creation. God's silence speaks tons! It is more like a pause in the musical notation; it is an essential part of the music, no less important than the sounds. In the Apocalypse, silence has its place: 'When the Lamb opened the seventh seal, there was silence in heaven for about half an hour' (Rev. 8.1).

So these hurtful, negative silences that wound the lives of our families, of our Church and the world, never need be final. They are discords in the music of our lives which God's grace wishes to gather into a final harmony.

What if I do not hear God addressing *me*? I wait in patient silence in the chapel, my ears open, but I hear nothing. Is there anyone there, or am I speaking to myself? More fundamentally than a word addressed to me, as if by an invisible interlocutor, the Divine word speaks me into being and, as St Augustine said so beautifully, is closer to me than I am to myself. In such moments I discover that it is not God who had been absent from me. I was absent from my deepest identity. St Augustine again: 'You were within me, and I outside ... You were with me and I was not with you.'[2] Then we discover that, yes, there is silence. The silence not of absence but of presence. My deepest identity is to *be* someone addressed by God. He speaks my name. My life can never be meaningless, swallowed up in empty silence, because I am spoken into being by the Lord *Philopsychos*, who 'loves the living' (Wis. 11.26).

Conversation with others whom I find incomprehensible, even distasteful, can catch fire if I recognize that they too are addressed by the Lord. Their very being, which may seem to me 'a waste of space', as we say in English, because of their politics or religion or way of life, springs from the same Lord who speaks them too into being. At the very core of their existence is also the God who is also closer to them than they are to themselves. How then can we not talk to each other? We are all fruit of the Divine Word which made the womb of Mary pregnant. Even if someone does not know God's name, the Lord knows his or hers and speaks it. This is the foundation of all dialogue, even when it seems to be impossible.

Fra Angelico OP, *Sacred Conversation* (the Annalena Altarpiece), 1438–40, Museum of San Marco, Florence

Abraham is summoned by name to leave his home for the Promised Land, and replies *Hinneni,* 'Here I am.' Moses is wandering in the soundless desert and hears his name called, 'Moses, Moses', and he too replies, 'Here I am.' The God who is within us is also *beside* us. When Moses wonders how he can fulfil his mission, God replies: 'For I am with you.' When Mary is startled by the appearance of Gabriel bursting into her life, she is greeted with the words: 'Rejoice, begraced! The Lord with you!' When the disciples flee Jerusalem, they meet a stranger who walks beside them. When the disciples go fishing after the resurrection, they see someone on the beach. 'It is the Lord,' says the Beloved Disciple. This is the beautiful refrain of our liturgies, 'The Lord be with you.'

So the climax of dialogue with God is not receiving some new data from Him but contemplation; that is, being *with* another Person. It does not serve as a means to anything else. St Augustine called it *bonum frui*, 'good to enjoy'.[3] It is not a staging point in a journey that leads further; it is the point of arrival! It is the place where my desires are fulfilled, where I repose, which I savour and in which I live. We experience some of it when we spend time with someone who loves us. It is like a moment of natural contemplation. With this person we are at home. This is also an experience of timelessness. Neither I nor he or she is looking over my shoulder thinking about the next thing on the to-do list.

So when we are called to dialogue with someone who seems alien and incomprehensible, the first step is to be with them. Not just as a physical presence, but abiding in their company, open to who they are, in expectant attention to what they might say or do. Not initially with any plan to negotiate agreements or seek to resolve conflicts. Just being there, as the Lord is with us and with them, in expansive silence. We are both Dominican brothers who live in community, and some of the most precious moments of our common life are just being there with the brethren, silent in the presence of the Lord.

If we are *with* people, attentive to their bodily presence, their vulnerability and sensitivity, how can it *not* be possible to find a word to share with them? If we learn to see their faces, we may catch a glimpse of the face which we long to see: 'Have you not seen him whom my heart loves?' If we dare to open ourselves to relish people, even in their oddness, the empty silence which goes nowhere may become the silence from which we do not wish to depart.

Then, like Jesus at the well with the Samaritan woman, a word may be given that resonates within them, a word they long to hear. 'She will bear a child,' the stranger speaks through the walls of the tent to the barren Sarah who longs for one; to the diffident Jeremiah he says, 'Do not say, I am a youth, for to all to whom I will send you, shall you go, and all that I will command you, shall you speak. Do not be afraid in face of them, for with you [it is] I to deliver you, the utterance of YHWH.' 'Give me to drink' he says to the woman who thirsts at the well. The Lord starts where we are. 'What are you talking about?' he asks the disciples, sharing their woes as they flee to Emmaus. He asks three times Simon, son of John, who is aching with the burden of his threefold denial, 'Do you love me more than these?' Most of the conversations we have looked at in this book begin with a question. Do we approach each other with questions that seek to understand what is in the other person's heart or with assertions that demand acceptance or rejection?

To find that fecund word, we need to make an imaginative leap into who they are, what they love and fear, what they suffer and cherish, the words that are the lodestars of their lives. Can I imagine why this person loves the Tridentine Mass, or longs for guitars at Mass? Or why this person hungers for the ordination of women, whereas another cannot imagine it? Or why this sulky teenager is at sea, not certain who she or he is? Or why my brother is downcast? Simply being with them, abiding in their presence, seeing their faces, catching their eyes and hearing their breathing, may unlock my imagination. For we are bodily beings and not disembodied minds.

For years both us have lived in international communities, Timothy in Rome and Łukasz in Jerusalem. Few things can be taken for granted: the sense of humour, ideas of hospitality, what it means to be poor or rich, what sort of food you consider tasty and how to speak of difficult things. One has to pray daily for the words that leap across cultural boundaries and chime in the heart and mind of the other and there bear fruit.

Even then we may find it hard to find the right word. Anything we say might unlock antagonism and provoke the other to say, 'You simply do not understand!' Then we pray for a word: 'Do not worry beforehand about what you are to say; but say whatever is given you at that time, for it is not you who speak but the Holy Spirit' (Mk 13.11). Words *will* be given if we are silently open to their gift. Indeed the word we need may be a silent one, just a gesture or a smile. Joseph, to whom Jesus is entrusted, appears to say little. Maybe all that we can do is stutter. But God chose the stuttering Moses and the young Jeremiah who could just say *Ahahah*. Łukasz shared how he was converted by a stuttering preacher. In the Temple, the Pharisee eloquently proclaims his virtues and gives elaborate thanks that he is not like the despicable man at the back. But it is he, who can do no more than mumble 'have mercy on me a sinner' (Lk. 18.13), who leaves justified.

Even when conversations fail, we should never give up. Cain seems to have locked himself forever into exile and despair; the conversation of Jesus with the Sadducees seems to crash without hope of resumption: 'You err greatly.' But this need not be the end for any of them. Peter, who denies his friend, finds healing words on the beach. Who knows the end of Pontius Pilate's questioning?

We both knew a famous Polish Dominican preacher, Jan Góra, who wrote a book on the priesthood the title of which was the motto of the French Foreign Legion, 'Marche ou Crève', 'Walk or Die'. This sounds like a commandment, and it truly is because it is the consequence of the most important commandment, to love. Faced with the breakdown of dialogue in the Church and in society and even in our families, we may be tempted to give up and retreat into our little bubbles or silos, in which those who think alike can console each other, reflecting on the presumed stupidity of everyone else. No, we must march or die, reaching out again and again to others as we journey to the Kingdom. God never gives up on humanity. 'Again and again you called us into covenant with you, and through the prophets you taught us to hope for salvation. You loved the world so much that in the fullness of time you sent your only begotten one to be our Saviour' (Eucharistic Prayer IV). If God never gives up, how can we?

Acknowledgements

We wish to thank Fernando Cervantes and Dominic White OP, for reading the book. Conversations with them helped us to clarify our conversations with each other. We are grateful to Patrick van de Vorst for help in choosing pictures, and to Pierre de Marolles OP for pointing us to the painting of the journey to Emmaus by Janet Brooks-Gerloff which we have used for the cover. We thank the brethren of our communities, the École Biblique et Archéologique Française of Jerusalem, and Blackfriars, Oxford, for their unfailing support and Robin Baird-Smith, our kind and patient editor, Fahmida Ahmed and all of the team at Bloomsbury for their encouragement and help.

Image Credits

All photos have been reproduced by permission of the copyright holders. Every effort has been made to contact copyright owners of the photos used in the book.

Page 6: Aneta Fausek-Kaczanowska, *Adam*, 2018, private collection, Kraków
Page 16: Julius Paulsen, *Cain*, 1891, Statens Museum for Kunst, Copenhagen
Page 31: Andrei Rublev, *Trinity*, 1411 or 1425–7, The State Tretyakov Gallery, Moscow
Page 50: *Moses before the Burning Bush*, sixth century, St Catherine's Monastery, Sinai, © Bridgeman Images
Page 62: Sieger Köder, *Elijah at Horeb* (*Elija am Horeb*), © Sieger Köder-Stiftung Kunst und Bibel, Ellwangen, www.verlagsgruppe-patmos.de/rights/abdrucke
Page 72: Detail of the Incipit of the Book of Jeremiah in the Winchester Bible, 1150–75, © The Dean and Chapter of Winchester Cathedral
Page 84: Jacob Steinhardt, *Jonah Has Pity on the Gourd*, 1965, © Israel Museum, Jerusalem
Page 131: Monika Sawionek, *Meeting at the Well*, 2010, private collection
Page 139: Annibale Carracci, *Domine, quo vadis?*, 1602, © The National Gallery, London
Page 148: *Three Patriarchs*, tenth century, church of Deir al-Surian, Egypt
Page 159: Rembrandt van Rijn, *Ecce Homo*, 1634, © The National Gallery, London
Page 170: Watercolour copy of *Christ as pilgrim received by two Dominicans*, Fra Angelico in the Museo di San Marco (Florence), Emilio Costantini, Arundel Society, 1889, © Victoria and Albert Museum, London
Page 176: James Tissot (French, 1836–1902). *Christ Appears on the Shore of Lake Tiberias* (*Apparition du Christ sur les bords du lac de Tibériade*), 1886–1894. Opaque watercolor over graphite on gray wove paper. © Brooklyn Museum, Purchased by public subscription, 00.159.343
Page 188: Bartolomeo Cavarozzi, *Dispute between St Peter and St Paul*, 1615–16, © Galerie G. Sarti, Paris
Page 199: Fra Angelico OP, *Sacred Conversation* (Annalena Altarpiece), 1438–40, Museum of San Marco, Florence, © Photo Scala, Florence – courtesy of the Ministero Beni e Att. Culturali e del Turismo

Plate section images:
FIGURE 1 Rembrandt van Rijn, Jacob Wrestling with the Angel, 1659, Gemäldegalerie, Berlin
FIGURE 2 Dante Gabriel Rossetti, The Beloved, 1865, Tate Britain, London
FIGURE 3 Gaston Petit OP, L'Etonnant Message, 1990, priory of St Sabina, Rome
FIGURE 4 Simone Martini, Christ Discovered in the Temple, 1342, Walker Art Gallery, Liverpool

Notes

PROLOGUE 'SPEAK, LORD, FOR YOUR SERVANT IS LISTENING'
(I SAM. 3.9)

1   Dei Verbum 2, promulgated 18 November 1965. In *The Basic Sixteen Documents: Vatican II: Constitutions, Degrees, Declaration. A Completely Revised Translation*. General Editor Austin Flannery OP. Dublin: Dominican Publications, 1996, p. 98.
2   Catechism of the Catholic Church 108: 'Still, the Christian faith is not a "religion of the book". Christianity is the religion of the "Word" of God, a word which is "not a written and mute word, but incarnate and living"' (St Bernard, Sermons, 'Missus est' homilia 4, 11; Patrologia Latina 183, 86). If the Scriptures are not to remain a dead letter, Christ, the eternal Word of the living God, must, through the Holy Spirit, 'open (our) minds to understand the Scriptures (Cf. Lk. 24.45)'.
3   Ludwig Wittgenstein, *Culture and Value*, trans. Peter Winch. Chicago: University of Chicago Press, 1984, p. 80.
4   *Politica*, Bk 8, vi, in *Opera Omnia*, vol VIII Paris, 1891, p. 804.

CHAPTER 1 'WHERE ARE YOU?' (GEN. 3.8–20)

1   'Maxims on Love, 21', in *The Collected Works of St John of the Cross*, trans. K. Kavanaugh and R. Rodriguez. Washington, DC: Institute of Carmelite Studies, 1979, p. 675.
2   *Il Dialogo*, ed. G. Cavallini. Rome, 1968, Chapter 165, p. 493.
3   'Simple Prayer', *The Clergy Review*, lxiii (February 1978), p. 43. Sister Wendy Beckett was Sister of Notre Dame de Namur, and a well-known spiritual writer and art historian. She died in 2018.
4   *De Virginitate*, XIII 1,15f, quoted by Simon Tugwell OP, *The Way of the Preacher*. London: Darton, Longman and Todd, 1979, p. 92.
5   M. E. Johnson, *The Prayers of Sarapion of Thmuis: A Literary, Liturgical, and Theological Analysis*, Orientalia Christiana Analecta 249. Roma: Istituto Orientale, 1995, cited in Tugwell, *The Way of the Preacher*, p. 92.

CHAPTER 2 'WHERE IS ABEL, YOUR BROTHER?' (GEN. 4.1–16)

1   John Steinbeck, *East of Eden,* with an Introduction by David Wyatt. London: Penguin Books, 1992, p. 268.
2   Marilynne Robinson, *Gilead.* New York: Farrar, Straus and Giroux, 2004, p. 66.
3   Jonathan Sacks, *Not in God's Name: Confronting Religious Violence.* London: Hodder and Stoughton, 2015, p. 453.
4   For the importance of the family dynamics in the narrative see André Wénin, *D'Adam à Abraham, ou les errances de l'humain.* Paris: Éditions du Cerf, 2007.
5   Founded by Frère Yousif Mirkis OP in 2006. He is now the archbishop of Kirkuk.

PART ONE INTERMEZZO: THREE ABSENCES

1   Herbert McCabe, *God Matters.* London: Geoffrey Chapman, 1987, p. 248.

CHAPTER 4 'WHAT IS YOUR NAME?' (GEN. 32.23–33)

1   Jonathan Sacks, *Not in God's Name: Confronting Religious Violence.* London: Hodder and Stoughton, 2015, p. 136.
2   Sacks, *Not in God's Name,* p. 141.
3   'Que tiernamente hieres', from *Llama de amor viva.*

CHAPTER 5 'AND IF THEY ASK "WHAT IS HIS NAME?", WHAT SHALL I SAY?' (EXOD. 3.1–14)

1   St Augustine, *Epistles,* 130.28; *Patrologia Latina,* ed. J. P. Migne, 33:505.
2   David Sanders OP joined the Dominicans in 1965, worked in Jamaica for many years, was editor of *The Pastoral Review* and died in 2020, of leukaemia combined with Covid.
3   *Summa Theologica,* II.II, Q 167.
4   'Par ce que c'estoit luy, par ce que c'estoit moy.' Michel de Montaigne *Essays* (1570–92), Book I, Chapter 27, 'Of Friendship'.
5   Josef Pieper, *Faith, Hope, Love.* San Francisco, CA: Ignatius Press, 1997, p. 170.
6   Cf. *Summa Theologica,* II.II Q 17.3.
7   Victor White, 'The Meaning of the Octave', Report of the Proceedings at the Church Unity Octave held at Blackfriars, 18–25 January 1942, pp. 7–16 [English Dominican Archives III, Ox 3].

CHAPTER 6 'WHAT IS IT FOR YOU HERE, ELIJAH?' (1 KGS 19.8–18)

1   John Henry Newman, Meditations on Christian Doctrine, 7 March 1848.
2   Terry Eagleton, *Radical Sacrifice*. New Haven, CT, and London: Yale University Press, 2018, p. 70.
3   This is a military tactic, technically known as 'rapid dominance', in which massive and spectacular use of force is intended to overwhelm the enemy and destroy their will to fight.

CHAPTER 7 'I AM YOUNG. I DO NOT KNOW HOW TO SPEAK' (JER. 1.4–10)

1   Letter to Monna Lodovica di Granello, *Letters of Catherine of Siena*, ed. Suzanne Noffke OP, vol. III, Letters 145–230, Medieval and Renaissance Texts and Studies 329. Tempe, AZ: Arizona Center for Medieval and Renaissance Studies, 2007, Letter 185.
2   Ben Quash, *Abiding: The Archbishop of Canterbury's Lent Book 2013*. London: Bloomsbury, 2013, pp. 41ff.
3   Leo Tolstoy, *War and Peace*, trans. Richard Pevear and Larissa Volokhonsky, Book 12, Chapter 12. Kindle edition Location 17723.
4   *The Sayings of the Desert Fathers: The Alphabetical Collection,* translated Benedicta Ward, preface by Metropolitan Anthony, Cistercian Studies Series 59. Dubuque, IO: Liturgical Press, 1975, p. 7.

CHAPTER 8 'IS IT GOOD FOR YOU TO BE ANGRY?' (JON. 4.1–13)

1   This translation of the Hebrew text comes from *Jonah*, La Bible en ses Traditions 5. Leuven: Peeters 2022.
2   *Vitae Fratrum*, I vi 6.
3   A brilliant American serial political drama television series created by Aaron Sorkin that was originally broadcast on NBC from 22 September 1999 to 14 May 2006.
4   James Finley, 'Ripening', *Oneing* 1, no. 2, *Ripening* (Fall 2013), 37–8.
5   Stephen Cherry, *Healing Agony: Re-Imagining Forgiveness*, London and New York: Bloomsbury, 2012, p. 190 and passim.

PART THREE INTERMEZZO: *FOUR* PROPHETS

1   Thomas Merton, *The Seven Storey Mountain*. New York: Harcourt Brace, 1948, p. 225.
2   St Bonaventure, quoted in *The Soul's Journey into God*, trans. Ewert H. Cousins. New York: Paulist Press, 1978, p.100; cf. William T. Cavanaugh,

'The City: Beyond Secular Parodies', in *Radical Orthodoxy: A New Theology*, ed. J. Millbank, Catherine Pickstock and Graham Ward. London: Routledge, 1999, p. 200.

CHAPTER 9 'HAVE YOU NOT SEEN HIM WHOM MY HEART LOVES?' (SONG 1.12–2.7)

1 Letter to Sano di Maco: 'You know that neither nails nor cross nor rock could have held the God-Man on the cross had not his love held him there.' *Letters of Catherine of Siena*, ed. Suzanne Noffke OP, vol. 1, Letters 145–230, Medieval and Renaissance Texts and Studies 202. Tempe, AZ: Arizona Center for Medieval and Renaissance Studies, 2007, pp. 76–7.
2 William Shakespeare *Macbeth*, Act V, scene v.
3 Commentary on 1 Cor. 15.
4 D. H. Lawrence, *Apropos of Lady Chatterley's Lover*. London: Martin Secker, 1931, p. 53.
5 In his Homilies on 1 Jn, Hom. 8, 5, Augustine also goes on about loving the smell of fish, which is rather more to my taste.
6 Antoine de Saint-Exupéry, *The Little Prince*, Chapter 21.
7 *Has Truth A Future?* London: BBC Publications, 1978, p. 16.
8 Rowan Williams, *The Body's Grace*, The Michael Harding Memorial Address. London: LGCM, 1989.
9 Quoted by William H. Shannon, *Seeds of Peace: Contemplation and Non-Violence*. New York: Crossroad Publishing Company, 1996, p. 63.

CHAPTER 10 'HOW WILL THIS HAPPEN?' (LK. 1.26–38)

1 St Augustine, *Confessions*, Book 1, Chapter 1.
2 William Blake, 'Auguries of Innocence', *Blake: Complete Writings*, ed. Geoffrey Keynes. Oxford: Oxford University Press, 1969, p. 432.

CHAPTER 11 'CHILD, WHY HAVE YOU TREATED US LIKE THIS?' (LK. 2.41–52)

1 Luke writes *pascha* in Aramaic; in Hebrew it would be *pesach*.
2 Neil MacGregor, *Living with the Gods*. London: Random House, 2018, p. 122.
3 C. Day-Lewis, 'Walking Away', *Complete Poems*. London: Sinclair Stevenson, 1992.
4 St Benedict, Rule, Chapter 3.3: 'The reason why we have said all should be called for counsel is that the Lord often reveals what is better to the younger.'

CHAPTER 12 'HOW CAN YOU, BEING A JEW, ASK FROM ME "TO DRINK", WHILE I AM A SAMARITAN WOMAN?' (JN 4.4–42)

1 The Greek participle 'One-who-sent' occurs a number of times in John's Gospel as a circumlocution for the Father: 5.23–4, 30, 37; 6.38–9, 44; 7.16, 18, 28, 33 etc.
2 Amélie Nothomb, *Soif*. Paris: Albin Michel, 2019 (our translation).
3 Targums are later translations and interpretations of the Hebrew Bible into Aramaic. Besides the translations they often contain early Jewish haggadah.
4 Theodore Zeldin, *An Intimate History of Humanity*. London: Vintage, 1994, p. 442.
5 Private email.
6 Evelyn Waugh, *Brideshead Revisited: The Sacred & Profane Memories of Captain Charles Ryder*. London: Chapman and Hall, 1945.

CHAPTER 13 'WHO DO YOU SAY THAT I AM?' (MT. 16.13–28)

1 Niall Williams, *This Is Happiness*. London and New York: Bloomsbury, 2019, p. 42.

CHAPTER 14 'WHOSE WIFE WILL SHE BE?' (MK 12.18–28)

1 The history of how this phrase came to be attributed to Tertullian is highly complex. Voltaire's contribution is to be found in his *Le Dîner du comte de Boulainvillier*, published in 1767.
2 Tertullian, *De carne Christi*, 5.
3 Alan Jacobs, *How to Think: A Survival Guide for a World at Odds*. New York: Currency, 2017, p. 110.

CHAPTER 15 'WHAT IS TRUTH?' (JN 18.28–19.16)

1 St Augustine, *Confessions*, Book 8, Chapter 7.
2 Francis Bacon (1562–1626), English philosopher and stateman. These are the opening lines 'Of Truth', the first essay in the final edition of *Essays or Counsels, Civil and Moral* (1625).
3 *Christ on Trial: How the Gospel Unsettles Our Judgment*. London: Fount, 2000, p. 90.
4 *Expositio in Canticum canticorum* (Exposition of the Song of Songs), 8; Patrologia Graeca, 44, 941C.
5 QAnon is a conspiracy theory, widely believed in the USA and elsewhere, that the world is ruled by a secret group of Satan-worshipping paedophiles.

CHAPTER 17 'DO YOU LOVE ME MORE THAN THESE?' (JN 21.1–22)

1   Rainer Maria Rilke to his sister, 4 September 1908. Quoted in Mark
    Patrick Hederman, *Dancing with Dinosaurs: A Spirituality for the Twenty-
    First Century*. Dublin: The Columba Press, 2011, p. 84.
2   W. H. Auden, 'The More Loving One', *Collected Shorter Poems, 1927–
    1957*, London: Faber and Faber, 1966, p. 282.
3   D. C. Schindler, 'The Redemption of Eros: Philosophical Reflections on
    Benedict XVI's First Encyclical', *Communio*, Fall 2006, p. 394.
4   Rowan Williams, *Tokens of Trust: An Introduction to Christian Belief*.
    London: Canterbury Press, 2007, p. 22.

CHAPTER 18 'I OPPOSED HIM TO HIS FACE' (GAL. 2.1–14)

1   See James Jeffers, *The Greco-Roman World of the New Testament Era:
    Exploring the Background of Early Christianity*. Downers Grove, IL:
    InterVarsity Press, 2009, p. 102. By the end of the second century
    Tertullian wrote that, although Christians used Jewish books, they refused
    to exist 'under cover of a very famous religion (and one certainly permitted
    by law [*licitae*])' and to share with Judaism rules on forbidden food,
    holidays and 'the bodily seal'. See Tertullian, *Apology*, 21.1, translated by
    T. R. Glover. London: Heinemann, 1931, p. 103.
2   Preface to the third edition of *Lectures on the Prophetical Office of
    the Church* (London, 1874) and the third edition of the *Via Media*
    (London, 1877).

EPILOGUE: 'FOR OUR CONVERSATION IS IN HEAVEN' (PHIL. 3.20)

1   Also so translated in the Douay–Rheims translation, that of the
    Webster Bible, the Geneva Bible of 1579, Coverdale Bible, Tyndale
    Bible of 1529 etc.
2   The Office or Readings for the Feast of St Augustine
3   Augustine speaks of the distinction between *res quibus fruendum est*, things
    which are for enjoyment, and *res quibus utendum,* things which are for use,
    in his *De doctrina Christiana*, Book 1, Chapter 3. Of course, God alone is
    to be loved for its own sake.